Of warriors, lovers and prophets

Of warriors, lovers and prophets

unusual stories from South Africa's past

Max du Preez

ZEBRA

Published by Zebra Press
an imprint of Struik Publishers
(a division of New Holland Publishing (South Africa) (Pty) Ltd)
PO Box 1144, Cape Town, 8000
New Holland Publishing is a member of Johnnic Communications Ltd

www.zebrapress.co.za

First published 2004

5 7 9 10 8 6

Publication © Zebra Press 2004
Text © Max du Preez 2004

Cover artwork © Doret Ferreira

PUBLISHING MANAGER: Marlene Fryer
EDITOR: Robert Plummer
PROOFREADER: Ronel Richter-Herbert
TEXT DESIGNER: Natascha Adendorff
TYPESETTER: Monique van den Berg
INDEXER: Robert Plummer
PRODUCTION MANAGER: Valerie Kömmer

Set in 11 pt on 15 pt Adobe Garamond

Reproduction by Hirt & Carter (Cape) (Pty) Ltd
Printed and bound by Paarl Print, Oosterland Street, Paarl, South Africa

ISBN 1 86872 901 X

www.imagesofafrica.co.za
IMAGES OF AFRICA
PHOTO LIBRARY

To Angela

Contents

Preface

I LOVE STORIES. I AM A STORYTELLER BY TRAINING AND profession – a journalist. But for some thirty years I was so obsessed with the stories of today that I didn't realise how fascinating and illuminating the stories of yesterday are.

And so my new passion for *history as storytelling* was born. I have learnt that it is important first to understand yesterday's stories before one can really understand today's. I have also come to realise what damage some teachers and academics and most ideologues and ethnic nationalists have inflicted on "history". The history I was taught at school was a boring pack of lies.

I hope this book will help South Africans realise that the stories of our past are more fascinating and riveting than any television soap opera or juicy novel. My own understanding of attitudes, mentalities and trends in South African society grew substantially with the research I have been doing the last few years.

This book is a collection of offbeat stories from our past that I have come across. The stories are not really "representative" of a time or a group, although I have tried to use stories spanning the time from the fifteenth century to the present. My idea was that anyone reading these stories would get the gist of how our history developed, but without finding it hard work.

Most importantly, I wanted to show readers that history can be fun. I hope this book will stimulate people's interest in the stories of our past so they will go on and read more about it. And I hope this will help South Africans from different backgrounds become more aware of their shared history. My attitude towards history is that we should stop looking for villains, for people and groups to blame and hate. Instead we should try to understand who the characters really were, what motivated them and what their legacies are.

My writing style is that of a journalist and storyteller rather than a researcher or historian. I have avoided using footnotes, because readers (like myself) tend to find them distracting, even irritating. Instead, where necessary, I have made what could have been a footnote part of the narrative.

I have also strictly avoided fictionalising events or inventing dialogue like some popular writers of history do, because I believe this would undermine the credibility and authenticity of the stories. Every story in this book is backed by solid and wide-ranging research.

For those who want to do further reading on specific stories, I have included a select bibliography at the end of the book. All the books mentioned are available at the National Libraries of South Africa – the most underutilised public spaces in our country.

I hope, once you have read this book, you will look at your surroundings and your fellow South Africans with new eyes and more understanding.

MAX DU PREEZ
SEPTEMBER 2004

I

Death on
the Beach

WHITE-SKINNED PEOPLE AND BLACK AFRICA. A
troubled interaction that has been going on for six
centuries or so – on the southern tip probably more so than the rest
of the continent.

The interaction, in what is now South Africa, started on
3 February 1488, when the Portuguese navigator Bartholomeu
Dias, the first European to set foot on South African soil, shot
and killed a Khoikhoi man with a crossbow on Mossel Bay beach.

Dias and his men saw the Khoikhoi as a threatening, savage and
curious species. We know that from the writings of the time. We
don't know what the Khoikhoi and the Bushmen of the fifteenth
century thought, but they could only have viewed the Europeans
as very strange beings with weird dwellings on the water, long hair
and bizarre clothes.

If only these people knew then that they were brothers, that
only the texture of their hair and the pigmentation of their skins
and perhaps the shape of their noses were different. If only they
knew that way back they had the same ancestral mother, and that
they all once lived not that far from Mossel Bay. If only the
Portuguese knew that the Khoikhoi and the Bushmen were the
people closest to what the original human beings were like –
indeed, what their own ancestors were like before they migrated to
Europe some hundred thousand years earlier.

It is strange, isn't it, to think these people originated in Africa, but five, six hundred years ago they had virtually no knowledge of it. To them it was a dark and mysterious place, and their main interest in it was the legend of a fabulously rich Christian ruler, Prester John, whose country had unimaginable deposits of gold. Their other interest, of course, was to stem the growth of Islam.

It was only after the Portuguese captured Ceuta in Morocco in 1415 that they decided to "discover" the rest of Africa: they reached Sierra Leone in 1460, Ghana in 1471 and the Congo River in 1483, and rounded the Cape in 1488 (four years before Christopher Columbus first sighted the "New World"). On the other side of the continent the Chinese, the Indians, the Egyptians and the Arabs had already sent their ships to Africa, but there is no record that they ever went further south than present-day Durban or rounded the Cape into the Atlantic Ocean.

In August 1487, Bartholomeu Dias was sent by King João II to find the southern tip of Africa, because that would open up the route to mystical India. On board he had four African women hostages who had been captured by the navigator Diogo Cão on an earlier trip to West Africa, most likely the Congo. The plan was to drop the women off at different spots on the coast so that they could praise the Portuguese and act as intermediaries with local chiefs. (This concept of "all Africans are the same" survived in Europe for five hundred years ...)

In December 1487, Dias's squadron of three ships sailed into Lüderitz Bay on the Namibian coast. They left their storeship there with a crew of nine, and sailed on. But somewhere south of the Orange River mouth they were blown into sea. They had no idea that during these torrid days in late January 1488 they had actually rounded the magical southern tip of Africa. The first land they saw was at the Gourits River mouth, and the next day they sailed into Golfo de São Bras, now Mossel Bay, to take in fresh water.

The local Khoikhoi were happy to trade sheep for trinkets and beads, but when the Portuguese went to their waterhole, they threw stones at them. This was when Dias shot one of the Khoikhoi with his crossbow, and he and his men hurried back to the ship. They sailed on to Algoa Bay, where they planted a wooden cross and put one of the African hostages ashore. It is not known what became of this poor woman. Two others were dropped off on the west coast north of Namibia and the other died at sea. Then the Dias party sailed back past Cape Agulhas and Cape Point into False Bay, and then back up the west coast back to Portugal. Dias was the man who named the Cape the Cabo de Boa Esperanca, the Cape of Good Hope.

But they first had to rendezvous with their storeship in Lüderitz Bay, where they found that six of the nine men had been killed by the Khoikhoi. The surviving three were overjoyed at the sight of Dias's ship – so overjoyed that one of them, Fernão Coloca, had a heart attack and died on the spot. (I'm sure his children lied to their friends when asked how their father had met his death. I would have.)

Nine years later Dias's countryman, Vasco da Gama, almost repeated Dias's act. On his way to the Cape, he anchored in St Helena Bay. One of his men got into an argument with the Khoikhoi, and Da Gama shot at them with his crossbow, apparently without loss of life.

On 16 November 1497 he rounded the Cape and then also sailed into Mossel Bay. Again the Khoikhoi were happy to accept the trinkets and little bells – they even played on their flutes, with the Portuguese trumpets joining in. But the Khoikhoi again protested when the Portuguese wanted to draw water from their watering hole. Da Gama ordered a cannon on his ship to be fired, and within minutes all the Khoikhoi had vanished.

This time, as far as we know, nobody was killed. But this visit to Mossel Bay brought about the first act of non-violent political resistance by the indigenous people of South Africa against the

Europeans. Da Gama's men put up a tall wooden cross and a *padrão* [marking stone] above the high-water mark. Albaro Velho, one of Da Gama's men, wrote in his diary: "Next day, when we were about to leave the said bay, we saw some ten or twelve blacks who threw down both the cross and the padrão before we sailed." It was an act laden with symbolism.

The word must have spread among the Khoikhoi of the Cape about this new danger to their land and lifestyle. Thirteen years after Da Gama fired his cannon, a Portuguese viscount and the first Portuguese viceroy in India, Francisco D'Almeida, sailed his ship into Table Bay to get fresh water and meat. (Table Bay was then known as Aguada de Saldanha, after the first European who sailed into the bay in 1503, Antonio de Saldanha.) This time, the Khoikhoi took no nonsense from the Europeans.

We know what happened on that fateful day in March 1510 from the diary of one J de Barros, published in Lisbon in 1552. The viscount sent some of his men to barter with the Khoikhoi for meat with cloth and pieces of iron. Some of the men went a few kilometres further to the Khoikhoi villages, and here the Khoikhoi took their daggers "and everything they fancied".

In an act of revenge, a servant of the viscount, Concalo Homen, lured two Khoikhoi men to the shore. De Barros recalled: "And since they, suspecting him of malice, were unwilling to come to the shore, and he somewhat forcibly tried to compel them to do so, they threw down what he had bought, and so misused him that he presented himself to the Viceroy with his face bloodied and some teeth broken." A nice way of saying they beat the hell out of the poor Homen.

This apparently also happened to some of the other Portuguese. The uppity savages had to be taught a lesson. D'Almeida took a hundred of his best men and rowed closer to the villages in the ship's boats, and ordered them to wait there. Then he sent his men into the village.

The men rounded up some cattle and captured a number of the Khoikhoi children, and started moving back to the boats. But then about eighty Khoikhoi men attacked them "like men who go to risk death to save their sons". It was eighty men against a hundred, but it was a very uneven battle, rather like a bunch of sissies from Rondebosch taking on a gang from Bonteheuwel. (The only firearm the Portuguese had at that time was the arquebus, a heavy and unwieldy weapon that didn't work efficiently.)

This is how De Barros describes the fight: "The blacks came on so furiously that they came into the body of our men, taking back the oxen. And by whistling to the oxen and making other signs (since they are trained to this warlike device), they made them surround our men like a defensive wall, from behind which came so many fire-hardened sticks that some of us began to fall wounded or trodden by the cattle. And since few of our men were in armour, and for weapons had only lances and swords, they could do little harm to the blacks in that manner of warfare."

The viceroy and his men hastily retreated to their boats, but because a heavy sea had since developed, the ship's master had taken the boats closer to the ships for safety. The Portuguese were trapped on the beach and had to run for their lives.

It didn't work, says De Barros. "When they began to reach the sands of the shore they became altogether unable to take a step, whereas the blacks went over the sand so lightly that they seemed birds, and came down on the gentlefolk who were holding out for the love of the Viceroy, the common folk having run ahead."

Viceroy D'Almeida had already been injured by stones and sticks, so his getaway was even further slowed down. The Khoikhoi caught him and killed him with a spear through his throat, then stripped off all his clothes. More than fifty Portuguese, including twelve captains, died with their viceroy, and all the rest were wounded.

When it was all over, Jorge de Mello, probably the ship's captain, took the wounded to the ships and went to look for the viceroy's body. "Finally, having buried him and others in this barbarous place, he returned to the ships and set sail for his kingdom."

There can be little doubt that those who remained behind in that barbarous place had a proper party to celebrate their victory over the invaders.

The violent conflict between black and white in South Africa would continue for another 484 years.

2

An African Chief in London

IT'S A QUESTION WORTHY OF A GOOD QUIZ: WHO WAS THE first South African to go overseas?

The answer is Coree, a Khoikhoi chief from the Cape Peninsula, who left our shores in 1613. (He was also the first South African to go on a hunger strike, a much-used weapon of resistance and protest over 380 years until the end of apartheid.) This is Coree's story.

Sir Thomas Smythe, governor of the English East India Company, was one of the most powerful merchants and financiers in England during the first half of the seventeenth century, and a personal friend of King James I. He had visions of establishing a settlement at the Cape of Good Hope, the place his countryman Francis Drake had, in 1580, described as "the finest cape that we saw in the whole circumference of the earth".

Sir Thomas had a sense of how important the southern tip of Africa could become as a port where the increasing number of trade ships sailing between Europe and the East could replenish their supplies of fresh water, vegetables, fruit and meat. And then, of course, there were those rumours that Africa had rich gold deposits.

Some of Smythe's ships had been to Table Bay, then still known as Saldania, but had failed to gather the information he sought from the local inhabitants. Smythe decided to find someone who could tell him all about the climate, plants and people of the Cape, and who could serve as his agent among the indigenous people. Someone to teach English to.

In May 1613, the *Hector* and the *Thomas* anchored in Table Bay on their return from the East. As Gabriel Towerson, the captain of the *Hector*, stepped onto Cape soil, he was met by Coree (some historians spell his name Quore, Xhoré or Kora). It was a friendly meeting, it seems, because Coree and his people exchanged some cattle and sheep for brass, iron and cloth, and allowed the English to pitch their tents alongside the stream that flowed down the mountain.

It was guessed at the time that Coree was about forty years old. He was described as "of average height, lithe, intelligent and physically strong". He and his wife had several young children. Some reports say that he was a chief, others that he was an ordinary member of the Khoikhoi group called the Gorachouqua.

Once the sailors had recovered from their journey and the ships were stocked with fresh water and meat, Captain Towerson and his men boarded. It is not known whether they were lured aboard with a promise or whether they were forced, but Coree and another Khoikhoi whose name is not known were on board when the *Hector* sailed for England.

One historian has suggested that the two men must have been restrained when the ship sailed, or "doped with strong liquor", because like all Khoikhoi living on the coast they were good swimmers and would otherwise have jumped overboard. Another source has Towerson inviting Coree to the *Hector* "for successive nights of drinking and eating", and when "Coree and his companion had fallen into a drunken stupor", the captain set sail. All records of the time mention that they protested violently at their kidnapping, and both men embarked on a hunger strike in an attempt to force the English to drop them off. It is said that Coree's companion later died of weakness and sorrow, but Coree started to eat again and survived the trip.

The *Hector* docked in London in the September of 1613. Coree stepped off the ship dressed like an English gentleman of the time: shirt, breeches buckled above the knee, stockings, buckled shoes, a cloak and a hat with a feather in it. Sir Thomas Smythe gave orders that Coree be well looked after and put him up in his own residence, one of the grandest in London at the time. Coree was shown the sights of London, and it is possible that he might even have met King James. Smythe personally tutored Coree.

We know most about Coree's London experiences from the records kept by Reverend Edward Terry (his *A Voyage to East India* was published in 1655). He wrote that Coree had "for his good entertainment made for him a chain of bright brass, an armour breft, back and headpiece, with a buckler, all of brass, his beloved metal".

Coree couldn't have had a pleasant time. London was a rather filthy, cramped city, and the English winter must have been as wet, grey and miserable as it has always been. Coree was accustomed to the beauty of the untouched Cape Peninsula; the crisp air, majestic Table Mountain and its fresh streams, the golden beaches. He was used to eating fresh fish and the meat of his people's cattle and sheep, cooked with herbs and roots from the veld. There were no Indian or Italian restaurants in London in 1613, so the poor man had to suffer grey, overcooked English food. I'm fairly certain Coree, like the rest of the Khoikhoi back home, loved to occasionally sit back and smoke a pipe of sweet, Cape-grown dagga – something not available to him in seventeenth-century England.

So, not unexpectedly, Coree was not a happy man. He had little regard for Smythe's "hospitality" – he hadn't wanted to be there in the first place. But the arrogant English were offended by his lack of appreciation, and called him "an ungrateful dogge".

In the words of Reverend Terry, "now one would think that this wretch might have conceived his present, compared with his former condition, as Heaven upon Earth; but did not so ... for never any seemed to be more weary of ill usage than he was of courtesies;

none ever more desirous to return home to his country than he; for when he had learned a little of our language he would daily lie upon the ground, and cry very often this in broken English, 'Coree home go, Souldanhia go, home go.'" (Souldanhia or Saldania being the name used for Table Bay at the time.)

An English historian, John Cope, offers this version in *King of the Hottentots*, published in 1967: "Every time Sir Thomas tried to question him about Saldania, Xhoré would prostrate himself on the floor, beating the carpet with his hands, and would cry: 'Xhoré go home – Saldania go!' The more English he learnt, the more eloquent became his pleadings to return to the sun-drenched country and the primitive community that were his own. But not one scrap of information would he impart about Saldania." Other sources claim Coree "played dumb", and only owned up to being fluent in English when he pleaded with Smythe to take him home.

Cope also states that Coree was "insatiably curious" about London and the strange culture of the local people. He was shown the Tower of London, and probably even taken to a performance of a Shakespeare play at the Curtain Theatre in Holywell Street, according to Cope.

Smythe eventually gave up on his pet project. Fearing that the English wanted to settle in the Cape permanently, Coree refused to give Smythe any information about his homeland. Smythe decided to send Coree home. It was 26 February 1614 when he boarded the *Hector*, the same ship that had carried him to London. It was an eventful trip: the *Hector* had barely left the Thames estuary when she ran into a sandbank. Two months later, her foremast split in a storm. Eventually the ship sailed into Table Bay in June 1614. Coree had been away from home for fourteen months.

To the astonishment of his people, who had long feared him dead, Coree stepped off the ship decked in his magnificent brass suit of armour. He walked to his village, leaving the crew of the

Hector behind him. They didn't see him again before they sailed on. Other Khoikhoi traded with the Englishmen, but this time they were not interested in iron or copper in exchange for meat. They insisted on sheets of brass.

There was an unintended consequence of Coree's cultural adventure in London: he got to see first hand how common and inexpensive copper, brass and iron were in England. These metals, contrary to what the Khoikhoi were led to believe, were not viewed as a sign of wealth at all. Coree made it clear: no more trinkets-for-cattle deals, the foreigners had to pay. Reverend Terry wrote that the consensus among the sailors was that it "would have bynn much better for us and as shall come hereafter if he had never seene Ingland".

Coree must have spent many an evening in his village telling the people about all his strange experiences. Now that he was back home, he seemed to be more forgiving towards the English, and had developed an apparent affection for his London host, Sir Thomas Smythe. When Sir Thomas Roe, King James's envoy to India, arrived with his fleet in Table Bay the following year, Coree welcomed him warmly and took a party to his village. There, according to the Englishmen present, the locals greeted them with joyous chants of "Sir Thomas Smythe English Ships!" Coree had obviously glamourised his miserable time in London, because several Khoikhoi expressed the desire to visit there.

Some historians believe that Coree became a chief of the Gorachouqua only after his return from London, and probably because his trip enhanced his status. True or not, we do know that his newfound friendliness toward the English was at least partly motivated by his desire to have their help in his fight with another Khoikhoi group, the Cochoqua.

The first group of Englishmen Coree approached for help was a rough bunch of ten criminals who had arrived at the Cape with Sir Thomas Roe in 1615. In London, they were convicted of such crimes as highway robbery, horse theft and pick-pocketing, and were sentenced to death. But Sir Thomas Smythe had made a deal with the king: he could select able-bodied condemned men "for service abroad", and they would escape the gallows. These chosen men were released from Newgate Prison and sent to the Cape.

Captain Walter Peyton left the ten in Table Bay and then sailed on to India. "We gave each man something for his own defence against wild beasts and men, weapons and victuals," the captain wrote in his diary.

The men chose John Crosse as their leader. He was a former "gentleman", born of an upper-class family, and had become a member of the elite King's Guard. But he lived a wild life of drinking and fighting, and when he was dismissed from the Guard, he took to being a robber on the highways outside the walls of the city of London.

Coree pleaded in vain for the Englishmen to help him ward off his enemies. Crosse's men clearly treated the Khoikhoi with little respect, and there are even hints of them molesting some of the Khoikhoi women. One of the men was killed by the Khoikhoi within a few days, so Crosse and the others fled to Robben Island in a boat left behind by Captain Peyton. They lived on seals and penguins. They were the second group of people who had ever lived on Robben Island – the first being a group of shipwrecked Dutchmen, who lived there for six months in 1611. (The Khoikhoi never went to the island before the first Europeans arrived, as they did not have boats.)

An English ship, *New Year's Gift*, arrived in Table Bay nine months later. According to the captain, Martin Pring, Coree told him on arrival that Crosse and his men were on the island, and he despatched a boat to fetch them. On the island they were told that Crosse and some of his men had just the week before tried to row to the mainland, and drowned when their boat overturned.

But Reverend Edward Terry, who arrived some three months

later, wrote in his book that Crosse had abused and quarrelled with the Khoikhoi, and that they had killed him.

Captain Pring rescued the last three survivors of the Crosse group, and took them back to England. The minute they got ashore, they stole someone's purse. They were caught, sentenced to death and hanged at Gallows Field near Sandwich. Bad karma, if you ask me.

Coree did not give up on his plans to persuade the armed white visitors to help him fight the Cochoqua. In 1617 he took a party of Englishmen to show them his assembled enemies: there were about five thousand men with ten thousand head of cattle. This was much more than Coree could muster, and the English refused to help him. Later that same year a group of Dutchmen came to his aid and helped Coree seize 120 head of cattle, 160 sheep and three Cochoqua as prisoners.

There is little mention of Coree in the years following this battle. But in 1627 a Welsh sailor reported that Coree had been killed by Dutch sailors the previous year, because he had refused to give them food.

And so ended the life of the first South African to go overseas and speak English.

But the stories of Coree's remarkable adventure, no doubt often embroidered upon, were kept alive among the Khoikhoi around the evening fires. Perhaps these stories led a young leader of the Strandlopers [Beachrangers], a small group of Khoikhoi who had no cattle or sheep, to volunteer for an overseas trip just six years after Coree's death.

In 1632, an English ship carried Autshomato to Bantam in Java. It is not clear why the English did this, but it seems it was purely to befriend him and to teach him English. They wanted Autshomato to be their postman at the Cape and to report on ships' movements – unlike Coree, he had no cattle or sheep to trade and no standing with the powerful Khoikhoi groups.

Autshomato returned, reasonably fluent in English. Later that same year the English took him and twenty of his followers at his own request to Robben Island, where they were joined a few months later by thirty other Strandlopers. Life on the island was much easier than on the mainland, where there were no seals or penguins. The English also left a few cows, pigs and chickens with Autshomato's party.

Autshomato and his people ran an efficient postal service for the English and the Dutch for years, keeping letters from the one fleet for the next. They lived on Robben Island for some eight years. Englishman Peter Mundy visited Robben Island in 1634, and reported that Autshomato was clothed in "English habit from head to foote". He called Autshomato the "governor of the island".

Autshomato returned to Robben Island in 1658, but this time against his will and known by a different name.

In April 1652, Jan van Riebeeck established the first permanent settlement at the Cape. Autshomato soon rose to the influential role of middleman and interpreter between the Dutch and the Khoikhoi. The Dutch named him Herrie de Strandloper, many later simply referring to him as Harry. Van Riebeeck banished him to Robben Island when he became too powerful and influenced the trade between the Dutch and the Khoikhoi.

Autshomato was the first of many political prisoners on Robben Island, the last being senior liberation fighters such as Nelson Mandela and Walter Sisulu more than three hundred years later. But unlike Mandela and Sisulu, who were released as part of a political settlement, Autshomato escaped from the island. In November 1659 he stole a leaky boat and rowed in the dark of night to Bloubergstrand.

3

Pacts with Lions

L ONG AGO, WHEN SOUTH AFRICA WAS SPARSELY POPULATED and nature was largely undisturbed, human beings' main enemy (apart from hunger and thirst) was the lion. Living in the open veld without firearms made humans easy targets for these beasts.

This is a story about how some of these ancient people made a "pact" with the lions not to attack them. We think we are awfully clever and sophisticated in the twenty-first century, but here is proof that as human beings we have lost a great deal of real knowledge on our journey to a "modern people".

First we need to find out who these people were and how their story has survived for four hundred years or more.

In 2003, archaeologists found jewellery and artistic engravings in the ancient Blombos Cave near Stilbaai in the southern Cape. These valuables have been dated to 77 000 years ago, proof that human beings with language and culture like ours lived there at the time. They are also the oldest cultural items to be found anywhere in the world. Of course, this is also proof that South Africa was never a "vacant" land – it has always been populated, from the very first days our species developed.

The people who lived at Blombos were the direct ancestors of South Africa's aboriginal people, the San, or Bushmen, and the Khoikhoi.

The Bushmen were hunters and gatherers who lived in small, mobile groups throughout southern Africa. In fact, all our ancestors lived this way during the early millennia of our species' existence.

People had few earthly possessions, and societies were therefore largely classless and without rigid hierarchies.

We know very little of Bushman life and culture. We do know that they had an astonishing knowledge of nature: plants, animals, seasons and climate. Other societies lost this knowledge when they stopped being hunters, but those who later moved into southern Africa regained some of this early knowledge from the San societies.

About three, four thousand years ago, a society developed around the broad region of the Great Lakes of Africa and the savannah of Zambia as they turned from hunting, gathering and fish-eating to planting millet and keeping domesticated animals. This society became less nomadic, grouping in larger settlements. They spoke a common language, later called Bantu.

Two thousand years later they had mastered the art of iron- and gold-smelting, and some started to move into southern Africa in different groups. By this time, they had developed different dialects, and the major language groups that moved south were later called the Nguni, Sotho, Venda and Tsonga.

By the early 1200s, a large group had formed a powerful capital at Mapungubwe on South Africa's northern border with Zimbabwe and Botswana. Following a serious and prolonged drought before 1300, Mapungubwe waned and Great Zimbabwe, about two hundred kilometres away, became the centre of power in the region. Many of the stone walls of this magnificent city still stand today.

It was from this civilisation, historians believe, that a fascinating small group of people left and moved south, probably around the middle 1400s, most likely to avoid conflict with some other group. (The way they made their clay pots and decorated them confirms their Zimbabwean ancestry.) They called themselves the Leghoya (also referred to as Lihoya or Coija). At some point the Leghoya adopted the hippopotamus as their *siboko* or tribal symbol, and many people knew them as the Bakubung – People of the Hippo.

The Leghoya were master stone builders who constructed low, round corbelled huts. They crossed the Limpopo and built their first peculiar and ingenious stone settlements in the region of Marico and Zeerust. Threatened by another group, they left, this time going further west, where they built a settlement at Lithako. They set off again, probably during the seventeenth century, moving further south to eventually settle over a large area in the northern Free State, in the regions of today's Winburg, Senekal, Steynsrus, Kroonstad, Vrede and Bethlehem. Although the white farmers after the Anglo-Boer War of 1899–1902 destroyed most of the Leghoya huts to use the stone for erecting walls and kraals, some ruins still remain.

Interestingly, identical round huts of unworked stone were built in ancient Britain and Ireland, and can still be found at Ty Mawr, the Holyhead Mountain and on the Skelligs off the coast of Kerry. These huts are very similar to igloos, with blocks of stone instead of ice. It took great skill to produce the domed roofs, because no mortar or clay was used. In 1993, I discovered a Leghoya village on my farm outside Rosendal in the Free State. For years I tried to restore some of the huts, often with the help of architects and specialist builders. We were not successful.

According to the oral traditions of the old people of the Free State and Lesotho, the Leghoya were the first black farmers to move across the Vaal River to settle in the Free State. They were followed by the Bafokeng, and then the Bakoena.

But the Leghoya were different from the Bafokeng and the Bakoena. Although they had ample cattle, they preferred to hunt. They hunted with spears, axes and bows and arrows, and also by capturing game in dugout pits. They were particularly peaceful and always preferred to move away rather than confront aggressors. Their timid approach made them the easy targets of many other chiefdoms and they lost their cattle many times.

But what really distinguished the Leghoya from other black groups was their approach to the Bushmen.

Like the European settlers in the Cape Colony, most of the Bantu-speaking groups looked down on the Bushmen. Some of these groups at different times encouraged their men to take Bushman wives, but did not allow their own women to marry Bushmen. Even the Bushmen's own close family, the Khoikhoi, regarded themselves as superior. The name *San* for the Bushmen originated from the Khoikhoi, and meant, freely translated, people of little consequence. I suppose the main prejudice against the Bushmen was that they owned no cattle and had no houses or villages.

But the Leghoya were different. In keeping with their peaceful political culture, they treated the Bushman communities they encountered with nothing but respect. All historical evidence points to the fact that the Leghoya clan chiefs and headmen always made agreements with the Bushmen so that the two communities could coexist in peace and cooperate to their mutual benefit in shared areas. It was unusual behaviour for the time. The norm was for different language and ethnic communities to be suspicious of and avoid each other.

During the eighteenth century, and possibly even before that time, an extraordinary thing happened. The Leghoya and various Bushman communities started to integrate. They learnt each other's language and intermarried. In some areas, the Bushmen even started to deviate from their age-old culture and kept cattle, rather than only hunting and gathering food from the veld. Some even learnt crop cultivation from the Leghoya.

George William Stow, the nineteenth-century author of *The Native Races of South Africa* who studied and documented the history of the Leghoya, wrote: "It has been revealed, to their honour, that they were the only race of men who came into contact with the Bushmen, that persistently attempted to improve the conditions of the latter, by their mutual intercourse. This had become so far ameliorated under the influence of the Leghoya that they had learnt the value of pastoral pursuits and had ... so far progressed beyond the occupations of their forefathers, and had fraternised to such an extent with their new friends that these old inveterate huntsmen had become possessed of herds of cattle."

Stow reported that one Mr Campbell, a European who visited the Free State region where some of the Leghoya were still living in 1820, reported that the Bushmen "not only abounded in cattle, but were more civilised than any of the other Bushman tribes of South Africa, and were evidently desirous of living, like the Leghoya themselves appear ever to have been, 'at peace with their neighbours'. From this, therefore, it would appear that, from the friendly relations which had sprung up between them and the intruding Leghoya, and the consideration with which the Bushmen were treated by the latter, that the two races had, from the very first, lived together, occupying the same country and coming into daily intercourse with each other, under conditions which proved more favourable, and mutually advantageous, than those of any other tribe with whom the aboriginal Bushmen were brought into contact."

Many historians and anthropologists who have studied the ruins of the Leghoya's huts have wondered whether they were a diminutive people, because the huts, especially the older ones, were very small and low with tiny entrances. Of course these people looked no different than any of the other black farmer groups they were related to. The answer is that these huts were not used as we would use houses today, but only for shelter against the elements and to sleep in. Walls were usually built around the huts to create communal space for social interaction and cooking.

But there is another explanation for the tiny entrances. The huts were a safe haven at night from prowling lion. Inside the village or group of huts, the Leghoya also built walls to keep their cattle from the clutches of hungry lion. Every cattle enclosure included a round hut even smaller than the rest. This served as shelter for the boy who played nightwatchman – shelter from rain and cold, but also from hungry lions on the hunt for a herd of cattle.

The plains of central South Africa were inhabited by large populations of lion up until the early nineteenth century. Their numbers started to decrease as human beings slowly diminished the game population by hunting and there wasn't enough food for them to eat.

The Leghoya, among the first people other than the Bushmen to move into parts of what is today the North West Province and the Free State, suffered many lion attacks, on their people and their cattle. The lions could not believe their luck when these slow, easy targets moved into their territory.

The Leghoya's answer was to build the impenetrable stone huts with entrances too small for a lion, and to bring their cattle into the kraal at night. Still, many of them and large numbers of their cattle became lion fodder. (Of course, it wasn't only the Leghoya who were attacked by lions. In the 1840s, one of King Moshoeshoe's wives was caught by a lion close to her hut on top of Thaba Bosiu.)

The Leghoya were astonished that their Bushman neighbours were never attacked by lions and did not seem to fear them at all. Their only explanation was that the Bushmen had supernatural powers. Well, they were perhaps not too far wrong, but these powers were applied in a very practical way.

The Bushmen were supreme naturalists. Over millennia they had studied the behavioural patterns of all the animals with which they came into contact. They knew that lions were territorial, and that each territory and each pride had a dominant male – an alpha male as we call it nowadays.

When the Bushmen moved into an area, they quickly identified the lion families and which were the leading males. They knew every member of the pride – male, female and cubs. They knew each lion's personality – some are more aggressive, or more playful, or more irritable than others. They kept a close eye on developments in the pride, waiting to see when the alpha male was getting older or weaker and when young males were ready to challenge him.

The Bushmen knew exactly when the alpha male was overthrown and which young male took his place. The first time the new dominant male had the opportunity to take a nap, three or four of the best hunters would creep up to him in a way only they understood and had mastered. And then they would jump on the sleeping lion and beat the hell out of him with their sticks, shrieking and shouting at the top of their voices.

The poor lion would get the fright of his life and flee in a hurry. And somehow, through this act, the lion understood that he and his subjects should never attack these people who scared but did not kill him. You don't mess with us, and we won't mess with you, was the understanding. Imagine the thought process of the beaten lion: from "king" of the open veld to scaredy cat in one sound beating.

We will never know if there was more to this pact between Bushman and lion, whether perhaps there was some kind of psychic connection between human being and animal. All we know is that this was more or less how they did it and that it worked.

I was first told this story by a highly educated anthropologist whose wife was a descendant of the Leghoya. He had heard the story from her grandparents who lived in Lesotho. He told me that he had come across a similar story, but this time regarding one of the aboriginal groups of North America. They had an identical relationship with the mountain lion of the region hundreds of years ago, also attacking but not killing the alpha male on the first day of his reign.

Between 1820 and 1830, the Leghoya were wiped out during the Lifaqane, the violent upheaval and restructuring of chiefdoms in Natal and on the Highveld. The remaining families and individuals moved into Lesotho and became integrated with the Basotho, although they never forgot their past. There are accounts from the last fifty years of Leghoya descendants living in Lesotho who still call themselves the "brothers of the Bushmen".

In 2002, I met two very old men in the Quthing district of Lesotho who, people had told me, were Leghoya descendants. They were very vague about their group's origins, but confirmed that they also believed their people were the first black farmers to move into the Free State and that it was they who built the corbelled huts which still lie in ruins in many places. I then asked them why their early ancestors had had so many problems with lions, whereas their Bushman neighbours had not.

"Because the Bushmen made arrangements with the lions which we did not understand," they told me. They confirmed that they were also told that this "arrangement" involved a vicious attack on the leading male lion.

George William Stow did not record this pact between human and beast, but he remarked several times in his writings on the Leghoya that they had a different relationship with lions than the Bushmen.

"We can easily imagine," he wrote, "that the first herdsmen, in their anxious desire to preserve the few animals which they had succeeded in domesticating, were doubtless the earliest men to attempt to form impenetrable fences to defend themselves and their charge from the savage and formidable brutes with which they were surrounded. Weak pioneer clans, carrying their herds with them, found themselves exactly in this position as they penetrated deeper and deeper into the lion-veld of southern Africa.

"It is true that the Bushmen, for unknown ages, had already been in possession, but he from his superior knowledge, roamed about with comparative impunity, while the newcomers, in every instance, found themselves suddenly and pertinaciously assailed by these ruthless and midnight prowlers."

Elsewhere Stow wrote that a very old headman of the Kroonstad area, Kachana, gave him a lot of information about the relationship between the Leghoya and the Bushmen and the Leghoya's troubles with lions. "The same authority further stated that it was a fact that the lions, which were then very numerous, used, without hesitation, to single out any newcomers to the land, and would forthwith lay wait for them, and thus the lions would kill and devour numbers of them; while the old inhabitants, the Bushmen, moved amongst them with perfect indifference, sleeping in the middle of the great plains, completely exposed, without the slightest apprehension."

But Stow sought another explanation than the fantastical story of the "arrangements". "It is stated," he wrote, "that this immunity on the part of the Bushmen was owing to their knowledge of the peculiar properties of a certain cryptogamic plant, which they powdered and sprinkled upon their night fires."

There may be some truth in that, but it wouldn't explain why the Bushmen also felt safe from lion attacks in daylight when they were not sitting around a fire or when they were hunting or gathering roots and fruits in the veld.

All these centuries later, we still haven't regained the intimate knowledge they had of the earth and the life on it.

4

A Fatal
Attraction

WAS IT LOVE? WAS IT RAMPANT LUST? PERHAPS A mixture of the two? We don't know. Anything we *do* know of this tragic tale is still stored in the Cape Archives in the records of the Court of Justice of the Cape of Good Hope. These records from the early 1700s do not reflect the players' emotions or motivations.

The story begins in the Dutch town of Deventer in 1695. The burgeoning Dutch settlement at the Cape had a need for a beer brewer (beer being the most important drink of Dutch society). They recruited the Deventer brewer Rutgert Menssink, who arrived at the Cape with his wife, Gerbregt, and his thirty-year-old son, Willem, in 1695. Rutgert died five years later and his widow and son kept the brewery going. Willem married Johanna Tas, sister of the famous Cape rebel Adam Tas, which gave him considerable social standing. But Johanna died in 1701 and Willem then married Elizabeth Lingelbach, the daughter of a doctor.

It did not take long for Elizabeth to realise that she had made a huge mistake. On her wedding night she walked in on her husband having sex with the slave woman Susanna. Elizabeth locked Susanna in at night, but Willem simply caught up with her during the day.

It was the beginning of Willem's many, and sometimes bizarre, tricks and cover-ups. The next time Elizabeth caught him with Susanna, he pretended to be beating her. When she caught him with two slave women in the stables, he explained that they were stealing and he was merely chasing them. But then Elizabeth woke up one night to find Susanna in bed with her and her husband. This time Willem was short of a quick excuse, so he lay absolutely still, drooling from the mouth pretending to be mad. Another time, discovered having sex in the attic, he put a basket over his head and ran off, later denying that it was him.

Elizabeth trapped Willem many times with Susanna and other slaves thereafter. On one such occasion he beat his wife, telling her that it was the custom at the Cape to live according to the Old Testament. By this he probably meant that the Old Testament sanctioned male slave-owners to have sex with their slaves, but this was not the policy of the VOC at the time.

After five dismal years of marriage Elizabeth couldn't stand it any longer, so she moved back to her mother's house. But there was no talk of divorce. Willem Menssink was a church deacon and a member of the Burgher Council, and thus a man of good social standing.

But things came to a head in 1709 when Elizabeth bought a new slave following her mother's death (she believed Willem had poisoned her mother). On arrival at the Cape, this slave was registered as Trijntje of Madagascar – slaves seldom retained their own names because the settlers struggled to pronounce the Eastern or African names and because they wanted to destroy their previous identities.

Willem was immediately smitten with the twenty-one-year-old Trijntje, and it took just two days after her arrival for him to get her into his bed. Evidence later submitted to the court suggested that the relationship wasn't against her wishes. Perhaps she loved Willem, perhaps she was hoping that their relationship was her best chance for freedom. Willem co-opted his own slaves, Isaac of Masulipatam and Gerrit of Tutucorijn, as go-betweens to assist him in his adulterous affair.

Once Elizabeth found out about her husband's new object of lust, she forbade Trijntje to leave the house. That same night

Willem jumped over his wife's wall and had sex with her slave right there in the courtyard.

Menssink and his antics would have made any psychoanalyst's eyes light up with fascination. He probably had a very low self-esteem, which encouraged him to function sexually only with women of a social standing lower than his own. He may even have had some cross-dressing desires – his favourite attire during his carnal escapades was a Japanese robe with a scarf bound about his head, and at least once he dressed himself in Trijntje's nightgown. Cape Town historian Nigel Penn, an expert on eighteenth-century history of the Cape, believed Willem was "dangerously addicted to Trijntje's sexual charms".

But Willem clearly also had major issues with his domineering mother and a rather bizarre relationship with his wife. Now, he persuaded Trijntje that they should have sex in her owner's house. Because she didn't trust her slave, Elizabeth forced Trijntje to sleep at the foot of her bed. That was exactly where Willem and Trijntje slept together for the next few months. To keep Elizabeth from waking, he told Trijntje to put a pillow filled with a certain powder at Elizabeth's feet. We don't know what this white dust consisted of, but Elizabeth later claimed it was ground-up human bones.

This went on for about a year, but when Elizabeth became suspicious again, she first made Trijntje sleep in a shed and later in the loft. Of course this didn't stop Willem. He had his slaves Gerrit and Isaac carry a ladder to the loft window, climbed in, and then told them to return the ladder at three in the morning.

It was the love-making in the loft that led to Trijntje's pregnancy. This time Elizabeth was determined to put an end to the scandal, and she ordered Trijntje to help her trap Willem in flagrante delicto. Willem's reaction was to urge Trijntje to run away. When Elizabeth got wind of this, she had Trijntje locked up in jail. But she heard that Willem had told Trijntje that he would buy her if Elizabeth ever sold her, so she eventually relented and took the heavily pregnant Trijntje back.

Three nights after the birth of Trijntje's baby boy, Willem secretly went to her bedroom window to inspect his child. He was desperate that it never became known that he was the father because it would undermine his social standing, so he made her promise never to tell. But Elizabeth knew, and she called the baby a "mongrel"; and clearly Willem's slaves, Gerrit and Isaac, also knew.

This is where the story becomes tragic. Trijntje, by now so traumatised at being caught in the hateful battle between her lover and her owner, started to resent the child. Perhaps it was a case of post-natal depression – we only know that she seriously neglected and even abused the baby.

Under instructions from Willem, Trijntje started to poison Elizabeth with seeds, roots and all sorts of unknown substances, and placing human hair and nails in her food. Willem had his slave Gerrit cut off the hand of a cadaver and told Trijntje to bury it under Elizabeth's bed. All this was too much for Trijntje and she ran away, hiding in a cave on Lion's Head for a while and spending some nights with Willem. But eventually she went back to Elizabeth.

This time Trijntje cracked. She stuffed goose feathers down her baby's throat and he died three days later. She was arrested soon after, but not for the murder of her baby: Elizabeth had become ill and told the authorities that Trijntje was poisoning her. The doctor who examined Elizabeth found goose down and human hair in her faeces.

The trial began in February 1713. The accused were Trijntje, Willem's slaves Gerrit and Isaac, and Elizabeth's slave Carel. They were charged with poisoning and bewitching Elizabeth. Willem Menssink was not charged with any crime nor called as a witness.

Most of what we know about Trijntje's tragic story and her

relationship with Willem Menssink comes from the records of that court case. Trijntje was found guilty of poisoning her owner, of adultery with Menssink, of cruelty to her child and conspiring with the other slaves against Elizabeth.

At the age of twenty-five, Trijntje of Madagascar was taken to a place of public execution in Cape Town, bound to a pole and strangled to death with a cord. Her body, if the sentence of the Court of Justice was indeed carried out to the letter, was fastened to a forked post and left to rot for the birds to devour.

Menssink's slave Gerrit was sentenced to stand beneath the gallows with a noose around his neck while being branded and having his back flogged. Further, he was sentenced to life in chains and with hard labour and banished to Robben Island. Isaac was also flogged and branded, but only sent to the island for two years. These sentences were handed down in March 1713.

The worst that happened to Willem Menssink was that he was kicked out of the Burgher Council for adultery and his wife was granted a divorce. This was justice at the Cape during the seventeenth and eighteenth century. Menssink died in October 1721.

A last word about this unsavoury man. In 1705 a group of wealthy farmers under Menssink's former father-in-law, Adam Tas, and his old friend, Henning Husing, organised a petition against Cape governor Willem Adriaan van der Stel. Menssink was an active co-conspirator and petitioner.

Part of their petition complained that whites were feeling insecure. The Khoikhoi would attack "the Christians" at the slightest opportunity, they said, as would the "Caffers, Moulattos, Mesticos, Casticos and all the black riff-raff". The petitioners, who included Willem Menssink, expressed their disgust at the number of racially mixed marriages and concluded that "Ham's blood" was "not to be trusted".

It was indeed forbidden at this time for white men to have sex with slaves or Khoikhoi women, but it was fairly common nonetheless. Marriages were permitted if the slave was freed and became a Christian. This is why a good chunk of the South African people's genetic make-up originates in India, Sri Lanka, Madagascar, the East Indies and African countries such as Angola, Mozambique and Guinea.

During the first 150 years following the permanent Dutch settlement at the Cape, some sixty thousand slaves were brought to South Africa. This is a lot, considering the small number of people who lived at the southernmost tip of Africa during this period. More than 1 200 marriages between white settlers and slaves or freed slaves or their offspring were recorded during this time. It is unlikely that there is a single Afrikaans-speaker, white or brown, alive today who does not have some slave ancestry, and there are many other South Africans who have some of this blood in their veins.

These are healthy genes to have. Only the strongest and most resourceful slaves survived the unspeakable conditions under which they had to live and the treatment meted out to them.

Looking back from the twenty-first century, it seems strange that the European settlers never tried to capture the indigenous Khoikhoi people as slaves – one couldn't be a slave in one's own country of origin, it seems. They did subjugate the Khoikhoi and at times treated them brutally; they did occupy the Khoikhoi's land and used them as farm labourers. But they could never be owned and sold or kept in chains.

It is even harder to comprehend the settlers' complex attitudes towards slaves. They were bought and sold at auctions like cattle, with potential buyers prodding at them and examining their teeth to assess if they were healthy. So fickle was the prejudice that when the slaves gained their freedom by buying it or being offered it by a European, they stopped being cattle and became human beings again. Many white men fell in love with slave women, often marrying them. "Free blacks", as freed slaves were known at the time, often became successful traders or farmers who owned slaves themselves and sometimes employed white settlers as labourers.

An interesting early example is Angela of Bengal, a remarkable Indian slave woman brought to the Cape by magistrate Pieter Kemp, and sold to Jan van Riebeeck. In 1662 Van Riebeeck sold her to Abraham Gabbema, who liberated her four years later "out of pure goodwill". She was only the third slave to be freed at the Cape.

Angela was given a small plot in what we today call Cape Town's City Bowl, where she grew vegetables to sell to passing ships. She soon became quite wealthy, even employing a slave by the name of Scipio Africanus. Angela complied with all the white community's minimum standards for entry into their society: she was baptised as a Christian, attended church regularly and spoke Dutch.

In 1669 she married the Dutch free burgher Arnoldus Willemsz Basson and bore him three sons, Willem, Gerrit and Johannes. Within a few years after her husband's death she had more than doubled the joint estate. All her children from her two marriages married white people and many living Afrikaner families have her as their ancestral mother.

Angela's apparent happy life at the Cape was surely an exception, as the treatment handed to Trijntje, Gerrit and Isaac has shown. Slaves were the first to carry the *dompas*: when they were away from their place of work, for instance when they were carrying messages, they had to carry a signed and dated letter from their masters. Cowherds and shepherds had to carry a lead medal with their master's name engraved on it. At night they were obliged to carry torches, and were not allowed to gather in groups of more than three.

But the worst was the punishment for transgressions. Just a few months after the first shipment of slaves arrived in 1658, a number escaped. When they were caught, the VOC's Council of Justice ordered that the ringleader be branded with a red-hot iron on the cheek. Fearing more escapes, Van Riebeeck ordered slave owners to stop beating and mistreating their slaves.

But it got a lot worse. In 1660 two slaves, Willem and Claes, were branded and severely flogged for killing the dogs of a Khoikhoi man. In 1669, a slave named Susanna was accused of killing the baby she had with a white VOC employee. She "confessed" after torture with thumbscrews. The Council ordered her breasts to be ripped off with red-hot irons and that she be burnt alive. Eventually the sentence was commuted and she was sewn in a sack and drowned at sea.

In the early 1670s the slaves Claes and Jan were found guilty of attempted burglary. Their cheeks were branded, each had one ear cut off and they were forced to work for twelve years in chains. In 1675 Domingo of Angola, owned by one Elbert Diemer, was hanged for stealing a sheep. That same year, two of Diemer's other slaves stole cabbages from the VOC garden. They were flogged, branded on their cheeks, had their ears cut off and had to spend the rest of their lives in chains. Cees, a fifteen-year-old slave, was hanged for stealing a sheep.

In 1681 Anthony of Coromandel, owned by the freed slave Louis of Bengal, was flogged, branded, the middle finger of each hand and the tip of his nose were cut off, and he spent the rest of his life in chains. His crime? He tried to run away. He was luckier than Francis of Batavia who was condemned to death by being broken on the wheel, or Ary of Madagascar who was burnt alive at the stake in 1679 for murder. In 1689 an Indian slave who stole silver buttons from his owner was hanged and his body left for the birds to eat.

These are just a few recorded examples of how slaves were punished. But the regular cutting off of slaves' noses, ears and hands became a problem. By the early 1700s the sight of large numbers of horribly disfigured slaves offended the white settlers, "particularly pregnant women", and in 1727 it was decided to scale down on these punishments and brand slaves on their backs rather than their faces.

No wonder so many slaves attacked their masters or tried to run away. At night the white inhabitants of Cape Town could see the fires of runaway slaves on the slopes of Table Mountain. But most were recaptured, many by the Khoikhoi, because the settlers put huge pressure on them to cooperate.

Once a group of slaves tried to regain their freedom even before they were delivered to Cape Town. This is their story.

There was a shortage of slaves at the Cape in 1765, so the VOC sent the *Meermin* to Madagascar to buy some. Captain Christoffel Muller quickly found enough slaves, and by 20 January 1766 he had 140 male and female slaves on board and sailed back to the Cape.

The rule of the slave trade at the time determined that male slaves on ships be chained. Since this could endanger the health of the slaves (they were only valuable if they were healthy), the ship's doctor warned Muller that he had no medicine to treat sick slaves. The chains were removed.

Captain Muller clearly ran a festive ship. He and chief mate Olof Jacobus Leij and pilot Daniel van Rostock threw fine parties with lots of wine and slave women dancing national dances.

So relaxed was the atmosphere on the ship that in late February the man in charge of the slaves ordered them to clean the firearms and some assegais bought in Madagascar. When he went to collect the arms, one of the slaves stabbed him in the chest with an assegai. An armed guard shot one of the slaves and killed him, but by now all the slaves were attacking. Captain Muller went to investigate and was wounded, but in the chaos he managed to escape down below. His crew fought back, but soon the slaves took control of the deck and most of the thirty guardsmen were dead. Armed slaves were guarding the entrances to below. Some guards climbed into the rigging, but the slaves told them that if they came down they would be allowed to join their comrades below deck. But as they reached the deck they were thrown overboard, and the slaves threw assegais at them into the water. Those who didn't drown became shark food.

Those who knew how to sail the vessel were now all below deck. They ate raw potatoes, but kept their spirits up by consuming a barrel of wine. On the third day they exploded a quantity of gunpowder, which scared the slaves. Chief mate Olof Leij, now in charge after the captain was wounded, sent a message via a female slave that they should negotiate. The slaves agreed.

The deal they struck was that the crew would be allowed back on deck and not harmed, but they had to turn the *Meermin* to Madagascar. The crew promised not to carry out their threat of blowing up the whole ship. Leij and his men then sailed west in daytime, but quietly turned the vessel around at night, trying to make for the African coast. They knew they were in the region of False Bay when the revolt had started, but they kept this from the slaves. When they saw land, it was near Cape Agulhas, although Leij convinced the slaves it was Madagascar. The *Meermin* anchored a few kilometres into sea.

Between fifty and seventy slaves boarded two boats and rowed ashore. The arrangement was that if all was well, they would light three fires and send the boats back to the ship.

Meanwhile, white farmers of the area saw the ship and noticed that it wasn't flying a flag, which indicated that there was something wrong. Word spread, and a number of them gathered behind the dunes on the shore. When the slaves landed, the farmers ambushed them. About fourteen were killed and the rest laid down their arms.

The nervous crew sent two messages saying that three fires should be lit immediately in order to mislead the slaves on board. They placed the notes in bottles and threw them overboard. Miraculously, a Khoikhoi man and a farmer found the bottles. The local landdrost was given the messages and ordered three fires to be lit. At the sight of the fires the slaves on the ship rejoiced. But they had no boats, so they cut the anchors and the *Meermin* drifted towards the beach.

The leader of the slaves got into a canoe with four others, but they were captured when they reached the beach. Anxious crew members jumped overboard and swam ashore. By now the remaining slaves on the ship realised what was going on and attacked the crew, who were still ensconced below deck.

The *Meermin* ran aground. The gifted negotiator Leij convinced the slaves that if they gave up their arms and surrendered, all would be forgiven. They surrendered and were immediately chained. The farmers on the shore cheered when the Dutch flag was again raised on the *Meermin*.

The *Meermin* soon began to break up and wrecked. All aboard were rescued. The surviving 112 slaves were taken to Cape Town. We can only imagine the life they lived.

An Iziko Museums team under Dr Jaco Boshoff has determined that the *Meermin* had run aground in the Heuningnes River estuary at the mouth of the Zoetendalsvlei Valley between Arniston and Struisbaai. This area is now a nature reserve called Die Mond. The Iziko team started their search for the wreck with magnetometers and metal detectors in 2004.

5

The Great Lover of the Mohokare Valley

BEFORE WE MEET THE LOVER OF THE MOHOKARE Valley, the Bard of the Bakoena, we need to make the acquaintance of his father, one of the proudest of the Basotho ancestors. Monaheng, who lived about 350 years ago, was a great chief of the Bakoena, a people who later became one of the important building blocks of the Basotho nation. It was Monaheng who led the Bakoena into the Mohokare (Caledon) Valley, which is now on the border of South Africa and Lesotho. He built his village at Fothane, known today as Fouriesburg, and soon became a powerful and influential man in the region.

Monaheng was first known by the name Kali. One day, when he was still a young chief, he met a Bushman who was desperate for a pipe of dagga, a crop grown by many of the black farmers of the time. He said to Kali: "*U mphe matakoane Mosotho oa ke me ke tla u nea monaheng oako o motle*" – "Give me some dagga, my Mosotho, and I will give you my beautiful country." (A bit like the biblical story of Jacob and Esau and the mess of potage.) Only, the Bushman had made a mistake – he didn't speak Sesotho very well, so instead of *monaheng*, he should have said *monaha*, meaning land. The Bakoena elders fell about laughing at the mistake, and from that day onwards Kali was known as Monaheng.

Before he led his people from the area today known as Gauteng to the Caledon Valley, his first wife bore him twin sons. Twins obviously ran in the family, because Monaheng's father, Tsoloane, also had a twin brother, called Tsolo.

It was a custom in those rough days to kill the weaker of twin babies to allow the other one a better chance of survival. It is not known why Monaheng's grandfather, Molemo, refused to kill either Tsolo or Tsoloane, but we know Monaheng looked at his two identical babies and they were so beautiful and healthy that he defied the advice of the elders and let them both live. As a compromise and to escape the wrath of the evil spirits, he gave them contemptuous names: Monyane [the insignificant one] and Mokheseng [scorn him]. In fact, Monyane's name was quite prophetic, because he turned out to be a rather mundane and boring man and is only remembered because of his very famous son.

Mokheseng, on the other hand, became one of the most flamboyant figures in South Africa in the seventeenth century.

Mokheseng was Monaheng's favourite son. He was an energetic, adventurous boy, one historian even calling him "happy and reckless". As a teenager he proved himself as an exceptional hunter and a brave and skilful fighter, and he soon became the head of his chiefdom's army.

The extroverted Mokheseng later established his own village in the area between what is today Lindley and Senekal, but he spent much of his time at his beloved father's village at Fothane. From there they planned expeditions and cattle raids or attacks on neighbouring chiefdoms.

By the time he was in his twenties, Mokheseng was already famous in the region as a poet and a singer – the Bard of the Bakoena. In fact, he wrote all the Bakoena's war and circumcision songs, many of which are still sung and recited in Lesotho.

But three centuries on, the old folk of Lesotho and the eastern Free State remember this early ancestor of theirs mostly for another reason: his insatiable appetite for women. Lots of them, maidens and married ones. Mokheseng was the ultimate ladies' man: he was a handsome, well-built fellow, a fearless hunter, a brave and accomplished warrior, a leader of men. On top of it all, he had the gift of the gab.

As is so often the case with men, his womanising was greatly admired by his father, the elders and his peers. Mokheseng became a bit of a legend in his own time; his conquests were the topic of many conversations around the late-evening fire or over a few calabashes of beer. His fellow warriors lived their fantasies through him. Many of them suspected that he had seduced their own wives, and more often than not they were right. But no one ever dared confront him.

But this weakness soon developed another side. Like so many powerful politicians before and since, he couldn't separate his political prowess from his sexual prowess. Mokheseng started lusting after other chiefs' wives. He would often go on visits to villages, ostensibly to pay the chief a courtesy visit, but actually to check out his wives. It became an obsession. He would stop at nothing to conquer the beautiful wife of a fellow chief. His father had begun the strategy of marrying the daughters of chiefs of other clans for political purposes, but Mokheseng did not have politics on his mind.

Dr David-Frédéric Ellenberger, a Swiss missionary who worked in Lesotho in the nineteenth century and who did more than anyone before him to meticulously record the history and traditions of the Basotho, wrote of Mokheseng: "He would conceive a desire for the wife of this or that chief, and would never rest until he possessed her by force or fraud. It is sad to relate that his personal advantages and reputation for gallantry were such that the ladies in question were not, as a rule, averse to his attentions."

Sad for whom, I wonder.

(Ellenberger was obsessed with recording Basotho genealogy, history and customs. Behind his back, people said his attitude was:

Do you want to know about God and Jesus? I'll tell you, but first you have to tell me who your ancestors were and where they came from.)

Mokheseng might have had many women, but, unlike his father, he only married twice and had four sons. It is not known how his wives felt about his philandering. His only son by his second wife was named Tlali, and so Mokheseng became known by a new name, Ratlali – father of Tlali.

As he became older, Ratlali's obsession became more serious. Two, three times a year he would lead his men into battle against another chiefdom, to take their cattle and, probably more importantly, to kidnap the chief's most beautiful wife. He built up quite a collection of these captured queens, and from time to time he would parade them to the envy of all the men in the region.

Of course, such an obsession was inevitably going to lead to trouble. One day Ratlali led his warriors to Makalane, probably in the region of today's Phuthaditjhaba, to attack his cousin Liyo, who was the chief of the Makhoakhoa. He had visited his cousin several times and his desire for Liyo's exceptionally beautiful wife, Matumane, was burning him up.

The attack was completely unexpected, because the two chiefdoms had a good relationship and the chiefs were, after all, related. Ratlali did not even tell his own men the real reason for the attack – his cover was he wanted to subjugate the Makhoakhoa on behalf of his father.

The Makhoakhoa were not prepared for an attack, and Ratlali's men drove them out of the village and captured all their cattle without much trouble. Ratlali could not contain himself and ravished the beautiful Matumane right there before leading his men back to Fothane.

It was just too easy. The Bakoena warriors were singing and dancing as they drove the captured cattle back home. But the Makhoakhoa and their chief were outraged. They quickly summoned the assistance of their neighbours, the Basia, and pursued the aggressors. Not even a day later they launched a surprise attack on the retiring Bakoena warriors. They took back all their cattle and killed many of the Bakoena, including one of Ratlali's other brothers, Motloang.

The Makhoakhoa and their Basia allies were relentless: they wanted to punish the arrogant Ratlali and free the wife of Chief Liyo – it was a question of honour. Ratlali and a few of his men who had travelled ahead with Matumane were soon overtaken by the Basia warriors.

The Basia chief, Tsele, himself stabbed Ratlali to death. Matumane was taken back to Makalane. For Ratlali she was one queen too many.

Chief Monaheng sent some of his men to fetch Ratlali's dead body for a proper burial. In a break with long-standing tradition, the Makhoakhoa attacked the men and killed several of them.

Ratlali's body was left in the open veld to be devoured by vultures.

As so often happens in life, Ratlali went from hero to villain in an instant. His behaviour was scandalous, people suddenly said – the same people who had revelled in the stories of his conquests. He had no respect, they said, and how did he think he was going to get away with it? Still, young men quietly kept his memory alive as an icon of Koena virility, and three centuries on people still talk about the Stud of Fothane.

The deaths of his two sons at the hands of the Makhoakhoa and the Basia were a heavy blow to the aging Monaheng, and to his prestige as a chief. To make matters worse, Monaheng's surviving sons started a bloody conflict over who had the rights to Ratlali's prize widows and concubines. Monaheng died soon after, a broken man.

His other sons, including Ratlali's twin brother Monyane, were mediocre men and insignificant chiefs. But Monyane's son Mohlomi would later restore the great name of the Monaheng family.

6

The African
Socrates

THE ABORIGINAL PEOPLE OF SOUTH AFRICA AND THE
black farmers who moved into the country from further
north around two thousand years ago did not read and write until
Europeans arrived in the seventeenth century. For many white
observers, it followed that they were backward.

The story of the man I call the African Socrates (or, as aptly,
Confucius) is just one powerful example to show that these early
societies were as advanced as those in Europe and the East, and
spiritually perhaps even more so. Reading and writing required
books and paper and writing instruments and libraries. The people
who first populated South Africa did not live stable lives in big,
permanent cities. They were hunters and farmers who lived a far
more temporary and immediate existence. In place of writing, they
developed a sophisticated oral tradition to record and transfer
information.

The philosopher of this story died years before his people
became literate, yet we know quite a lot about his extraordinary
life. He was the nephew of Ratlali, the Lover of Mohokare, and
the grandson of Bakoena chief Monaheng. Let's pick up the story
from there.

Old Chief Monaheng had one last day of joy before he died – a
day that was later celebrated not only by the Bakoena, but also by
the other peoples of central South Africa.

On that day, Monaheng sent his grandson, Tlali, to punish the Basia chief Tsele for killing Ratlali. Tlali was successful, to Monaheng's great satisfaction. But that wasn't the great event. On that very same day (it was 1720 or thereabouts), Ratlali's twin brother Monyane's wife gave birth to a son. Grandfather Monaheng rushed to Monyane's hut to welcome the baby and named him Mohlomi, meaning the Founder or the Builder.

"This boy is going to be a great chief one day," Monaheng said proudly. "He will be the founder of many new villages."

Mohlomi was true to his name and his grandfather's predictions, and then some. He became the greatest philosopher, prophet and healer southern Africa had ever known. Towards the end of his life he instructed and anointed a young man who would later change the face of South Africa through his wisdom, diplomacy and extraordinary nation-building. His name was Morena Moshoeshoe, the founder and king of the Basotho nation.

Mohlomi's unusual life as a mystic began one night at the age of thirteen or fourteen, while he was undergoing the initiation process to reach manhood. There are several versions of this event – not one of them by any means ordinary.

After his death in 1815, Mohlomi's widow, Maliepollo, told the French missionary Thomas Arbousset: "My husband used to have communion with heaven. Once, when he was about thirteen years old, during the months which he passed in the circumcision lodge, after nightfall when his companions slept, he saw the roof of the hut open wide and he was carried up to the skies, where there was a great multitude of people assembled. There it was said to him, 'Go, rule by love, and look on thy people as men and brothers.' He brought back with him a heart honest and wise."

Another, more elaborate version comes from Ntsu Mokhehle, who later became the independent Kingdom of Lesotho's prime minister. From 1941 onwards, Mokhehle interviewed many of the old people of Lesotho who had the gift of remembering the past.

Many of them were in their nineties, so they lived just a few decades after Mohlomi's death. In a booklet published in 1976, *Moshoeshoe I Profile*, Mokhehle used the recollections of these elders to construct Mohlomi's own version of this event. This is how they told the story of his legendary, life-changing experience.

In his vision, Mohlomi said, there was a strong hurricane and it became very dark. Then he saw a ball of very bright light descending on the *mophato* [initiation hut] in which he slept. The roof opened and an eagle landed in the hut. The eagle put Mohlomi on its back and flew over the highest mountains to the highest peak, where it dropped him off. He noticed that he was surrounded by old men and women.

One of these elders then spoke to him. "My child, be not afraid, because at this place where you are now, you are meeting with your departed ancestral souls, the *Balimo*. You are in the presence of those who care and protect you while on earth." The old man continued: "You will grow to be a chief, you will rule over men. We, your *Balimo*, say to you: go and rule your people well. Always temper your actions with justice and sympathy. Care for the needy, especially children. The elderly men and women must be so looked after in your rule that the unbearable burden of old age shall not be a source of discomfort for them."

Another missionary, JP Bruwer, wrote in a fascinating book published in the early twentieth century, called *Manne van die Bantoe*, that the Balimo told Mohlomi to "go and rule your people with wisdom and love. Let all people be your brothers and sisters." All the versions of Mohlomi's vision, including that of Professor LBBJ Machobane of Roma University in Lesotho, published in 1978, state that the Balimo instructed Mohlomi to immerse himself in the study of medicines, to learn how to treat sick people.

Mokhehle stressed that according to Mohlomi he did not have a dream, called *toro* in Sesotho, but a *pono*, a vision. He had "joined the spiritual configuration of his Balimo", who then spoke to him through a dream. "I clearly recollected – even as I do to the present – the whole event and clearly remembered the things they said to me. Their orders and their directives remained fixed in my mind in their clarity and proper sequence," Mokhehle quoted Mohlomi through the versions of the old people he interviewed.

Mohlomi's psychic powers were soon given expression. Not long after he had the vision, his father, Chief Monyane, conspired with two other chiefs, Liyane and Ramokhele, to raid the cattle of the Leghoya chief Mahoete. Very early on the morning of the raid, the young Mohlomi awoke his father and said: "My father, I lay awake last night. And although I did not sleep, I dreamed, and in my dream I saw you dead. I beg you, do not go on this raid. Please, leave it and stay right here."

Monyane reacted angrily and called his son a girl: "Go, draw water with the other girls."

Perhaps Monyane *did* wonder whether his son's dream was true, because he withdrew from the raid at the last minute. But after the successful raid he realised that among the cattle captured by the other two chiefs was Moupello oa Likhomo, the ox famous throughout the land. This was a magnificent beast, larger than any other, and pure white, with a proud black head. Monyane just had to have it for himself, and he set about doing just that.

Liyane and Ramokhele wouldn't part with their bounty, especially not the famous ox, so Monyane launched a war against them. During the fierce battle he was hit in the leg with a poisoned arrow from the bow of a Bushman fighting with Ramokhele.

Monyane, as his son had predicted, died on the spot.

After this incident, people started to take Mohlomi more seriously, and his stature grew. He became a respected chief in the area around Hlohloane (white people who could not pronounce it, later renamed it Clocolan), with his main village at Ngoliloe, now a commercial farm just north-west of the present town of Clocolan. He chose this place because of the Bushman rock paintings in the rock overhangs – the name came from the phrase *"ke melimo e ngolileng moo"* – "the spirits have written there".

Mohlomi quickly became a popular and wealthy chief. But he left much of his duties as a chief to his counsellors, because he travelled a great deal and was much in demand in the region as an adviser, healer and psychiatrist.

If Mohlomi lived today, he would be world famous not only as an original thinker, but probably as something of a New Age guru. He was an ascetic with a high degree of self-control. He was extremely fit and ate very little, certainly no rich foods. He only ever drank water and milk. He never smoked tobacco or dagga – in fact, he lectured everybody with whom he came in contact against smoking and drinking. He wore large earrings and a brass collar around his neck. Later in life, admittedly after fathering a number of children, he opted for celibacy so that he could purify his spirit – he did not even have sex with his favourite wife, Maliepollo. He loved spending his time with children – "the young are the better", he used to say, explaining that their minds had not yet been corrupted and that they could still understand the natural truths.

Mohlomi loved to have long philosophical discussions with other wise men. Long after his death, people remembered that he often pondered these questions: Where does the universe begin and where does it end? What is life, and how is it created? He argued strongly that there had to be one Creator of all things and believed that souls were immortal.

His beliefs were similar to oriental philosophies and the law of karma, although he never came into contact with anyone but indigenous Africans. Conscience was man's only guide, Mohlomi said. "Conscience is the faithful monitor of man; she invariably shows him what is his duty. If he does well, she smiles upon him; if he does evil, she torments him. This inward guide takes us under her guidance when we leave the womb, and she accompanies us to the entrance of the tomb."

Love and you will be loved, hate and you will be hated, Mohlomi said. If you are kind and generous to others, especially the unfortunate and weak, fate will be your friend. If you are selfish and cruel, misfortune is sure to cross the path of your life sooner or later.

Mohlomi was also a pacifist. According to Ntsu Mokhehle's interviewees, he had disbanded all his chiefdom's fighting units. This was unprecedented in those troubled times. He instructed his warriors to go home, to till the land and to look after their wives and children.

Mohlomi's teachings were directed at the society he lived in and its most pressing problems. These problems included the abuse of power by chiefs and kings, armed conflict between chiefdoms and clans, the abuse of alcohol and dagga, witchcraft, and the ill-treatment of women and children. His maxims became part of future Basotho morality.

"It is better to thrash the corn than to shape the spear," was a Mohlomi proverb that was repeated long after his death. As was "Peace is my Sister", a sister being a person who was in a fragile position in society and to be looked after, protected and cherished. Another version of this philosophy was: "A knobkerrie is far more valuable when used to harvest the grain than to kill men on the battlefield." His advice to chiefs and headmen was: "When you sit in judgment, let your decisions be just. The law knows no one as a poor man."

But possibly his most famous saying of all, now proclaimed by many a Mosotho historian as a call to democracy, was: "A chief is a chief by the grace of his people."

Even the early European Christian missionaries of the nineteenth century, most of whom saw the indigenous people of South Africa as primitive, or, at best, as children needing education, spoke highly of Mohlomi. The Swiss missionary Dr David-Frédéric Ellenberger, to whom we owe much of the written records of Mohlomi's life, reflected that some men are born great and others have greatness thrust upon them, and said: "Mohlomi was born great." Elsewhere he wrote that Mohlomi was famous for his love of peace, his charity to all and his wisdom. "He was a teacher of men, and his teaching had far-reaching effects in humanising all the Basotho tribes. He established confidence between man and man, and chiefs and people with one voice sought to honour Mohlomi for his wisdom and for the love he bore to all men."

The Afrikaans missionary JP Bruwer called Mohlomi "a counsellor with deep wisdom". The French missionary Eugéne Cassalis referred to him as a chief of great benevolence "whose name is often invoked in times of public calamity".

Mohlomi took it upon himself to spread his message of peace, love, tolerance and good governance to the other peoples of the African subcontinent. At the same time, he studied these societies and analysed what made them peaceful and prosperous or struggling and failing.

With only a walking stick and a calabash of water, and accompanied by a few unarmed men, he regularly traversed the areas north and south of the Vaal River. He walked as far as present-day KwaZulu-Natal, Transkei, Northern Cape, Mpumalanga and Limpopo, even visiting parts of Botswana and possibly Zimbabwe. On several occasions he undertook journeys that kept him away from home for several years. He must have travelled tens of thousands of kilometres in his full life of about ninety-five years.

Mohlomi could be called southern Africa's first Africanist. Other African chiefs of the time rarely, if ever, visited other chiefdoms, especially those who spoke different languages. Mohlomi revelled in discovering the different cultures and customs of the other groups in southern Africa. He saw all African people as one, and proclaimed all as his brothers and sisters. It was a very unusual attitude for the eighteenth century. (It is unlikely that Mohlomi ever met a white person during his life. The first white travellers and missionaries only reached the central parts of South Africa in the years after 1815, when he died.)

Mohlomi's reputation and positive attitude were such that he never feared for his safety during his travels. He was well received everywhere and was consulted as a kind of oracle.

Around 1782, Mohlomi was on a long visit to the Limpopo Valley area, where he had several interactions with Venda chiefs. There are also accounts of a visit Mohlomi made to the far end of the Kalahari Desert, where he met a tribe called *Ma-ya-ntja*, "eaters of dogs". These people measured their wealth by the number of dogs, rather than cattle, they owned. One couldn't keep cattle in the desert.

While visiting here, he accumulated a large number of dogs, probably as payment for healing people and advising them about their problems. He married a young woman from the tribe and paid her dowry in dogs. He even had a son with her, a man named Moriri, who died in Lesotho in 1883.

Marrying young women or the daughters of the chiefs he visited became Mohlomi's strategy for ensuring peace and good relation-ships. It is generally believed that he had forty wives – the norm of the time was for a chief to have four or five – but that number excludes the wives he did not take back to his village. He would pay such a woman's dowry and build her a hut, but allow her to choose her own "protector" and sexual partner in her village. In other instances, he would find wives for men who could not afford to pay a dowry, and pay it on their behalf.

In both cases Mohlomi had made a good investment: the children of these couples were legally his and the dowries paid to their daughters had to be paid to him. Some say he never claimed these benefits, but regardless, it was in his interest for so many people to be indebted to him. It is said that, before he died, the number of wives and children he had accumulated far exceeded a thousand souls.

The white missionaries of the time never fully comprehended this strategy, later emulated by his anointed successor, Moshoeshoe.

Dr Ellenberger remarked that it was "to be regretted that a man otherwise so enlightened as Mohlomi should have shown an example of sexual irregularity, and have given rise to a polygamy which killed the consciences of those who gave themselves up to it".

Mohlomi brought back many cultural and artistic items from his travels. His most prized acquisition was a cotton handkerchief he was given by a man somewhere in the north who had bought it from a Portuguese trader in Mozambique. Mohlomi's love of this piece of strange, woven cloth reminds us of Kenneth Kaunda, another proud African leader, who became president of Zambia 150 years after Mohlomi's death: he always clutched a white handkerchief in his hand when he appeared in public. It was as if Mohlomi realised that this cloth symbolised a completely different world and culture of which he had no real knowledge.

Mohlomi was also famous as a healer and medicine man. He had a thorough knowledge of the herbs, leaves, roots and bark that had healing properties. It was said that he even had a cure for leprosy. But, as one with a deep knowledge of people, he knew that many sicknesses had their roots in an unhappy mental state and treated this at the same time.

The black farmers of the time often asked the Bushman shamans to bring rain in time of drought. But not when Mohlomi was around: he was the most successful *moroka*, rainmaker, of the time.

Dr Ellenberger, who had studied medicine as well as theology in Switzerland, almost wanted to believe that Mohlomi actually had the power to bring rain. He wrote: "His process is not known in detail; but in times of drought he would shut himself up in his secret place and manipulate herbs, roots, etc., stirring up a concoction of them with a reed, and invoking the aid of the Supreme Being through the intercession of the shades of his ancestors. It may be that, being a good judge of the weather, like most intelligent natives, he used to occupy himself in this manner just when rain was probable; it may have been pure coincidence; or again, that the

Almighty did indeed hear and answer the prayers of this untaught old heathen: the reader must choose the explanation which suits him. But the fact remains that rain did come certainly on one occasion, probably on more, for Mohlomi's fame in this respect was very great."

But Mohlomi never threw the divining bones, and wherever he went he warned against witch doctors. Once, he hid a shield, and then reported that it had disappeared mysteriously. Several witch doctors from the region were called in. They threw their bones and then started to accuse some of the people present. Mohlomi then produced the shield, calling the witch doctors liars and deceivers.

At the times that Mohlomi was home at Ngoliloe, there were usually long queues of people waiting to be healed or advised or wanting disputes settled. On one such occasion, around 1804, when he had returned from a long journey and was seeing patients at a neighbouring village, an important event took place.

We must first go back to 1786 or thereabouts, to the small village of Menkhoaneng, northern Lesotho, where a boy was born to Mokhachane, a petty chief of the Mokoteli clan of the Bakoena, and his wife Kholu, a member of the Bafokeng. Mokhachane's father, Peete, was the son of one of chief Monaheng's brothers, Motloang. The new baby, named Lepoqo, was thus a distant cousin of Mohlomi.

Lepoqo was a troubled boy. He had a violent temper and believed from a young age that he was going to be a great chief. This was odd, because the Mokoteli clan was small and insignificant. Lepoqo bossed his young friends around and once killed five of them for not show- ing him proper respect. But he proved his physical and leadership skills during his initiation, and because of this he was renamed Tlapule, the Busy One, while others called him Letlama, the Binder. But a few years later he would get a new name, a name which would make him famous all over southern Africa and beyond: Moshoeshoe.

The young man's father and grandfather were concerned about his temper and odd behaviour, and so took him to Mohlomi to be given medicine. Those waiting in line to see Mohlomi were surprised to see the wise old sage welcoming the two men and the teenager as if he knew they were going to come. He made special time over the next three days to consult with them.

Grandfather Peete introduced the troubled young man to Mohlomi, and Lepoqo, as he was then still known, confirmed that he had a burning ambition to be a chief over chiefs, a powerful man with many subjects and cattle. That was why he was so aggressive, he explained, because "wasn't it true that many ordinary people have become chiefs by intimidating, bullying and inspiring others with fear?"

According to Mokhehle's reconstructions, Mohlomi replied: "It is often so. But you have to know that chieftainship founded on people's fear of someone who becomes their chief, and not based upon peace, justice and *botho* [humanism], such chieftainship never goes far; it never stands the test of the difficulties of governing; and even if it holds it never brings benefit to anybody … If you drive people away from you by inspiring people with fear for you and by killing some, whom then are you going to rule? Experience I have gained as a chief as well as also through my extensive travels among other small and great chiefs in different parts of the world has brought me a clear realisation of the fact that a chief becomes and remains a chief only by the people's will, recognition and support."

Lepoqo then begged Mohlomi to give him a talisman or medicine that would enable him to become a powerful chief. Mohlomi answered: "*Motse ha o na sehlare: sehlare ke pelo*" – "Power is not acquired by medicine: the heart is the medicine."

On the second day, Mohlomi explained his personal philosophies in detail and related the experiences of his long journeys. On the third day he gave the young man his final advice. It was a pity Lepoqo could not accompany him on his travels, he said. "You would then learn how men are won by truth and justice and not by the use of spears. If you were to go around with me, you would find where, by justice alone, I established peace; and by genuine and effective healing, love abounds where hatred and suspicion reigned before."

Mohlomi seemed to know when the three men from Menkhoaneng arrived that Lepoqo was destined to become a great leader of people. He would certainly not otherwise have spent three days with him, what with so many other people queuing for his counsel. And when he said farewell to the three, he told Lepoqo: "One day you will truly be a chief and ruler over men. Learn to understand men and know their ways. Learn to bear with their human weaknesses and shortcomings. Always determine to direct them along the paths of truth and purity. In their disputes, adjudicate with justice and sympathy. You must not allow elements of preferences based on wealth, status or prestige to influence and tarnish any of your decisions."

Then, according to Mokhehle's interviews with the elders, he spoke words that became the basis of Moshoeshoe's building of the Basotho nation: "You must be a friend and helper to all those who are in tribulation, the poor and the needy. Travellers of all types should be fully protected throughout the areas of your chiefdom. Fugitives escaping death and persecution in their own homelands should find a ready sanctuary in your land. You should protect them. The land you shall rule should be a home to travellers and fugitives."

Then Mohlomi took off one of his earrings and fixed it to Lepoqo's ear as a symbol of authority. He gave him a black cow, a symbol of hospitality, and a knobkerrie as a symbol of power. He took Lepoqo's head in his hands and rubbed his forehead against the teenager's, saying: "All the experience, knowledge and wisdom with which Molimo [the Supreme Being] and our Balimo have endowed and enriched my mind shall also be nurtured in, inhabit and enrich your intellect for the great work you are to perform."

With that, Lepoqo, Peete and Mokhachane left and went home. Within weeks the elders of the Bamokoteli remarked how radical the change in Lepoqo's behaviour was. Barely fifteen years later he started a remarkable process of accumulating clans and chiefdoms fleeing from the great upheaval that afflicted South Africa from about 1820 onwards, called the Lifaqane in Sesotho, or Mfecane by Nguni-speakers. From the top of his mountain fortress, Thaba Bosiu, he built a new nation out of all these groups and called them the Basotho. If he had not stabilised central South Africa at that time of war and misery, the country's history would probably have been a lot different – and more violent. He could quite rightly be called the Nelson Mandela of the nineteenth century.

(Lepoqo became Moshoeshoe when, shortly after his visit to Mohlomi, he raided the cattle of an opposing chief, Ramonaheng. On his return a praise singer made the sound of a shaving blade, *shwe, shwe*, and chanted that Lepoqo had shaved off Ramonaheng's beard. He thus became Mo-shwe-shwe, or Moshoeshoe as it is spelt in Sesotho.)

According to Peter Becker, author of *Hill of Destiny, the Epic Story of Moshesh*, Moshoeshoe visited Mohlomi again, this time in 1811. After a long conversation, Mohlomi gave his precious handkerchief to him. "Presenting it to Moshoeshoe," writes Becker, "he said there were white-skinned people living in the south of the Maluti mountains, and he advised him to solicit their friendship and to start trading with them." Becker claims the two met again in 1814, and that Moshoeshoe rushed to Mohlomi's deathbed in 1815 and was present when the old man died. Lesotho University historian LBBJ Machobane insists that Moshoeshoe spent a few weeks with Mohlomi.

Ntsu Mokhehle said of Moshoeshoe: "It is not overstretching the point to state that what Jesus Christ was to Paul or Matthew, what Karl Marx was to Lenin or Mao, so was Mohlomi to Moshoeshoe. Jesus, Marx and Mohlomi laid down new principles for the recasting of human society. And Paul, Lenin and Moshoeshoe, each in his own field, built up new societies, state structures and religious institutions to make human society a surety for man's humane existence in this world; to ensure man's security and survival in man's own society-complex."

Mohlomi died in about 1815, several years before the Lifaqane, or even signs that a great upheaval was about to happen. But he predicted it on his deathbed, when he said: "After my death, a cloud of red dust will come out of the east and consume our tribes. The father will eat his children." The cloud from the east was later interpreted as the groups who fled from the land of the Zulu on the east coast and overwhelmed those groups living on the Highveld. The father who eats his children was seen as a reference to the phenomenon of cannibalism that occurred during and after the Lifaqane.

Mohlomi was dead, but perhaps his immortal soul rested peacefully in the knowledge that his dreams for his people were being realised by the young man he had anointed a decade earlier.

7

The Graves
Are Alive

I T SEEMS THAT THE OLD SAGE MOHLOMI HAD ANOTHER
foreboding regarding Moshoeshoe. When he greeted the young
man after their first consultation, he told Moshoeshoe that his
grandfather, Peete, the man who had brought him to Mohlomi,
was his special responsibility.

According to a reconstruction by the Basotho elders interviewed by Ntsu Mokhehle, Mohlomi said: "Young man, my last
words to you are: always keep close to old Peete. Cherish his
friendship and protect him from harm. This old man is endowed
with immeasurable psychic gifts and could serve to keep those
whom he loves in touch with the most illustrious ancestral souls
of our clan. Old Peete still has many years to live. But when the
time comes for his departure from earth to a higher plane, you
must take charge of his corpse. Look after his grave, for you
alone are capable of performing the ritual rites necessary for
assuring his disembodied spirit safe conduct to the domain of his
ancestral souls."

The young Moshoeshoe was indeed close to his grandfather.
Peete's actual name was Motsuane, but he was nicknamed "pete-
pete", someone who repeats everything, and that became Peete
(pronounced *pee-heh-teh*). He was so called because his father,
Mualle, from the Hlubi clan, a Zulu-speaking Nguni group, spoke
Sesotho haltingly and with an accent.

In 1820, the young Chief Moshoeshoe moved his clan from Menkhoaneng to the flat-topped mountain at Botha-Bothe further west. This was at the beginning of the great social and military upheaval on the east coast and in the interior. It wasn't long before the Tlokoa, a Sotho group who lived in the area of modern-day Harrismith, were displaced by the marauding Ngwane and Hlubi groups. The Batlokoa in turn attacked the Bamokoteli and laid siege to Moshoeshoe's mountain.

After the siege ended in June 1824, Moshoeshoe decided to relocate south to an almost impenetrable mountain fortress his scouts had discovered, called Thaba Bosiu. It was a long journey, an arduous route in the bitter cold. Horses were still unknown to the people of central South Africa at the time, so the party had to walk in single file along the footpaths through the mountains.

At the back of the group of travellers were Moshoeshoe's sister, Mamila, who was ill, two of his wives, Maneko and Mamakhobalo, who were pregnant, and the ageing Peete.

This slow-moving group fell behind when they had to traverse the rugged Lipetu Pass near Malimong. Suddenly a band of men jumped out of the bushes and attacked them and tried to capture the women. Men from the main party heard their screams and saved them, but the attackers had succeeded in taking old Peete and a few others with him.

The attackers were cannibals under the leadership of one Rakotsoane. They duly ate Peete and his companions for supper.

Moshoeshoe and his main party had meanwhile pushed on and arrived at Thaba Bosiu that night. The chief was only told of Peete's capture once he had reached the mountain. He was outraged and heartbroken. He was also deeply troubled, remembering that the great Mohlomi had given him the special task of burying Peete with dignity and performing all the necessary rituals. How would he fulfil his task now that his grandfather's body had been consumed by cannibals?

The Bakoena had very strict burial customs. The women of the village would gather round the hut of the deceased and, wailing loudly, praise the dead person. Inside, the man responsible for the burial would bend the corpse's legs and arms, and, using grass ropes, tie him up into a fetal position. If rigor mortis had already set in, the corpse's tendons would be cut and the limbs forced into position. The gall bladder of a specially slaughtered ox would be tied around the wrist of the man preparing the deceased's body. Sandals would be put on the feet and a skin mantle folded over the body.

The corpse would then be placed in a circular hole in a sitting position, facing east. Seeds of grain and pumpkin, bits of thatching grass, the person's pipe or snuff-box and the pot used for milking would be placed with him in the grave for use in the afterlife. The meat and intestines of the ox would be used to purify the grave and the family of the dead person. A flat stone was placed over the corpse and the grave was then filled with earth. The deceased's cattle were then driven over the grave, and the meat of the ox would be consumed by all present.

Moshoeshoe knew he had to do something to ease Peete's passing into the next world, but the absence of a body and a grave presented something of a problem. The elders of his clan, egged on by Peete's son Mokhachane, had no doubt about what had to be done: Rakotsoane and his men had to be captured, brought to Thaba Bosiu, and killed.

As soon as things had settled down at Thaba Bosiu, Moshoeshoe had Rakotsoane and his cannibals brought there. And then he informed his stunned subjects that he wasn't going to kill them. The cannibals, he declared – somewhat like the biblical Solomon – had consumed Peete's flesh and had thus become the living graves of his grandfather. To kill them would be to desecrate Peete's grave.

Moshoeshoe told Rakotsoane and his men to undress and lie down in a row. He then took the ritual purification offal from a specially slaughtered ox and rubbed it over their bodies, so purifying Peete's grave. He sent Rakotsoane and his men away, imploring them to change their ways. Later, he sent them two oxen as a gift.

Rakotsoane did eventually stop eating human flesh and subjected himself to Moshoeshoe's jurisdiction. Eugéne Cassalis, the French missionary stationed with Moshoeshoe from 1833 onwards and who became the king's closest adviser, wrote in 1861 that the king's first priority was to suppress cannibalism. Most of his people despised the cannibals and wanted them to be killed, but Moshoeshoe thought there had been enough killing and he realised that the cannibals themselves found their lifestyle repugnant.

"He therefore answered that man-eaters were living sepulchres, and that one could not fight with sepulchres," Cassalis wrote. "These words were sufficient to rescue the wretches whom he wished to bring to repentance. They saw in the clemency of their chief an unhoped-for means of restoration to their former position, and resolved to avail themselves of it. From that time cannibalism was gradually discontinued. There are critical moments in the fate of nations, when a word suffices to introduce a new era."

Many South Africans, as well as historians and anthropologists worldwide, nowadays reject most accounts of anthropophagi or cannibalism in the past. It is a healthy cynicism. For a long time European travellers and adventurers described the indigenous peoples of Africa, the Americas, the West Indies and the Pacific Islands as man-eaters. In most cases, this was stated without any evidence; in others it was based on hearsay. These Europeans saw their own culture and race as superior, and indigenous peoples as primitive savages. They expressed their superiority and disgust by ascribing the basest human behaviour to these people.

In fact, the word *cannibalism* was derived from the West Indian Carib people. Christopher Columbus was the first European to meet them, and reported that they ate human flesh. No evidence has ever been presented to prove that the Caribs were indeed cannibals.

The accusation of cannibalism was also often used to stress the necessity of civilising foreign peoples, or to demonise others. Medieval Christians, for instance, spread the story that Jews loved to eat Christian babies.

Of course, non-Christians have long remarked that the Christian sacrament of the Eucharist, when believers eat a piece of bread as a symbol of the "body of Christ", is a form of cannibalism.

But cannibalism has existed in different forms worldwide since the birth of the human species, and still exists today. When practised for the sake of survival, it appears to be acceptable to most cultures. A modern example is the case of the Uruguayan rugby club's aeroplane crash in the Andes in 1972. The survivors ate their dead teammates in order to stay alive. This was not frowned upon, because it was accepted that they had little choice.

In 2003 and 2004, United Nations and Doctors without Borders aid workers reported that the devastating famine in North Korea had driven some people to eat human flesh.

Aboriginal peoples in Papua New Guinea and Australia are said to have consumed the flesh of relatives or friends who had died. This ritual, called endocannibalism, was meant to ensure that the dead person's spirit would live on.

The ancient Aztecs are believed to have practised exocannibalism, the ritual eating of enemies. In 2003, a Fijian tribe apologised to the descendants of the missionary Thomas Baker, who was eaten by the tribe a century ago – his offence was that he touched their chief's head. And in 2003, the United Nations accused rebels in the war-ravaged Democratic Republic of Congo of eating body parts of their enemies.

I have come across one confirmed example of this kind of cannibalism in South African history. It took place on 15 August 1865 and also involved Moshoeshoe.

A force of about three thousand men of the Free State Republic under Louw Wepener attacked Thaba Bosiu on that day. Most members of the force, which included a thousand black auxiliaries, rode around the base of the mountain in a show of strength. Late that morning, Wepener and a few hundred of his men started to move up the main pass to the top of the mountain, with the protection of a cannon that shot shells right on top of the mountain.

The Free Staters had not learnt the lesson Moshoeshoe's men had earlier taught the armies of the amaNgwane under Matiwane or the British under George Cathcart. Their attacks on Thaba Bosiu had failed: the mountain was simply impenetrable. They had no answer to the Basotho warriors' tactics of rolling boulders onto their attackers or hiding behind huge rocks and shooting at those who were climbing the mountain.

Wepener and his *agterryer* [afterrider] made some progress up the pass, but the moment he was spotted in a clearing by the Basotho soldiers, he was shot and died on the spot. Shortly afterwards the Basotho charged, and the Boers fled in a hurry. Eleven of them were killed and about thirty injured.

The loss of Wepener was a huge blow to the Free Staters, because he was a popular leader and regarded as a very brave man. Later that night, two of his followers, Carl Mathey and Chris du Randt, quietly sneaked up the side of the mountain to look for his body. When they found it, they dragged it into a shallow trench next to another fallen Boer, Adam Raubenheimer, and went back to their camp.

The Basotho rejoiced at their victory and were especially proud that they had killed the famous Louw Wepener. According to several versions, Moshoeshoe had Wepener's heart cut out and told all his young commanders to eat a piece of it so they could become as brave as Wepener was.

Long after his death, one of the Basotho warriors who had witnessed Wepener's last moments visited his sister, Catherina van Rooyen, on her farm near Harrismith. According to Peter Becker, author of *Hill of Destiny*, the man said that Wepener's heart was first hung in a cave and later eaten. He said Moshoeshoe was present, but did not take part in the eating.

During a visit to Thaba Bosiu in April 2004, I asked a local chief, and Tsediso Ramakhula Sr, one of Lesotho's most respected historians, whether it was true that Wepener's heart had been eaten. Both men said they had no doubt that it happened.

Eleven months after Wepener's death, his son Dick and four friends went to Thaba Bosiu to collect his bones for a proper burial. The young Wepener was greeted warmly by King Moshoeshoe, then almost eighty years old, because he was a great admirer of Wepener's bravery. But Dick Wepener was angry and refused to shake the king's hand. Some sources even allege that he called Moshoeshoe a "kaffir" and demanded to know where his father was buried.

The king was upset at the insult, but showed more patience than usual with the son of the dead hero. Dick apparently regretted his outburst, since most versions of the incident say he apologised to Moshoeshoe. The king's son, Tladi, took Dick Wepener to where his father was buried, at the place where his two young admirers had left his body. Tladi apparently told Wepener that his father's heart had been eaten by the warriors. Wepener nevertheless thanked the king and took his father's bones to be buried on the family farm.

Modern historians have expressed serious doubt regarding the earlier accounts of cannibalism among the indigenous peoples of South Africa. Dr David-Frédéric Ellenberger, the missionary who recorded so much of the Basotho history, wrote that Mohlomi once visited a group of Venda cannibals in northern South Africa, and stated that it was widely known that many Venda had been man-eaters for generations. Researchers could never find any proof that there were ever any cannibals among the Venda.

But few historians contest the stories of cannibalism in the Free State and Lesotho areas during the 1820s and 1830s. These were good examples of survival cannibalism: the social and military upheaval of the time, the Lifaqane, had caused such serious famine that some people's survival was dependent on eating human flesh.

In his book *The Basutos*, Eugéne Cassalis published a transcript of an interview he had with an old Mosotho named Mapike about his experiences among the cannibals of Rakotsoane at the infamous Malimong cave. Mapike was sent to the cave to negotiate the release of his chief's wife, who had been captured by the cannibals. This is what Mapike said: "We … climbed the steep ascent that led to the cave of the anthropophagi. But hardly had we reached it when our legs began to tremble, and a thrill of horror ran through our veins: nothing was to be seen but skulls and broken bones. A woman uncovered a pot that stood upon the hearth, and we saw in it a hand swollen by cooking. The men, they said, were gone a-hunting.

"It was not long before we understood what that meant, for they soon arrived, armed with clubs and javelins, bringing a captive with them, and shouting, Wah! Wah! as the Basutos do when they drive a herd of oxen. This captive was a tall, well-formed and handsome young man; he entered with a firm step and was ordered to sit down in the centre of the cavern. He heard us explain the object of our visit, but seemed not to heed what we said.

"A few moments afterwards a cord was put round his neck, and he was strangled. I hid my face in my cloak, but when I supposed that the poor young man was dead I looked up again, in order not to offend my hosts. The cutting-up was performed just as if it had been an ox."

One of the most fascinating books on central South Africa during the early nineteenth century is Thomas Arbousset's *Excursion Missionaire*. It was recently translated into English, edited by David Ambrose and Albert Brutsch and published under the full title of *Missionary Excursion into the Blue Mountains, being an account of King Moshoeshoe's Expedition from Thaba Bosiu to the Sources of*

the Malibamatso River in 1840. It is essentially the diary that Arbousset, a colleague of Eugéne Cassalis, kept when he went on a long expedition with Moshoeshoe.

On 15 February 1840, Arbousset and Moshoeshoe went to the very place where the king's grandfather had been eaten by Rakotsoane's cannibals sixteen years earlier: Malimong. They went to visit Rakotsoane himself in the huge cave with the waterfall in front of it where Peete's flesh had been consumed, the cave Mapike had told Cassalis about. Rakotsoane was now a vassal of Moshoeshoe, and it appears that he and his group had been rehabilitated from their cannibalistic practices.

On the second day of their visit, a Sunday, Arbousset gave a sermon and held a prayer meeting. The next morning, he sat down with Rakotsoane to question them about cannibalism. The chief's explanation was as good a definition of survival cannibalism as you'll find anywhere. He told Arbousset: "Hunger was the first cannibal. It devoured us. Although we were numerous, we were without cattle, without millet, there was little game on the plains, and the plains were occupied by our enemies. What was to become of us? Each one ate his dog; then the sandals he was wearing on his feet; next his old antelope kaross; finally his leather shield.

"After six or eight days of suffering our limbs seemed to grow bigger, the joints would swell, our heads became drowsy, our bodies in general and particularly our necks became numb; terrible dysentery forced everyone to leave the cavern frequently; and outside a hyena would take us and drag us to her cubs. Those who were courageous enough to go hunting or gathering were liable to become the prey of ferocious beasts, which in those days of great famine waited for us, and finding us very weak, would feed on our limbs, in the fields, and also at home, like animals possessed.

"It was then that we started to rush upon people and began to devour them."

One of the other chiefs of the group told Arbousset: "Many preferred to die of hunger; but others were deceived by the more intrepid ones, who would say to their friends when they saw them returning from the fields worn out and famished: here is some daman [dassie] meat, recover your strength. However, it was human flesh. Once they had tasted it, they found it was excellent. Yet perhaps it was cursed, because after eating it for several days, many people died of the dysentery it caused."

Arbousset asked the chief: "And what did you feel in your heart in the midst of all these atrocities?" Rakotsoane answered: "Our heart did fret inside us; but we were getting used to that type of life and the horror we had felt at first was soon replaced by habit. Besides, conscience in times of famine is different from the conscience of today. It is now, especially, that I feel ashamed of myself. I look at my limbs and I shiver. What! I tell myself, it was as eating ourselves! We have all purified ourselves extensively, but our conscience is still there, gnawing away at us."

But it wasn't only the indigenous Africans who were sometimes forced to practise survival cannibalism in South Africa. There are at least two documented cases of European visitors to South African shores eating human flesh. The first happened almost 300 years before Rakotsoane's time, on the coast of what is now KwaZulu-Natal, and the second 131 years before Peete's death, this time on the Cape west coast.

The Portuguese ship *São Bento* under the command of Captain Fernão d'Alveres Cabral left Cochin on the west coast of India in February 1554 with a heavy load of slaves and trade goods. Its steering mechanism broke in heavy seas near the African coast and it drifted onto the rocks south of Port St Johns on the Eastern Cape coast. Some 140 people drowned, but 224 slaves and 99 Portuguese seamen made it to shore, many of them injured.

They did not know exactly where they were, but thought that if they walked far enough along the east coast, they would reach

Delagoa Bay, where Portuguese ships occasionally traded. Carrying a crucifix fixed to a lance, they set off on their journey.

On the third day their spirits were dealt a severe blow when they came upon the wreck of the *São João*, a Portuguese galleon that had run aground two years earlier, in June 1552. The *São João* was the first known shipwreck off South Africa. The crew and passengers had walked up the coast, and only twenty-two were still alive when they were found at Inhambane in May 1553.

But the *São Bento* survivors found that more people had survived their sister ship's misfortune. Near the present Port Shepstone they met an Indian slave who had settled with the local indigenous community, near the Umkomaas River they came across a Moor named Gaspar, and where Durban is today they met a Portuguese sailor, Rodrigo Tristão, naked, well tanned and a successful hunter. The Indian refused to accompany them because he was happy living with the Xhosa, but Gaspar offered to be their interpreter and Tristão also joined them in their quest to return to "civilisation".

The *São Bento* party did not do well. Some became ill and died, some drowned crossing the substantial rivers in their way, others were killed by lion or hyena or by hostile locals. Captain Cabral drowned in the Tugela River. The boatswain, Francisco Pires, took over as leader after the captain's death.

They were desperately hungry. Manuel de Mesquita Perestrello, whose diary reveals most of what had happened to the *São Bento*, wrote that sometimes friends or relatives fought tooth and nail over a locust, beetle or lizard that had been found. Once they found white crabs on the beach and devoured them raw and "in such a hurry that often when we put them in our mouths they held on to our lips with their claws, and stuck fast, while the rest of them, half-masticated, were wriggling down our throats".

When they reached the Mkuze River, four sailors who were in the advance party became so desperate that they killed one of the local black people, and consumed his flesh. Unfortunately for them, the victim's friends came upon them enjoying their feast and killed them. The tribe then attacked the rest of the *São Bento* party. After a battle that raged for two hours, the Portuguese successfully broke away and fled further north, but not before twenty more were killed.

On 7 July 1554 the survivors, fifty-six Portuguese and six slaves, arrived in Delagoa Bay. But they had to wait until 3 November for the first Portuguese ship to arrive, and by then only twenty Portuguese and four slaves were still alive. The naked hunter, Rodrigo Tristão, and the scribe, Perestrello, were among them.

Interestingly, only four decades later, in 1593, another Portuguese ship, the *Santo Alberto*, ran aground at almost the same spot as the *São Bento*, and the survivors again decided to walk to Delagoa Bay. But this time they had a clever and strong leader, Nuno Velho Pereira, one of the passengers. He was a nobleman and had earlier served as Portugal's Captain of Mozambique.

Pereira knew what had happened to the *São Bento* survivors, and opted to travel inland rather than along the coast. He took enough copper, beads, nails, chains and silk to trade with local chiefs for food, and he carefully avoided conflict with the indigenous people.

Pereira's party arrived at Delagoa Bay in July 1593, ninety days after leaving the wreck. Of the 125 Portuguese and 160 slaves who survived the shipwreck, 117 Portuguese and 65 slaves made it to Delagoa Bay. The other 95 slaves did not die, but chose to stay with the local black farmers they encountered.

What a pity we don't have information about what happened to all these foreigners who came to live among the local black farmers of South Africa at the end of the sixteenth century.

The other case of cannibalism occurred in 1693, and this time involved the crew of a Dutch ship, *De Gouden Buys*. It sailed from Holland on 4 May 1693, but by the time it reached the tropics many of the crew were suffering from scurvy. It got so bad that when the ship reached St Helena Bay on the Cape's west coast on 11 November, more than a hundred crew were dead and only seven men were strong enough to row ashore.

Their teeth were too loose from the scurvy to take some of the last food on the ship – at least, that was their excuse for only taking a bottle of wine and a bottle of brandy. After three days, and losing one of their number, they went back to the place where their ship was anchored, but their boat had been smashed by the waves and they could not row back. They tied a shirt to an oar and waved it, screaming and shouting, but no one on the ship noticed. So they resumed their quest to find someone who could give them food and water.

It is interesting to note that the men, at least those who survived the ordeal, reported seeing large numbers of elephants, hippos, eland and hartebeest, even the occasional lion – we're talking about the areas of today's Dwarskersbos, Velddrift, Vredenburg and Hopefield.

The bookkeeper, Jacob Lepie, fell ill the next day, and the carpenter, Laurens Thys, decided to stay with him while the others moved on. But Lepie died, and Thys set off and eventually met with a group of Khoikhoi, who welcomed him in their midst and fed him. They sent a messenger to Saldanha Bay, where there was a Dutch presence, and he was soon rescued.

The other three did not do so well. They were walking in circles, three Dutchmen in the African bush, desperately hungry and thirsty. Drinking seawater made them very ill, so they started drinking their own urine.

The day after Christmas 1693, one of them, Jan Christiaanz, died. The two remaining survivors looked at each other. Here, at last, was some meat for them to eat. The military commander of the ship, whose name has not survived in the records, eventually made the argument to his companion, Daniel Sillerman: "If we eat Jan, we will live. If we don't, we will die. God knows that, He will not think it a sin."

Sillerman agreed, but could not face carving up his friend's body. If the commander cut the meat, he would make the fire, he said. They roasted Jan's flesh on the fire, and started eating. According to Sillerman, the meat was almost too tough to eat – Jan Christiaanz had been without food and water for a long time. After their meal they packed some of the meat in their bags to eat later.

The next day they were discovered by a group of Khoikhoi, who gave them food and water. They wanted to take the two men to their village, but the men were too weak to walk. When the Khoikhoi grabbed Sillerman by the arms to drag him, he (perhaps mindful of what he had done the previous day) was convinced they were cannibals and wanted him for lunch. When he took out his knife to fight them off, the Khoikhoi abandoned them. The commander died a few days later.

Sillerman eventually made it back to the beach where the *Gouden Buys* was anchored. To his utter joy he saw that two other ships had arrived to save the *Gouden Buys*, and he was rescued forty-two days after he had first gone ashore. If he had not eaten his friend Jan Christiaanz, he would probably have died too.

The ships that came to the rescue of the *Gouden Buys* discovered only one man alive on the ship, but he died the next day. Of the 189 men who started the voyage, only two survived.

8

The Scoundrel
Pioneer

THE TREKBOERS, THE WHITE SETTLERS WHO TOWARDS the end of the eighteenth century moved further and further eastwards away from the Cape, were pious, ascetic Calvinists faithful to God and family. And they were deeply racist. Right? Well, not exactly. Not all of them.

This is the story of one of those trekboers, who spoke the bastardised, simplified Dutch from which the Afrikaans language grew, and who fathered many children but never consorted with white women. He was married to the mother of a great Xhosa chief and the sister of a famous Nguni warrior. He was a giant of a man, often accepted as a leader, but rarely by white people. At different times he was a de facto chief of the Xhosa, Bushman, Khoikhoi, Sotho, Tswana and Venda groups, and was repeatedly declared a dangerous enemy of the state by the Dutch and British colonial authorities. He was the first white man to settle in the northern parts of South Africa.

His name was Coenraad de Buys.

Coenraad was the great-grandson of an original Huguenot, Jean du Buis, who arrived from Calais in 1688. Coenraad's father, by now called Jan de Buys, married Christina Scheepers in 1752, and Coenraad was born in 1761 on his father's farm in the Montagu district of the Klein Karoo. His father died a poor man when Coenraad was only six years old.

It is not known where he spent the remainder of his childhood years, only that his own family employed him as a labourer with the promise that he would be paid for his work when he came of age. During his teenage years Coenraad went to live with his half-sister, Geertruy Minnie, who married David Senekal of the Swellendam district. Coenraad helped Senekal produce butter in exchange for a share of the profits. But Senekal cheated him, never delivering on the promise of payment for his years of work, so the young Coenraad took his family to court and won. This is the first sign we have of his often belligerent and obstinate personality. Perhaps it ran in the family: his uncle, Jacobus de Buys, had been jailed for a year after he cursed and assaulted the Swellendam landdrost.

Coenraad later left Swellendam and wandered further east to rent a farm for a year, probably in the region of present-day Willowmore, and established himself as a farmer at the ripe age of twenty-two. During this time there were only three magisterial districts in the Cape: Cape Town, Stellenbosch and Swellendam. But the settler farmers quickly moved further east in search of grazing and agricultural land, and in 1786 a new magistracy was declared on the banks of the Sundays River. It was called Graaff-Reinet.

It took a certain type of man to survive in this frontier region: tough, independent, often wild, uneducated and in perpetual conflict with the colonial authorities. They were far away from settlements where they could buy provisions and sell their produce, and had to contend with lion, leopard and elephant. Their farming activities threatened the lifestyle of the Bushmen, who often had little choice but to slaughter the farmers' cattle. Around the time that the Graaff-Reinet drostdy was established, they also came into contact with the black Nguni-speaking farmers who had farmed in the Eastern Cape for many generations. The Xhosa were comprised of the Gcaleka and the Rharhabe, although later groups such as the Thembu, Mondo, Mpondomise, Bhaca, Hlubi and Zizi were also called Xhosa. Conflict was inevitable: both groups wanted more and more land. This clash between the white settlers and the Xhosa had a profound effect on later political developments in South Africa.

During the mid-1780s, Coenraad de Buys moved to the farm Brandwacht on the eastern side of the Bushman's River, and a little later he acquired another two farms on loan. He clearly wasn't a very good farmer, and in 1792 it was recorded that he had not paid rent on any of the three farms. He apparently convinced the authorities that his debt should be written off, due to his losses of cattle stolen by the Xhosa. Successful farmer or not, by this time the young Coenraad had become notorious throughout the colony as a wild man who knew no fear and entertained no opposition, and as a renowned hunter.

Lady Anne Barnard, wife of the British colonial secretary, wrote of the frontier Boers in one of her famous letters from the Cape to her friend Henry Dundas, the British Minister of War: "They are very fine men; their height is enormous; most of them six feet high and upwards; and I don't know how many feet across; I hear that five or six hundred miles distant they even reach seven feet."

Well, she was certainly correct when it came to Coenraad de Buys. Henry Lichtenstein, who met Coenraad at least once, wrote in his *Travels in Southern Africa, 1803–1805*: "His uncommon height, for he measured nearly seven feet; the strength, yet admirable proportion of his limbs, his excellent carriage, the confident look of his eye, his high forehead, his whole mien, and a certain dignity in his movements, made altogether a most pleasing impression. Such one might conceive to have been the heroes of ancient times; he seemed the living figure of a Hercules, the terror of his enemies, the hope and support of his friends."

The area nestled between the ocean, the Bushman's River and the Fish River was called the Zuurveld, and for years it was an area of great conflict between the Xhosa and the settlers. Coenraad's clash with the Xhosa began almost as soon as he moved there. His uncle Petrus also lived in the district, and wrote him a letter on 21 March 1788, which survives in the records, about an altercation with Chief Langa of the Mbalu clan: "Respected Cousin Coenraad de Buys, I have to inform you that Langa let you know that he desires payment from you for beating his caffre, otherwise he will immediately come again because that is a challenge and the Christians must not think he is afraid to make war. This he made known in presence of Gert Knoetze. With compliments from us all, I am your uncle Petrus de Buys."

In August 1788, Coenraad forged the signatures of four other farmers in a petition to the landdrost complaining that the Xhosa were stealing their cattle, and demanding that a commando be called up to deal with them. In reality, it seems, it was Coenraad who did all the stealing. The secretary at the Graaff-Reinet drostdy, one Wagenaar, wrote later that the "Boers, particularly C. Buis, under the pretence that the Caffres had committed depredations, continually insisted to form a commando against the Caffres". The farmers' complaints were found to be groundless and "merely advanced for the purpose of enriching themselves with the plunder from the Caffres".

In March 1789, Chief Langa and a group of his men had had enough, and they invaded the Zuurveld and recaptured some of their cattle. The colonial authorities in the Cape ordered the landdrost to not send a commando against them, because they wanted to avoid a war with the Xhosa. But conditions did not improve, and war was inevitable. In September 1792, Cornelis van Rooyen wrote to the landdrost that unless he settled the ongoing quarrel between Coenraad de Buys and the Xhosa, there was going to be bloodshed. That bloodshed came in 1793, when commandos clashed with the Xhosa.

Landdrost Honoratus Maynier, who investigated the causes of this war, called the Second Frontier War, was a very unpopular man among the white farmers because, unlike his predecessors, he considered both sides of the story. In his monumental work on Xhosa history, *Frontiers*, Noël Mostert says of Maynier: "He marks the beginning of the moral debate about relations between whites and blacks in South Africa that within a decade was to come before world attention as a subject of popular passionate indignation, which it remains to this day. He was the first man to try to administer the South African frontier through powerful humanitarian principles, and he was vilified for it."

Maynier blamed the war on Coenraad de Buys. He cited the evidence of two Xhosa headmen who stated that Coenraad had stolen their cattle and kidnapped their wives. Chief Langa told him that the only reason he attacked the whites was the behaviour of Coenraad de Buys, who had, among other things, "taken his wife with violence and used her as his own". A Khoikhoi man, Gerrit Coetzee, testified that Coenraad used the pretext of elephant hunts to raid the Xhosa's cattle, and that he had killed some of the owners.

Some white farmers were also sick of Coenraad's wild behaviour. Veldwagtmeesters Gerrit Rautenbag, Hendrik Janse van Rensburg and Johannes Botma told Maynier that the Xhosa who attacked the commando had called out that if Coenraad and two other farmers, Coenraad Bezuidenhout and Christoffel Botha, were removed from the area there would be no war. They also claimed Coenraad had stolen their women and "used them as his own property". Maynier started to build a serious criminal case against Coenraad, but in February 1795 the burghers expelled the landdrost from the drostdy.

Agatha Schoeman, a historian, researched Coenraad de Buys's life for her PhD thesis in 1937. Her research was published in 1938 as a little book titled *Coenraad de Buys, the First Transvaler*. Schoeman was rather sympathetic towards Coenraad (and hostile towards Maynier) and questioned the credibility of Maynier's witnesses. She concluded: "[De Buys] was undoubtedly violent, but he may have had much provocation." But, she adds, "The charge of taking kaffir women was made by different chiefs, and, judging from his later career, seems very likely to have been the truth."

The war laid waste the Zuurveld and Coenraad de Buys lost all his property. Maynier led a commando against Chief Tshaka of the Gqunukhwebe and Chief Langa of the Mbalu and drove them across the Fish River. But there, an old foe, Chief Ndlambe, lay in wait. His men killed Tshaka and captured Langa. Chungwa succeeded his father as chief of the Gqunukhwebe and Nqeno his father as chief of the Mbalu. Many of the Khoikhoi who fought with the whites went to live among the Xhosa because of the harsh treatment they received on the farms. There were no victors in this mini-war caused mainly by one renegade settler.

The Dutch East India official sent to investigate the unlawful unseating of landdrost Maynier, OG de Wet, was himself forced to flee Graaff-Reinet by aggressive Boers, Coenraad de Buys among them. The burghers promptly declared Graaff-Reinet an independent republic, and Swellendam did the same soon afterwards. Both republics cited the French Revolution of the time as an inspiration.

But shortly afterwards, on 11 June 1795, nine British military ships under the command of Major-General James Craig arrived at the Cape. On 16 September the British officially took over from the floundering, corrupt Dutch East India Company, and General Craig became the first governor. For the next century (apart from another Dutch stint between 1803 and 1806), the British were the colonial masters. WA de Klerk writes in his *The Puritans in Africa: A Story of Afrikanerdom*: "The emergent Afrikaners, for so long out of the age, were being brought back to it, haltingly. They were now facing black Africa in the form of the Xhosa; the world in the form of the British."

The Republic of Swellendam gave up its "sovereignty" within a month, but the frontiersmen of Graaff-Reinet were more stubborn. The new landdrost, FR Bresler, was kicked out of town and the

British flag he had hoisted was unceremoniously pulled down. Graaff-Reinet governed itself for another year before submitting to British rule.

Landdrost Bresler was sent back to Graaff-Reinet, and in 1797 he gave Coenraad de Buys two months to leave the Cape Colony, citing complaints that he had killed Xhosa men, kidnapped Xhosa wives, and assaulted and incarcerated Khoikhoi men on his remote farm.

Of course, Coenraad did not comply. He continued to live in the Graaff-Reinet district for some time, but now as an outlaw. Late in 1797 his cousin and arch-enemy in the district, Hendrik Janse van Rensburg, reported to Bresler that Coenraad had crossed the Fish River and was living among the Xhosa. He was, Van Rensburg alleged, instigating the Xhosa "to rise against the Christians", to seize the land along the Sundays River and to capture Bresler and the British officer in the region, John Barrows.

Earl Macartney, the British governor of the Cape Colony, ordered Bresler to summon Coenraad to appear in court. Naturally, again Coenraad did not comply. Bresler put up a notice announcing that anyone who brought Coenraad in, dead or alive, would receive a reward of one hundred rixdollars.

Hermann Giliomee writes in *The Afrikaners: Biography of a People* that Coenraad, a poor man after the Xhosa burnt down his homestead and stole his cattle, "suddenly acquired a new lease of life" when he was invited to live at the royal homestead of the Rharhabe chief Ngcika (known to whites as Gaika). The young chief needed an adviser from the colony who could also help him get his hands on guns and horses. Ngcika probably chose Coenraad because he was also an enemy of his Xhosa enemies, but surely also because he spoke Dutch, Xhosa and English fluently and had close contact with the burghers. Coenraad had a thorough knowledge of Xhosa customs, culture and protocol – and a deep affection for nubile young Xhosa maidens. The Xhosa called him *Khula* – The

Big One. According to Jeff Peires in *The House of Phalo: A History of the Xhosa People in the Days of their Independence*, Coenraad promised Ngcika his fifteen-year-old daughter: "Ngcika hoped to marry Buys's daughter to cement the alliance between himself and the Dutch."

Towards the end of 1798 the burghers of Graaff-Reinet planned to overthrow British rule and "renew the old Graaff-Reinet patriotism". These plans got a kick-start when local farmer Adriaan van Jaarsveld was imprisoned at the drostdy for fraud. The leader of the rebellion, Marthinus Prinsloo, organised the farmers into an armed commando with the aim of unseating the landdrost. But he needed a strongman. He sent for Coenraad de Buys.

Prinsloo and De Buys called the burghers to a meeting on 10 February 1799. The meeting resolved "to deliver the landdrost into the hands of Coenraad de Buys". At his subsequent court trial, Prinsloo declared that Coenraad's plan was "to join the Caffers to the Burghers and retake Graaff-Reinet, and all those that would not participate in their proceedings would be put to death and their cattle would have been served out to the Caffers for provision".

Wisely, Coenraad realised that it was dangerous for him to operate in the Graaff-Reinet district, because as a declared outlaw he could be shot on sight, or captured and deported. So he and his friends forced landdrost Bresler to write a letter to the colonial governor in Cape Town, requesting that his outlaw status be overturned. We don't know how they forced him, but Bresler later said that he had written the letter to save his own life. It read: "The Burgher Coenraad de Buys has also appeared in the Village and requested that it may please Your Excellency to repeal the order given by the Earl of Macartney to the Landdrost by an Instruction bearing date 14th February 1789 by which he was declared an outlaw, we therefore beg leave to join our request to this that it may please Your Excellency to reinstate him in his former Burgher Freedom, he promising to conduct himself as becomes a good Burgher and to answer this favour, and we being able to assure Your Excellency that the behaviour of the said de Buys has in every respect appeared to us to be more than worthy of this exoneration."

The governor indeed pardoned Coenraad, but the order was soon revoked. When the rebellion fizzled out without a shot being fired, a price was put on Coenraad's head and those of the other rebels: a thousand rixdollars, dead or alive. Shortly after this episode another war between the Xhosa and the settlers erupted, and again some blamed Coenraad, this time for inciting the Xhosa to attack.

By this time, it appears that Coenraad had written off Graaff-Reinet and was planning to move further up the east coast with his motley band of fellow travellers: some burgher rebels, a few Englishmen who had deserted from the colonial army, and his extended family of Khoikhoi and Xhosa women and their children. He had had enough of the colonial government. He hated the British as much as he had hated the Dutch authorities. In fact, he did not want to live in a land where there was any government at all. When he wasn't stirring up his fellow burghers against the colonial authority, he did so with the Xhosa or the Khoikhoi.

He told Xhosa chief Ngcika that the English were the "Bushmen of the sea", which to the Xhosa meant that they were sneaky thieves. The acting governor at the time, General Francis Dundas, wrote later about De Buys and his fellow troublemakers who lived among the Xhosa: "I have always been persuaded that the people from Graaff-Reinet who have taken refuge in Caffraria have scattered the seeds of future mischief, by falsely representing us to the savages, and although the fruits are not yet developed, it is most certain that the source of any serious interruption of the present tranquillity will be found on the other side of the Great Fish River, so long as that gang of ruffians remain there."

By the end of 1799, Coenraad was happily living with Chief Ngcika at his settlement called The Great Place. He helped the chief write letters to the Graaff-Reinet landdrost and the colonial authorities, and acted as his interpreter and adviser. Although he had at least one wife, a Khoikhoi woman named Maria, he also had several Xhosa concubines and many children.

But now Coenraad increased his influence over Ngcika by marrying the chief's mother, Yese, the Queen Mother of the Rharhabe, a woman described as "vastly corpulent". According to the colonial official Dr Henry Lichtenstein, "a sort of marriage was concluded between them after the manner of the Caffers, and in a short time he shared with this woman the almost unbounded influence which from her rank as well as her prudence she obtained over the whole nation". The traveller John Campbell reported that Coenraad "was a man of amorous disposition. Like Solomon he had many wives or rather mistresses and concubines. The mother of Gaika was one of them." Coenraad also had a home among the neighbouring Tembu, where he had at least one wife and several children.

It was at Ngcika's Great Place that Coenraad de Buys became a close friend of Dr Johannes van der Kemp of the London Missionary Society. With his colleague John Edmonds, Van der Kemp was the first missionary to cross the Fish River and work among the Xhosa. Van der Kemp's journal is the source of much of what we know about Coenraad during this time.

Coenraad became Van der Kemp's protector, and on several occasions interceded on the missionaries' behalf with the Xhosa chiefs. Coenraad attended his sermons and prayer sessions, and told the missionary he was convinced God had sent them. This demonstration of friendship from the bearded giant moved Van der Kemp to write in his journal, "How inexpressibly wonderful are thy ways, O our God!"

The two men probably liked each other because both were outsiders and a little eccentric, with forceful personalities. Van der Kemp, who was born in Holland, refused to wear shoes or a hat – something no Boer and few Xhosas would do in the hot, rugged veld of the Eastern Cape. This was so odd to Ngcika that he asked him why he renounced such protection. Van der Kemp replied that it was God's wish. Later he wrote: "What does it signify to walk barefoot, as I now have done for almost two years, if my feet may be shod with the gospel of peace? What if I had no hat to cover my head, if it may be protected with the helmet of salvation?"

Noël Mostert writes of Coenraad's relationship with Van der Kemp: "The unusual friendship that developed between this egregious frontiersman and the missionary balanced in a curious way the one he already maintained with the youthful Xhosa chief. The age gap between Ngcika and Coenraad de Buys was roughly the same as that between De Buys and Van der Kemp. The Boer stands as an intermediate figure between the two cultures of Europe and Africa and, as the eighteenth century passes into the nineteenth, there is something touching about this link. At the threshold of the new century and the new age beyond it, the three men form a strange trio bonded by odd intertwined and interdependent relationships, which become symbolic of what already was over and what was begun."

It was during this period that Coenraad was offered another pardon, this time by General Dundas. The only reason for Dundas's offer was to get him back into the colony and away from Chief Ngcika, because the British believed, quite rightly, that Coenraad was poisoning their relations with the Xhosa. This time Coenraad refused.

In her 1937 PhD thesis, Agatha Schoeman had this explanation for Coenraad's refusal to be pardoned and thus end his life as an outlaw: "Perhaps he considered it better to live as the leader of his band and a valued councillor to Gaika than to live in the colony as a poor struggling farmer, who would be scorned for his relations with native women. In Kaffirland he could live a free and easy life and by hunting he could no doubt obtain sufficient to trade with the colony for gunpowder and other necessities."

But Coenraad's friendship with the missionaries came at the expense of his influence over Chief Ngcika. His marriage to the chief's mother, Yese, was already turning sour because of the wife he kept among the Tembu, and now she was angered because Coenraad's friends, the missionaries, were threatening her position as the best rainmaker in the region. (On Christmas Day 1799, Ngcika had asked Van der Kemp to pray for rain, which he did. The rain started a few hours later, breaking a serious drought. Ngcika was impressed with Van der Kemp's God, but his mother was not amused. Coenraad immediately demanded a few head of cattle from Ngcika as "commission" for introducing him to the new rainmaker ...)

The chief, caught in the intrigue between all these white people who had invaded his world, became increasingly suspicious that the renegade burghers and the British just wanted to use him. He began thinking the missionaries were British spies and blamed Coenraad for bringing them into his kraal. Suspicion and fear pervaded The Great Place, and Ngcika refused to let Coenraad near his hut.

Coenraad sent a messenger to the chief, informing him that he was going to leave The Great Place because of this treatment. To show that he was serious, he gathered his oxen and saddled his horse. As he predicted, Ngcika arrived to demand an explanation. Coenraad told him: "You have declared that you would consider me as your father, but your conduct to me, in these last days, denies these feelings." He explained that Ngcika's threats and rudeness towards Van der Kemp were an insult to him personally. Ngcika apologised and granted Van der Kemp the permission he had long sought to travel further into the interior.

Despite the chief's apology, the atmosphere at The Great Place did not improve, and Van der Kemp and the other whites came to fear for their lives. On 31 December 1801, Coenraad, Van der Kemp, five English deserters, four other burghers and all Coenraad's wives, concubines and their children left The Great Place under the pretence that they were going on an elephant hunt (they believed that Ngcika would have killed them all if he knew they were on their way back to the colony). They trekked eastwards, but turned north near the Kei River on a long route back towards Graaff-Reinet. They were attacked by Bushmen several times and at least five of their party were killed. Van der Kemp nearly drowned crossing a river, but Coenraad bravely saved him. In May they arrived in Graaff-Reinet, where Van der Kemp remained to work among the many Khoikhoi assembled there. But Coenraad de Buys returned directly to The Great Place to patch up his relationship with Chief Ngcika.

It must have been during this time, the second half of 1802, that Coenraad went to Natal. His son Michael later told people that he went with his father to the people beyond the Xhosa where his father won over the hand of the sister of the feared chief and ferocious warrior Mzilikazi of the Ndwandwe (also called the Ndebele and Matabele), brought her back to the colony and legally married her. Agatha Schoeman noted that Coenraad for the first time mentioned a wife, Elizabeth, in an official document in 1813, and speculated that this could have been Mzilikazi's sister. But this "Elizabeth" could also have been a Khoikhoi woman from the Gonaqua tribe east of Algoa Bay to whom Coenraad was very attached.

On 1 January 1803, the Batavian Republic of the Netherlands again took over the control of the Cape Colony from the British, with Commissioner-General Jacobus Abraham de Mist and Lieutenant-General Jan Wilhelm Janssens as joint governors. Their first priority was to sort out the dangerous chaos on the eastern frontier. They pardoned all political offenders and released the Graaff-Reinet rebels from the Castle in Cape Town, where they had been imprisoned. Next they wanted all the Boers living with the Xhosa to return to the colony, and to this end arranged a meeting with Coenraad de Buys and Chief Ngcika. After the meeting, Janssens referred to Coenraad both as "the most dangerous man in the colony" and "intelligent and striking".

This change in events was a turning point for Coenraad, and soon afterwards he returned to the colony and settled on the farm d'Opkomst in the Swellendam district. This is where Dr Henry Lichtenstein, the colony's medical officer, met him in 1804. Coenraad, he wrote, was "the living figure of a Hercules", and if this wasn't praiseworthy enough, Lichtenstein had more to say: "We found in him ... a certain modesty, a certain retiredness in his manner and conversation, a mildness and kindness in his looks and mien, which left no room to suspect that he had lived several years among the savages, and which still more even contributed to remove than his conversation the prejudice we had conceived against him. He willingly gave information concerning the subjects upon which he was questioned, but carefully avoided speaking of himself and his connection with the caffres. This restraint, which was often accompanied with a sort of significant smile, that spoke of the inward consciousness of his own powers, and in which was plainly to be read that his forbearance was not the result of fear, but that he scorned to satisfy the curiosity of anyone at the expense of the truth, or of his own personal reputation, made him more interesting to us, and excited our sympathy much more than it would perhaps have been excited by the relation of his story."

By all accounts Coenraad tried his best during his time in the Swellendam district and later the district of George to settle down and live within the law. He formally petitioned the colonial authority in Cape Town to revoke his outlaw status and declare him a legal citizen. It was so granted. The records reflect that he even had three of his children baptised.

Coenraad's good intentions and efforts to be a solid citizen lasted a whole ten years. But when he rebelled again, he did so with greater abandon than ever before. Unfortunately, we have much less information about his whereabouts for the next decade, because he roamed where there were few white officials, travellers or missionaries to keep official records or travel journals.

We don't know what triggered his final departure from the Cape Colony in 1814, at the age of fifty-two. Of course his white neighbours didn't like him, mostly because of his black and Khoikhoi women and many coffee-coloured children, but also because he had testified against a white woman who was accused of abusing and murdering some of her mixed-blood ("bastaard") servants. She was charged before the Circuit Court, known as the "Swarte Ommegang" among the burghers, with Coenraad's old friend Johannes van der Kemp and his fellow missionary, James Read, presiding. Perhaps Coenraad was frustrated by the introduction of strict new hunting laws, which curtailed one his favourite activities. The missionary John Campbell wrote in his journal that he heard that Coenraad had left because the Dutch had again ceded the Cape to the British, but there is no other source that suggests this was his motivation.

The way I choose to understand Coenraad de Buys, after much research some two centuries later, is that the mundane, regimented life among his fellow burghers – and under the colonial whip – was so against his character and his love of freedom and adventure that he simply couldn't stand it any longer. I also get the impression that he didn't like most of the white people in his society. Noël Mostert agrees: "After his childhood experiences, one is inclined to believe that he never really liked or trusted his fellow Boers, or even much respected them. His contempt for their gullibility, credulousness and panic was often apparent; he knew well, too, their jealousies, bitter quarrels and tawdry recrimination. His life had been one of scorn for the ordinary and conventional even on that unconventional frontier, and he drew a line of evident disdain between himself and the rest."

This time Coenraad went to the northern frontier around the

Gariep (Orange) River, a frontier even more violent and chaotic than the east. The people who lived on the northern frontier were Bushmen, a Khoikhoi group called the Kora or Koranna, the Griqua, and black farmers who spoke Setswana and Sesotho. The Griqua, known at the time as the Bastaards, were a group mixed of Boer, Khoikhoi and slave blood who had fled the colony. They spoke Afrikaans and, unlike the Khoikhoi in other regions or the black farmer groups, dressed in European clothing and used fire-arms and horses. They, and not the later Voortrekkers who followed in their footsteps, were the real pioneers of the Orange River valley and what was called Transorangia, the area north of the Orange River. They named themselves after the ancestral chief of the Charigurigua, Griqua.

This was the region to which Coenraad and his great entourage of concubines, sons and daughters and their families trekked. He was one of the very first white settlers to visit the region. While the eastern frontier had some law and order and stability brought by the age-old Xhosa societal structures, the north was a frontier without rules and law. Here society consisted of a collection of private armies. A Boer named Petrus Pienaar employed a powerful army under a German deserter, Jan Bloem, and when Bloem started his own army, he was replaced by an Oorlam Khoikhoi with the name of Klaas Afrikaner, who eventually murdered Pienaar and his family. A Xhosa-speaking man named Dantser headed a band of Xhosas who raided and pillaged for a living, and there were several Griqua commandos that did the same. Coenraad de Buys linked up with Dantser and started his own commando of escaped slaves, deserters, Griqua, Khoikhoi, Xhosa and Bushmen.

By mid-1815 the colonial authorities in Cape Town started to receive the first complaints about Coenraad in a long time. The missionaries among the Griqua and Bushmen complained that he was telling the people that the missionaries would betray them to the colonial government and that they would be forced into the colonial army. The missionaries also reported that Coenraad had gone to the region of today's Kuruman and influenced the local Setswana-speaking group to reject the missionaries. In a report on Coenraad's behaviour addressed to the colonial secretary, he was referred to as "a Colonist long known for his rebellious disposition and bad habits, who has for many years been a distinguished character among the disaffected on the frontiers".

Andries Stockenström, the colonial commissioner-general of the frontier, discovered that Coenraad was living in the region where Kimberley is today. He was very concerned that Coenraad would cause conflict and war in the region, but there was little he could do except put a price on his head. Again.

Stockenström was right to worry about Coenraad. Many Griqua started to accept him as their leader and raided Tswana cattle under his command. Stockenström travelled himself to the Gariep River to deal with the De Buys problem. There, the missionary William Anderson told him that Coenraad had instilled in the minds of the local people "that they should consider themselves entirely independent of the Government, as a separate nation, strong enough to defend themselves".

Stockenström persuaded the Griqua chiefs with a combination of threats and promises to capture Coenraad and deliver him to the colony. In 1818 they sent a commando to find him, but he heard of it and fled further north. Because his party of wives and children were slow moving, the Griqua commando caught up with him. They tried to ambush him when he and one of the runaway slaves, Arend, went down to a watering hole, but the two managed to escape. The Griqua did not pursue him further, because his band of men had a terrible reputation.

But Coenraad got the message that he wasn't welcome in Transorangia any longer, and during late 1818 he and his party started to move even further to the north. Coenraad was now fifty-seven years old. Some eighteen months later, Stockenström was again sent after him, this time to offer Coenraad a pardon in exchange for information about the interior. But he never got near to the De Buys party. Stockenström wrote in his report: "All I could collect about Coenraad Buis that can be considered authentic is, that after flying from the Griquas in 1818, he remained for some time with a Bootchuana [Tswana] chief called Sibbenel [the Barolong chief Sebonella], who, understanding that he got his flock of 1 400 cattle by plunder from the Goka, took the half; and Buis flying, on the second report that the Griquas were pursuing him, went so far up the country that he had easy and frequent communication with the eastern coast."

Stockenström added: "I was sorry I could not see this wanderer. He has travelled a great deal, and can give the most useful information. He is quite worn out by the restless life he has been obliged to lead, hunted from one tribe to another after his ammunition was exhausted, exposed to the inclemency of the weather and extreme fatigue, without a single horse. He has lost the use of one side, and is really wretched."

The missionary John Campbell also believed the gossip and wild rumours flying throughout southern Africa about Coenraad, and wrote in his journal: "Buys, the Africaner, is reported to sleep little, being always afraid of an attack upon his life. He has three guns, which he keeps beside him, and has taught his wife how to load them that, when attacked, he may only have to fire. He is a miserable man, and his family are captives with him."

These reports were in part wishful thinking by the missionaries and colonial officials, who hated Coenraad. Between 1818 and 1824 numerous rumours were spread, often told as the first-hand truth, among them that Coenraad and his family had been murdered.

According to Noël Mostert's research, after 1818 Coenraad was "moving from one Sotho chieftain to another as he went northwards, offering his military services to some and raiding others ... On one occasion De Buys himself reigned as paramount chief over various black chiefdoms."

The escaped slave Arend, who had survived the Griqua attack with Coenraad, told the traveller George Thompson that "the notorious outlaw Conrad Buys was living in ease and safety in Makabbas' dominions and had received from him, on arrival, a present of fifty head of cattle".

Most sources agree on one point: eventually Coenraad ran out of ammunition and started to hunt expertly with bow and arrows. He also ran out of Western clothes, so he wore skins like the local people. Imagine this giant, over two metres tall, with long hair and a flowing beard, half-naked and sun-browned in the African bush.

The last official account of Coenraad's whereabouts came from the missionary Stephen Kay, who wrote to Stockenström in August 1821 that he had heard that Coenraad's wagon broke down "six or eight days journey" north of Chuenyane, and that he was determined to travel further north. What we can deduct from these last accounts is that Coenraad travelled through the present-day provinces of the Free State, North West, Mpumalanga and Limpopo.

Following this, there are no further records of Coenraad de Buys, excepting the information offered by his son Michael fifty years later. He said that they had been travelling along the Limpopo River when his mother died of fever. "My father was grief-stricken over the loss of our mother and told us in his grief that he was leaving us there, we were not to go further or back. He said that white people would eventually come [and find us]. The Lord would look after us. The following morning we could not find him, he left during the night."

So the grief-stricken Coenraad de Buys walked into the night and was never seen again. Did he commit suicide? Was he killed by a lion, or perhaps by the same fever that killed his wife? We do not know.

The clan he left behind heard rumours that he walked all the way to Mozambique. The husband of one of his daughters apparently went to look for him there, and reported that he heard that his father-in-law had married a woman in Sofala. There is no way of testing this. Perhaps his clan could simply not believe that this indestructible man could die, and would believe any story to confirm that he was still alive.

Agatha Schoeman believed it was "more reasonable to surmise that, feeling himself unable to fend for his family any longer, he intended to do what his son did in 1838 for Louis Trichardt's fever-stricken party of Voortrekkers, namely, to fetch help from the Portuguese at Delagoa Bay, which Coenraad had been trying, periodically, to reach ever since 1798. One is more tempted to believe that he was overcome by fever and died far from aid rather than that he raised a new clan of Buyses in Portuguese territory."

Perhaps it is fitting that this enigmatic man's flamboyant life ended in mystery; alone and in the wild of Africa.

My history teachers in my hometown of Kroonstad never told me about Coenraad de Buys. As Noël Mostert remarks: "Coenraad de Buys would have been a legend on any frontier, in any situation anywhere that offered power and brigandage, but in the gallery of traditional Afrikaner heroes, De Buys has no place. He is a footnote in all history books, someone who cannot be passed without a pause and some reflection; a minor figure, but one who provides magnificent illustration. An embarrassment he might be, and as he surely was to be to many Afrikaner nationalists, but he is impossible to ignore, for he was the embodiment of all that was different and interchangeable on that early frontier."

Coenraad de Buys left behind a clan – they were later called the Buysvolk – made up of virtually every genetic strain that ever existed in South Africa. The Buyses were the real Afrikaner pioneers of the Transvaal, which not long thereafter became the bastion of racially exclusive white Afrikaner nationalism. For years the Buyses lived among the Venda people, acting as interpreters and guides to all kinds of hunters, adventurers and trekkers who visited the area. They spoke Afrikaans and viewed themselves as Afrikaners, and Coenraad's sons made common cause with Voortrekker leader Hendrik Potgieter against some of the black chiefdoms of the area. Venda chief Ravele granted the Buys people a piece of land near Kranspoort, but Transvaal president Paul Kruger gave them the land between today's Vivo and Makhado (previously Louis Trichardt), where their descendants still live today. It is called Buysdorp.

At least the man who has never had more recognition than being a footnote in the Afrikaners' history books has a town named after him.

9

Shaka's Women

KING SHAKA OF THE ZULU IS PERHAPS THE MOST legendary figure in South Africa's history: the genius militarist who rose from humble beginnings to forge a nation and change the history of an entire subcontinent. But few people know the story of the two women in his life: his mother Nandi and the woman who dedicated her life to him, Pampata.

Nandi was the beautiful, strong-willed daughter of the chief of the small eLangeni clan of the Nguni people on South Africa's east coast. One day (it was probably 1786), she began an affair with Senzangakona, chief of a small neighbouring clan called the Zulu, whom she fancied. (Some versions suggest he made a pass at her when he saw her bathing in a stream.) She couldn't have been planning marriage, because her beau's mother came from the eLangeni, which meant that they were cousins and a relationship would be frowned upon. But she was a woman with a very independent mind and a flirtation suited her just fine.

Actually, it became a bit more than a flirtation. The Nguni had a custom whereby men and women could engage in sexual play and genital interaction which stopped just short of penetration. This was what Nandi and Senzangakona were doing. Only, at least once their self-control must have slipped.

The next thing Chief Senzangakona knew, a messenger arrived to tell him and his elders that he had made Nandi pregnant. It was a bit of a scandal. He knew that Nandi was off-limits, and as a chief he should have controlled his urges better. So the annoyed elders of the Zulu clan sent the messenger back with the insult that Nandi's condition could clearly only be the work of *uShaka*, an intestinal beetle that sometimes interfered with a woman's menstrual cycle.

About seven months later the eLangeni messenger returned to the Zulu chief's settlement. With a touch of sarcasm he told the elders that their chief could now send for Nandi and her *uShaka* – she had just given birth to a boy. And that's how Shaka got his name: he was named after a parasite.

Any romantic notions Nandi might have had about her relationship with Senzangakona quickly disappeared. The chief had no choice but to make her his third wife, but because of the scandal they could not even have a wedding feast. Not only was she treated as a harlot by the rest of the Zulu clan, she also discovered that her husband was not a nice man.

Although they had another child together, a daughter named Nomcoba, it was a tempestuous relationship. Nandi, it seemed, was something of an early feminist and didn't meekly accept Senzangakona as master of her mind and body. As punishment, he sent her to live in several different kraals, which made her even more unpopular with the rest of the clan.

When Shaka was six or seven, he became a herdboy. His father had a pet goat he was very fond of, and this animal was Shaka's responsibility. But one day disaster struck. Shaka let the goat out of his sight and a dog killed it and ate it. Senzangakona had had enough of his troublesome wife and her stupid little boy, so he sent them and baby Nomcoba back to the eLangeni and claimed back the lobola he had paid for her. Needless to say, this didn't make Nandi very popular with her own clan. There she was, a single, disgraced mother of two, with no man to look after her, in a society where that meant everything to a woman's status. To make matters worse, all this misfortune failed to transform Nandi into a demure young lady: she still had a will of iron and a tongue like a razor.

The fact that his mother was unwanted in the clan, and constantly gossiped about, not only hurt her young son deeply; it also led to other eLangeni boys bullying him quite cruelly. He was constantly mocked about his father not wanting him. According to some of the surviving stories, the boys sometimes forced him to lick his porridge spoon after they had thrown it in the fire, or put boiling food in his hands and when he dropped it they forced him to eat it from the dirt like a dog.

And all this time the young Shaka knew that his father was a chief and his mother the daughter of a chief, which made him royalty while his bullies were plebs. His own hardship and that of his mother forged a deep bond between the two – perhaps even unhealthily so. He was only a boy, yet he had to be the man in her life, and in turn she was his only solace in a hostile world.

But an even crueller fate befell the little boy. Young Nguni boys of that time didn't wear any clothes until puberty. Several historians have recorded the fact that Shaka had very small genitals as a boy, and in the macho Nguni society this became a source of particularly hurtful taunts. Donald Morris wrote in *The Washing of the Spears* in 1965: "To add to his other burdens, he seems to have had undersized genitals until he reached puberty, and since herdboys wore no clothing at all, he was not allowed to forget it for an instant." In his book *Shaka Zulu, The Rise of the Zulu Empire*, published in 1955, EA Ritter describes an event that took place when Shaka was eleven years old. Two older herdboys pointed at him and shouted: "*Ake ni-bone umtondo wake, ufana nom sundu nje!*" – "Look at his penis, it looks like a little earthworm." Shaka nearly killed the two boys.

Nandi was the only person he could talk to about this. She called him her Little Fire, and constantly reminded him that he had the courage of a lion and would one day be the greatest chief in the land. "I can see it in your eyes," Zulu historians report her telling him. "When you are angry they shine like the sun, and yet no eyes can be more tender when you speak comforting words to me in my misery."

Two other women also understood how humiliated Shaka felt because of his small penis: Mkabi and Langazana, his father's other wives. They both told him that he shouldn't worry about it; that they had known other boys who had small penises when they were young, but as adults their penises were as big as or bigger than other men's. (After Shaka became a powerful ruler, he elevated these two women to senior positions in his military kraals.)

At fifteen, Shaka had to go to the royal kraal of Senzangakona to undergo the puberty ceremony with the other boys of his age. Zulu historians insist that Mkabi and Langazana were right and that Shaka's penis had indeed developed formidably. So much so that the proud owner refused to wear the *umutsha*, the loin girdle he received after the ceremony – he wanted everyone, especially the bullies, to see for themselves that he had outgrown his earlier shortcoming, and he wanted them to be envious. His father and the elders were outraged when he refused to accept the girdle, and he returned to his mother. Under pressure from the clan he agreed to start wearing the *um-ncedo*, a tiny cover for the foreskin, which would still show off the size of his manhood.

Nandi and Shaka's lonely and miserable life soon got worse. In 1802 a serious famine afflicted the eLangeni, and mother and son were unceremoniously kicked out of the clan so that others would have more to eat. Like vagrants, Nandi and her children wandered off, eventually to settle with Gendeyana, a man from another neighbouring clan, the Mbedweni. This man loved her and made her happy (she already had a son with him by this time, called Ngwadi), and she stayed for a while.

But Shaka, now sixteen, had no position in this new village. They left again, this time to Nandi's sister, who was living among the Dletsheni clan, part of the Mtetwa people of King Jobe. The Dletsheni headman, Ngomane, was very kind to Nandi and her children, and there they stayed. A man called Mbiya acted as Shaka's foster father, becoming his very first positive male and father figure. But it was a bit late in life.

Nandi and Nomcoba were happy, and Shaka blossomed for the first time. With his now powerful physique, alert mind and strong personality, he quickly became the leader of the young men in the village. Nomcoba made a new friend, Pampata, who had a crush on the handsome Shaka from day one, although she was only eleven and he sixteen. Shaka achieved local hero status among the local villagers when, at the age of nineteen, he single-handedly killed a leopard with an assegai and a club. Pampata told everyone who would listen that Shaka was going to be the greatest chief her people had ever known. Her hero-worship of Shaka continued without waning until his death.

But the Mtetwa people had their own intrigues. One of King Jobe's two sons who conspired against him was killed and the other, Godongwana, fled. When Jobe died, this son returned, now calling himself Dingiswayo, the Wanderer. When Dingiswayo became chief of the Mtetwa, Shaka was drafted into his army, and his life changed forever. Shaka immediately excelled as a soldier and became Dingiswayo's star warrior as the chief usurped clan after clan into his chiefdom. Shaka abandoned the long, throwing assegai of the time for a short, stabbing one, fought without sandals so as to be faster and more agile, and strategised successful attacking formations. These genius innovations later made him the most feared warrior-king in southern Africa.

After his first kill during battle, it was expected of Shaka, as of all soldiers, to "wipe his axe" – to have sex. The custom dictated that he should have intercourse with the first maiden he came across after the battle. Shaka arranged that the first maiden to cross his path be none other than his sister's friend Pampata. But there are different versions of what actually happened. Many Zulu chroniclers say that Shaka found Pampata a beautiful and intelligent woman and that the two made passionate love on his oxhide shield. But other historians maintain that Shaka had been celibate all his life, and that he had organised for Pampata to be the one he met after battle because she would not tell the others that they didn't actually have intercourse.

Whatever the truth, Pampata now began a life of devotion to Shaka. By day, he was making a name for himself as a warrior, and she went to his hut to clean it and light a fire. She spent everything she had buying medicine and charms from the sangomas to ensure his safety. She was the one waiting for him when he came back from a military campaign, ready to dress his wounds.

It was during this period that Shaka, newly appointed as commander over Dingiswayo's army, was reported to have told his mother that the time was near for her to become the greatest chieftainess of their people; that he had longed since childhood to give her all the power and privilege she deserved. He also told her then, to her shock, that he wasn't going to marry Pampata, as everybody expected. He did add that Pampata was, after Nandi, the woman "closest to my heart". His explanation was that he did not want heirs, because the son of a chief was always in danger. But this may not have been the whole truth.

When Shaka was about twenty-eight, his biological father and chief of the Zulu clan, Senzangakona, died. Before his death he appointed the son of his eighth wife, Sigujana, as his successor. Shaka and Dingiswayo were outraged, and Shaka sent his half-brother Ngwadi to warn Sigujana to leave the area, but the two got into a fight and Sigujana was killed – or perhaps Shaka had instructed Ngwadi to kill Sigujana. Dingiswayo then told Shaka to seize the chieftancy and sent a crack regiment with him to announce this to the Zulu.

Shaka was now the chief of the Zulu, but the Zulu were still just a small clan. His first task was to bring all those in the clan who had insulted or mistreated Nandi and himself before him in a kind of one-man tribunal, with Nandi in attendance. He started with his uncle, Mudli, the one who had said that Nandi wasn't pregnant but merely plagued by the *uShaka*. Shaka was reported to have shouted: "Know all people, whosoever is not kindly to Nandi here, my mother, is already as good as dead and they shall die the hard way." Mudli was stabbed to death and about ten others clubbed to death.

A little while later, once his new Zulu army was up to scratch, he went to take revenge on the eLangeni, who had caused his mother and him so much sorrow. Again he held a public hearing and brought before him all those who had bullied or mocked him and who had caused his mother pain. He recounted all the events, then condemned them to death. As if to remind his taunters of how his manhood had developed, he undressed in front of them and washed himself, saying that the mere sight of them contaminated him. The worst offenders were impaled on sharp poles and left for the birds to devour – "as testimony to all what punishments await those who slander me and my mother". Those who were still alive were burnt and lesser offenders were clubbed to death.

Shaka's next undertaking was to subjugate the Buthelezi clan, after their chief, Pungashe, had insulted him. During this battle he used his revolutionary new tactic of attacking in a horn formation for the first time, and with great success. Shaka's quest to forge a new nation under the name of his father's clan, the Zulu, had begun in earnest.

It was also the beginning of Shaka's collection of maidens, whom he kept in the royal court. At the height of his power there were more than a thousand of them. He started with about a hundred Buthelezi maidens, whom he divided among his mother and his father's wives. These older women had the task of seeing to it that all the maidens remained virgins – he called them his sisters – and appointed the ugliest men he could find to guard them.

But the force of nature was often stronger than fear, and some of the virgins didn't remain so. Several historians recorded that, if he suspected them of having sexual relations with other men, Shaka had the women and their lovers murdered — he was even reported to have killed some of the babies born of these "sisters" with his own hands. Some oral versions of that period's history maintain that this was Shaka's harem and that he regularly satisfied all his women sexually.

Shaka's biggest remaining opponent after the Buthelezi clan was Zwide, chief of the Ndwandwe, who had killed Dingiswayo in 1818. The story is told that when the inevitable battle between Shaka's army and the Ndwandwe loomed, Pampata was deeply worried that the man she was so obsessed with would be hurt. She approached Shaka with a strange plan. She would dress as a married woman and walk alone towards the Ndwandwe army, then take off all her clothes. This shock tactic would confuse and unnerve them, she explained, and even if they did attack and kill her, it would make the Zulu army's job easier. She said it would make her feel as if she were Shaka's bride. Shaka was deeply moved by her proposal to risk her own life, but declined the offer, saying the Zulu would never be able to hold their heads high if he sheltered behind a naked maiden.

In the ensuing battle, more than seven thousand Ndwandwe and just over a thousand Zulu were killed. But it took another great war between the two armies, some time later, before the Ndwandwe were finally defeated. Shaka became the chief of virtually all the northern Nguni chiefdoms and the successor to Dingiswayo.

A great deal of what was written about Shaka during this time came from an Englishman, Henry Francis Fynn. Fynn worked as a surgeon's assistant in London, but in 1809 joined his father and brothers in Cape Town. He became fascinated with the indigenous people and quickly learnt to speak Xhosa. In April 1824, he and a small party sailed to what is today Durban and followed one of Shaka's impis on their way home from battle in the hope of meeting the legendary warrior-king. Fynn spent a lot of time with Shaka in the ensuing years. He kept a journal, but at one point lost all his records and had to reconstruct them later from rough notes and memory. These reconstructions were later published as *The Diary of Henry Francis Fynn.*

We will never really know how reliable Fynn's memoirs were. He was clearly very proud of being one of only a handful of whites ever trusted by Shaka and loved to tell the stories of his experiences with the king. We do not know how much he embellished what he saw and heard, nor whether he might have misunderstood the customs, rituals and behaviour of the people under Shaka. But the stories he told were fascinating.

When Fynn arrived at Shaka's royal kraal, the chief was addressing a group of thousands of warriors and women. He was putting on a show for the white people, certainly to impress them but perhaps also to scare them a little. The maidens of his royal court danced, the warriors marched, and some of his vast herds of cattle were paraded past them. According to Fynn, Shaka gave a hand signal and several of his subjects were killed on the spot. This happened every time whites visited, and was seen as Shaka's way of demonstrating his absolute power.

Fynn and his friends were also told to attend the royal bath: Shaka had the habit of making his daily bath a public ceremony. Watched by his subjects, male and female, he would slowly disrobe, smear his body with a paste of fat and ground meal, rinse it off with water, and then rub himself with fat and ochre.

In October 1827 Fynn was with Shaka on an elephant hunt when a messenger brought word that Nandi was very ill. They rushed back and arrived just before her death. Shaka put on his full military regalia and stood next to his mother's corpse for twenty minutes, crying quietly. Then, according to Fynn, he was overcome by his emotions.

Shaka let out a primal scream, and this was a signal for mass hysteria of almost unimaginable proportions. Tens of thousands of his people came rushing to the scene, all uttering "the most dismal and horrid lamentations". It went on through the night, as warriors and women arrived from further afield.

At noon the next day, Fynn recorded, the assembled masses formed a circle around Shaka and sang war songs. "At the close of it, Shaka ordered several men to be executed on the spot; and the cries became, if possible, more violent than ever. No further orders were needed; but, as if bent on convincing their chief of their extreme grief, the multitude commenced a general massacre ... those who could no more force tears from their eyes – those who were found near the river panting for water – were beaten to death by others who were mad with excitement. Towards the afternoon I calculated that not fewer than seven thousand people had fallen in this frightful indiscriminate massacre."

On the third day after her death, Nandi was buried. The legs and arms of ten of her maiden servants were broken, and some say that they were buried alive with her to keep her company. Shaka ordered twelve thousand men to guard her grave for a year. "I have conquered the world but lost my mother," he was quoted as saying. "Bitter aloes fill my mouth and all taste has gone out of my life."

But Shaka did not want to mourn alone, and he issued an edict setting out how his people had to mourn with him. No one was allowed to plant crops for a year. No one was allowed to drink milk, the Nguni staple food of the time. Instead the milk from the cows had to be poured on the ground. No one was allowed to have sex. All women who fell pregnant that year would be killed, along with their husbands. Shaka's regiments roamed his territory of jurisdiction to enforce these rules, and many thousands more were killed in the process. This madness lasted for three months, until a man called Gala confronted Shaka and pleaded with him not to destroy his nation. Strangely, Shaka not only listened to the man, but gave him some cattle as reward and called off the edicts. But his behaviour became increasingly bizarre after his mother's death.

It seems that this whole bloody episode had to do with more than Shaka's trauma at the death of his mother. Fynn got the impression that Shaka was sending a message to potential enemies that if such a bloodbath followed his mother's death, his own death would have even graver consequences. Professor John Laband of Natal University writes in *Rope of Sand: The Rise and Fall of the Zulu Kingdom in the Nineteenth Century* that it was clear "that Shaka deliberately used the opportunity to rouse popular feeling against his enemies and political opponents ... in order to justify eliminating them".

The most peculiar thing about Nandi's death is that most recorders of Zulu history make mention of the rumour that Shaka himself had killed her. Donald Morris's sources told him that Shaka's father's sister, Mnkabayi, was convinced that Shaka had poisoned his mother, and took her evidence to his half-brothers and other elders. EA Ritter says Nandi's death had "generally, though falsely, been attributed to Shaka himself". Laband writes that "the persistent Zulu tradition" has it that Shaka killed his mother. But he adds: "There is the possibility that this was Mnkabayi, Shaka's king-making aunt, who first spread that malicious story in order to turn people against Shaka, whose assassination she had in mind."

Shaka undoubtedly had some peculiar, obsessive attitudes towards sex. He attempted to regulate every aspect of his subjects' sex lives, and on numerous occasions used enforced celibacy as a weapon of control. His soldiers were forbidden to marry, usually until they were in their forties, and his female guilds were not allowed to have sex at all. There are numerous accounts of how he had the women attached to his royal household, the *isigodlo*, killed if they were caught having sex or became pregnant.

These edicts, combined with his deprived childhood, the trauma about the size of his genitals as a boy, his strange custom of parading his manhood and bathing in public, his intense relationship with his mother, the absence of any positive male figure during his formative years, and the fact that he never married, have inevitably led to speculation among scholars that Shaka was gay. Some writers, such as Donald Morris, have no doubt about it: "He was unquestionably a latent homosexual, and despite the fact that his genitals had more than made up for their previous dilatoriness, so that he always took great pride in bathing in full public view, he was probably impotent." Morris clearly didn't seem to get the point that impotence does not equal homosexuality.

Zulu-speaking historians and Zulu traditionalists mostly insist that Shaka was a virile sex machine, and accept the explanation Shaka himself gave, that he didn't want an heir because his or her life would be under threat. EA Ritter, discussing the abilities of Zulu chiefs to sexually satisfy many wives by witholding their own orgasms, states: "For a very potent and virile man, with a harem of 1 200, he established something of a record in self-control, for he only caused one authenticated pregnancy ... he too glories more in the satisfaction he was able to give rather than which he received".

Yet the same EA Ritter records a conversation between Shaka and Nandi, when she expressed unhappiness that he would not produce an heir. "Shaka defended his celibacy with the usual arguments and, when Nandi saw that she was still to be denied grandchildren, she wept. Shaka tried to console her but she became angry and, among other things, accused him of folly in trying to keep more than a thousand young and unsatisfied women in purdah. She ended her tirade with a deadly sneer: 'Sometimes,' she said meaningly, 'I wonder if there is not something in the jibes the herd-boys made at you concerning your sexual development. Perhaps you do lack potency.' Shaka was stung to the quick, for it was still a sore point with him. For a moment or two his face became distorted with rage. After a long pause, Shaka took his leave."

The "one authenticated pregnancy" Ritter refers to is also mentioned by Fynn. According to these versions, there was an occasion when Nandi was playing with a baby boy when Shaka visited her. When he asked her who it was, she said it was his child, born of a young girl named Mbuzikazi. Ritter says Shaka's reaction was: "You don't say so? How could that have come about?" The baby, according to Ritter and others, was later taken to "Tembeland" and was never heard of again. Other versions have it that Nandi so wanted a grandchild that she took a baby from one of Shaka's harem, fathered by one of his soldiers, and declared that it was Shaka's. Shaka confronted the child's mother in front of his mother and others, insisting that he had never been near her.

The Basotho of Moshoeshoe also suspected that there was something odd about Shaka's sexuality. More than one old Mosotho has told me that Moshoeshoe knew that Shaka preferred receiving softened skin of jackal, otter, buck or dassie, and pretty feathers of birds like the ostrich, crane, secretary bird and the black widow bird, rather than the usual gifts of cattle. Moshoeshoe constantly sent Shaka such gifts, because he knew the Zulu chief had a powerful army and he preferred to be on his good side. "What kind of a man would prefer skins and feathers above beautiful Basotho cattle?" one Mosotho elder asked me. "And where were his children, the pride of every man of his time? He was such a powerful king, why didn't he see to it that the royal line continued with a son? Our king had more than a hundred wives and many children – that's what real men did in those days. Shaka didn't even have one wife or one child."

Ritter tells the story that some of the young boys attached to the royal court "had developed the habit of peeping into the King's hut while he fondled his girls". Shaka ordered the boys to be caught, but they always succeeded in running away and blending in with the other boys. So Shaka ordered that all the young boys in the royal kraal be clubbed to death. One would think this was a bit extreme for a man who loved to show off his male prowess. Could it be that the boys were trying to see if their king indeed had sex with the women, or if the rumours among the herdboys, which Nandi had earlier referred to, were untrue?

John Laband does not examine the issue of Shaka's sexuality in his book, but seems to accept that he had sex with the women of his *isigodlo*: "Shaka was said to have habitually put to death any of the women of his *isigodlo* he made pregnant to prevent the birth of a rival to the throne."

Laband also gives credence to another rumour mentioned by many historians, namely that Shaka once viciously assaulted his mother. This incident, the story goes, had to do with the boy Nandi wanted to keep as a grandchild. "Enraged with Nandi over her denials of being at fault," Laband writes, "he stabbed her with the sharp shank of a spear through her leather skirt and up her anus, as she stooped to feed the fire." He adds that Shaka "suffered great remorse" when Nandi died.

I'm afraid that we will never know the real story of Shaka's sexuality – over and above the fact that it was out of the ordinary, that is. It is of course quite possible that he was a heterosexual man and that his childhood experiences and his relationship with his mother resulted in his dysfunctional attitudes (for the time) towards women, sex, marriage and fatherhood.

But his relationship with Pampata makes me doubt this. Every historian who makes mention of her states that not only did she devote her life to Shaka, but that he was very fond of her, indeed loved and admired her, thought she was beautiful, listened to her counsel often, and spent a great deal of time with her. There is no mention anywhere of any other woman Shaka liked, admired or spent time with. So why did he not have a sexual relationship with Pampata? Why didn't he marry her, even if he didn't want children?

Her loyalty to him was epic. It began when he was sixteen and

lasted until after his death at the age of about forty-two. It ended
in a way that makes the story of Romeo and Juliet look as dull as
an American television soap opera.

The historian who wrote most about Pampata was EA Ritter.
His father, Captain CLA Ritter, was a British soldier and the first
magistrate in Natal. Captain Ritter's court orderly, Njengabantu
Ema-Bovini, was the son of Mahola, a Zulu warrior who had fought
with Shaka under Dingiswayo. The author's maternal grandfather
was the Reverend CW Posselt, one of the first missionaries among
the Zulu. The author himself was born in 1890 and brought up by
Zulu women, daily listening to Njengabantu's tales of Shaka. Ritter's
principal Zulu source for his book on Shaka was Chief Signanda
Cube, who had served Shaka as a boy and became one of the most
important Zulu chroniclers. Learned scholars have often attacked
Ritter's version of events as overly romanticised and unscientific,
but I think one can accept that he reflected the oral history of the
Zulu closely.

Shaka became increasingly unpopular because of his violent
actions and authoritarian attitude, and in September 1828 he was
stabbed to death in the royal settlement of Dukuza by his two half-
brothers, Mhlangana and Dingane. In shock, all the people living
in Dukuza fled. Ritter paints a dramatic scene of what happened
next. When Pampata heard of her hero's death, she rushed to the
deserted settlement, not knowing where his body was. She ran
through a fierce electric storm, and "as Pampata approached, an
almost blinding flash illuminated the scene – and there, a few yards
away, she saw the body of the King.

"With a sob she threw herself beside the beloved figure and,
as her fingers began to caress his face, she could not, and would
not, believe that her lover – the Titan of her world – was dead.
Presently the lightning lit up his face, and as she beheld his glazed
eyes, and as the inescapable truth was forced upon her, she uttered
a piercing cry of anguish."

Pampata guarded Shaka's body throughout the night, fighting off hungry hyenas with a pole she took from a fence. "Robbed of their prey," Ritter records, "they formed a circle around Pampata and set up a hideous howling, like cackling, demented laughter." But she held out until dawn, when the hyenas left.

Pampata camouflaged her footprints around the dead body and hid in a nearby hut, contemplating suicide. But she decided against such a course, because she had to see to it that Shaka was given a proper burial, and she knew he would have wanted her to go and warn his brother Ngwadi and his other allies of Dingane's treachery.

That morning, Dingane, Mhlangana and their co-conspirator, Mbopa, arrived back at the scene of the assassination to see how much the hyenas had left of Shaka's body. They were "thunderstruck" when they saw the evidence of a large number of hyenas circling the body, but Shaka's corpse completely intact. It was probably in awe that Dingane was moved to slaughter a black ox, wrap Shaka's body in its skin and bury him in an empty grain-storage pit. (This burial site became part of a white farmer's land soon afterwards, and Shaka's grave is today somewhere under the streets of the town of Stanger.)

As soon as she was satisfied that Shaka had been buried properly, Pampata grabbed the toy spear which Shaka was famous for carrying with him, and ran to the kraal of his most loyal ally, Ngomane, some sixteen kilometres away. She warned him that Shaka was murdered and that Mbopa's army was sure to come for him too. Ngomane gave her a young man to accompany her to warn Ngwadi, and then he fled into the mountains with his family.

Pampata set off to Ngwadi's kraal some 160 kilometres away. As she and her young male companion crossed the Tugela River, they saw the glistening spears of Mbopa's army in the distance. "She had no illusions about the marching power of Zulu warriors," Ritter writes, "but woman though she was, she was determined to out-distance them. All that day she kept up a steady jog-trot, pausing only to drink a very little water." Every time she was stopped by Zulu elders, because by now "the two utterly exhausted runners looked more like fugitives than anything else", she whipped out Shaka's toy spear, which everybody knew belonged to the great king, and they let her pass.

And Pampata kept running. "Only her will-power kept Pampata running now," Ritter goes on, "for she was in a grievous state. All her toes were battered, and her feet were swollen. She was afraid to stop and rest, for she felt she would not be able to get up again." To make matters worse, she lost her way several times. Eventually her male companion gave up – "human nature could endure no more, for he lacked the almost supernatural will-power of Pampata".

Pampata kept running, until she reached Ngwadi and told him the devastating news. He immediately had his small army take up position, and the next day Mbopa's regiments fell upon them. Ngwadi and his men fought bravely, but they were seriously out-numbered. Ngwadi retreated with Pampata and all the women and children to the cattle kraal in the middle of the settlement, but soon Mbopa and his men were approaching. Mbopa urged his men to kill them all, and capture Pampata alive. It is said Ngwadi killed eight of his attackers before he was himself killed.

I will let Ritter describe what happened next. "As Ngwadi fell, at last Pampata knew her time had come, and taking the little toy spear she placed the point between two ribs opposite her heart; then she gave a vigorous push and with a cry collapsed dead, just before the massacre of the women and children took place.

"Some say that her last cry was *U-Shaka*!"

10

The Case of
the Pink Slips

THE DISCOVERY OF MASSIVE DIAMOND AND GOLD deposits in South Africa during the last decades of the nineteenth century changed the course of the country's history dramatically. It also unleashed a period of overwhelming, naked greed and callousness as powerful men built enormous fortunes. Some of the empires created then survive to this day.

This is a story that provides a glimpse of the avarice and abuse of power of the time. Two famous men, British imperialist Cecil John Rhodes and his sidekick, Leander Starr Jameson, are the main actors in the drama.

The story comes to us from the colourful Hans Sauer, member of the prominent and well-connected Sauer family. His brother, JW Sauer, was an influential Cape politician and cabinet minister, and JW's son, Paul, was a cabinet minister in the first National Party government and author of the report on which its policy of apartheid after 1948 was based. Hans was born in Smithfield in the Free State, and qualified as a medical doctor at Edinburgh University in 1881.

When he returned to South Africa in 1882, the young doctor went straight to the diamond fields of Kimberley to work as a GP. The very day after he arrived, the sanitary inspector of the town, Denis Doyle, paid him a visit. A violent epidemic of smallpox was ravaging the Cape, and the diamond mine owners feared that if the disease spread to Kimberley, "there would be a sudden and complete flight from the Fields of all the natives working in the mines". Doyle wanted Sauer to stop people from entering Griqualand West unless they had a medical certificate stating that they were free of the disease and had been vaccinated.

The next day Sauer, accompanied by a company of police, set up camp at the confluence of the Modder and Riet Rivers, near the present town of Ritchie on the N12 highway, which was the main access road to Kimberley. Sauer asked Doyle what legal right he would have to stop people from crossing the Modder River or put them in quarantine. Sauer writes in his book *Ex Africa*, published in London in 1937: "He pointed to the troop of mounted police and said, 'There's your law, and behind them is the Kimberley Town Council.' He might have added, but did not, 'And behind the Town Council is a certain Mr Cecil Rhodes.'"

For more than a year Sauer and his policemen stopped, vaccinated and quarantined many thousands of people on their way to Kimberley, and no case of the dreaded disease got through to the diamond fields. "At certain times," he recalls, "I had as many as eighteen hundred people in quarantine in a large camp formed for the purpose – all of them detained, fumigated, disinfected, and vaccinated without any legal authority whatever. There were, of course, many who objected violently, but force was always employed to make them submit, with the result that at one time I had as many as nineteen actions for assault, battery, and interference with persons on the Queen's highway, but somehow none of these actions came to anything; they all mysteriously faded away and died out. I only knew the reason for this twelve months later."

Sauer found the lawyers and judges whom he had to stop the most difficult. His encounters with the men of the law resulted in two High Court actions against him, "but these actions also faded away under the mysterious influence of some hidden force". On his return to Kimberley after fourteen months, Sauer found out that "it was Rhodes, and Rhodes alone" who had conceived of the plan and pulled all the strings. Three years later Rhodes amalgamated all the main diamond concerns into the De Beers Company, which still dominates the world diamond trade today.

It was also during this time that the diamond bosses had the possession of and trade in uncut diamonds by unlicensed persons criminalised to protect their trade. The large number of black mineworkers were forbidden to leave the mine for the entire term of their employment, to stop them from smuggling diamonds. Police and mine security set traps for suspected smugglers on a daily basis, and soon all the jails and labour camps were overcrowded. People guilty of IDB, as it was called – illicit diamond buying – were regularly sentenced to twenty-five years' imprisonment with hard labour.

For a while, Sauer lived a life of leisure in Kimberley, hunting and socialising with the mining magnates – Rhodes and Jameson, Alfred and Otto Beit, George Goch and Barney Barnato. In 1883 he went on an extended hunting expedition into today's Mpumalanga province, and paused at Mac Mac near the present Sabie, where alluvial gold had just been discovered, before travelling to Lourenço Marques (now Maputo), capital of the Portuguese colony Mozambique.

Sauer and Dr Oscar Sommershield, a partner in Dr Jameson's medical practice, took a boat to Inhaca Island in Maputo Bay. They got the Portuguese officer in charge drunk, locked him up in their boat, and annexed the island as a British possession, to the amusement of the black Mozambican troops. It lasted a full two days. They were informed that a Portuguese gunboat had been despatched to recapture the island. Hans and Oscar fled up the Maputa River and then proceeded to walk back to South Africa, but were captured by a Portuguese patrol and incarcerated in Lourenço Marques. They were released after many weeks of diplomatic wrangling between Cape Town, London, Paris and Lisbon, and walked back to Mac Mac.

Here Sauer again met Leander Jameson, who was buying up gold mining rights. A little while later, in neighbouring Lydenburg, Sauer and Jameson played a game of poker, which became famous at the time. Sauer had four kings in his hand, and thought that could not be beaten. He recalls that he "bragged up to 800 pounds, which represented all my cash resources at the time". But Jameson kept raising him, so Sauer added his wagon, all his oxen, his guns, all his medical equipment and his boots to the pot. Then Jameson revealed his hand: a straight flush. "I rose from the table broke to the wide world," Sauer writes. Jameson later returned his surgical instruments and his boots. The two men parted friends, but would not long afterwards face each other acrimoniously in civil court in another matter.

Shortly after the poker game, Sauer received a telegram from Kimberley with the news that the dreaded smallpox had broken out and requesting him to return immediately. He arrived a few days later, travelling by postal coach.

As the coach came into town, Sauer noticed young boys running around, handing little pink slips of paper to everyone. Printed on them were the words: "The disease at Felstead's farm is not smallpox, it is a bulbous disease of the skin allied to pemphigus." It was signed by Sauer's poker friend Jameson and four other doctors. Sauer had never heard of this condition, but soon heard that a group of Mozambicans had been stopped by police on a farm called Felstead, outside Kimberley, on suspicion that they were sick with smallpox. Dr Jameson and a deputation of six other doctors went to investigate, and reported to the Cape government that it was indeed smallpox. That was when the authorities sent for Hans, because he had a lot of experience with the disease. But a week later Jameson changed his story and declared it was pemphigus, an extremely rare but entirely curable skin condition.

Sauer went to Felstead to investigate, and found that the men were suffering from "smallpox pure and simple, with nothing abnormal about it". He reported this to Cape Town, and was appointed Medical Officer of Health of the district to deal with the epidemic.

Within days the epidemic spread, and people, especially black mineworkers, started dying. Not one of the doctors who had signed the pink slips – Sauer refers to them as "the pemphigus men" – ever reported a case to him, but the other medical practitioners did so on a daily basis. Sauer was denied permission to enter the mineworkers' compounds, where, he was told, many were ill and dead bodies were lying around. When he eventually forced his way into the Du Toit's Pan compound outside Kimberley, he found "a disgusting state of affairs": many dead bodies and many patients in the final stages of the horrible disease. He had no idea how many workers had already been buried under false death certificates.

"My report on this incident produced an outburst of hostility so extensive and virulent that I was obliged to have some of the armed sanitary police with me whenever I made my rounds," Sauer wrote. The mining magnates and businessmen hated him most, but so did shopkeepers and other white business people, even the white miners.

The reason for the conspiracy was simple: if it became known that there were cases of smallpox in Kimberley, the black workforce would flee and go back home, and all mining activity would come to an end. The mining bosses and their henchmen would rather see hundreds of men die than see their profits diminish.

Despite Sauer's reports to the Cape government and reports published in the Kimberley newspapers that the disease was indeed smallpox, Jameson and his masters continued their conspiracy of deceit for two years, while every day people died, mostly black but also some ordinary white folk. As fast as Sauer could vaccinate the population, more black workers came from outside to seek work and were employed to replace the sick and the dead. He was denied access to their places of living, so they were inevitably also attacked by the disease. For as long as Jameson and the other doctors insisted that there was no smallpox on the diamond fields but that the prevalent disease was a harmless skin disorder, the public did not feel it necessary to be vaccinated or isolated, or even notify the authorities of cases of the disease.

Sauer campaigned for a new, wide-ranging Public Health Act, which would make smallpox a notifiable disease to be promulgated by the colonial government. Eventually, after lobbying by his brother and another prominent Cape politician he knew well, John X Merriman, the law was passed.

"The passing of this excellent law made me the most unpopular man on the Diamond Fields," Sauer wrote. "High Society turned its back on me, and as for the ruck of the population, it simply spat when I passed."

As part of the campaign against Sauer, a rumour was spread that he only called the disease smallpox because he made money out of it. Then one day someone told him that the secretary of the civil commissioner had made this accusation in his presence. Sauer bought "a beautiful horsewhip" and went to see this man in his office. Sauer told him that his statement was slanderous and, unless he wrote an abject apology for publication in the press, he was going to beat him up. "On hearing this, he seized a long ruler and made a lunge at me. I warded off the blow and had no difficulty in getting him down on the floor and giving him a sound horsewhipping."

The slanderer, identified only as Mr B, then sued him in the High Court of Griqualand West. Sauer was forced to pay him a hundred pounds. "The judgment was wrong, as the plaintiff in the box admitted the slander. As a matter of fact, the influence of the diamond trade was so great that it was difficult to obtain justice for the side that was in conflict with it," Sauer remarked. It wasn't his last appearance in court during his battle to counter the smallpox epidemic.

A young Irishman told Sauer that a friend and countryman of his had died of smallpox at Kimberley hospital, but before his death he had been operated on by Dr Jameson and an associate, Dr Wolff. Sauer told the police to cordon off the hospital and forced his way in. He found that all nurses and staff had recently been vaccinated against smallpox.

Then Dr Wolff arrived and threatened to throw Sauer out, but in turn Sauer told the police to "throw that man out into the road", which they did. During Sauer's further inspection of the hospital he found the bodies of men who had died of smallpox, and several patients with the disease freely mixing with other patients, with no attempt to isolate them. He found the corpse of the young Irishman, who had died of a severe attack of smallpox, his whole body covered in pustular eruptions and his face and head hugely swollen. He also found, as the dead man's friend had said, that a tracheotomy had been performed on him. Sauer remarked that the operation was "useless, needless and verging on criminality".

The next day he made a full report to the authorities, accusing the doctors and their associates of gross unprofessional conduct. "The publication of my report created a sensation not only on the Diamond Fields but throughout the whole South Africa. Strong protests were made by the medical men scattered over the country and public opinion was aroused."

Two days after the report was published, Dr Leander Jameson sued Sauer for defamation in the High Court. He also repeated the slander of the horsewhipped man that Sauer only diagnosed smallpox because he was making money out of it, so Sauer counter-sued him for the same amount. The court told Sauer to pay Jameson damages of two thousand pounds, and Jameson to pay Sauer two thousand pounds. Another case of judges who couldn't resist the pressure of the diamond bosses, Sauer remarked.

(Sauer was also deeply annoyed by Jameson's statement that, as the only doctor who had graduated from London University, his opinion should be given more weight than the other Kimberley doctors. The University of Edinburgh, Sauer protested, was the best medical school in Europe at the time.)

Sauer wasn't done yet with the doctors who were involved in the conspiracy. He found out that Dr Wolff had visited a patient, a Mrs Greenhough, in the neighbouring town of Bultfontein. When he left, her friend, a Mrs Sarsfield, asked him what the matter was with her, and Wolff replied that she had a mild form of pneumonia. She asked whether it would be safe to visit her friend, and Wolff solemnly assured her that she could visit her without fear.

When Mrs Sarsfield saw her friend, she fainted: her whole body was festering with pus-filled blisters. Twelve days later, the precise incubation time of smallpox, Mrs Sarsfield also showed the symptoms of the disease. Sauer had no doubt that she'd contracted it from Mrs Greenhough, and had Dr Wolff charged with murder. But in the witness box Sauer could not completely rule out the possibility that Mrs Sarsfield caught the contagion from someone else, and Wolff was found not guilty.

Eventually, after months of Sauer's lobbying, the colonial government sent a Dr Saunders (he graduated from London University) to investigate the disease that had struck the diamond fields. His verdict, after many weeks of delay, was clear: "The disease at present prevailing in Kimberley is smallpox."

Once the public were convinced of this, most came forward to be vaccinated, and by the end of 1885 the diamond fields were clear of the disease.

Sauer doesn't give a definitive death toll, but several times in his book he talks about "many thousands of people, mostly natives" who died during the epidemic. He concludes: "I must state my conviction that many people contracted and died of the disease as the direct consequence of the action taken by those who signed the pink slip."

The scandal had little or no impact on the future fortunes of Cecil Rhodes, Leander Jameson and other diamond magnates and their tame doctors. In fact, they were up to much more mischief. When gold was discovered on the Witwatersrand in 1886, that's where they all went – as did tens of thousands of other foreigners from all over the world, which meant they soon outnumbered the burghers of the Transvaal Republic of President Paul Kruger.

By the mid-1890s the tension between Kruger's government and the Uitlanders [foreigners] had reached breaking point. Cecil John Rhodes, with Leander Jameson again right beside him, desired the fabulously rich reef of gold, the biggest deposit in the world, to belong to Britain. Rhodes believed the Transvaal held the key to the whole of southern Africa, and he dreamt of the entire subcontinent being British. The easiest way to make this plan work, they figured, was to transfer political control to the Uitlanders.

Rhodes, then prime minister of the Cape Colony, and leaders of the Reform Committee, a political lobby group consisting mainly of Uitlanders, hatched a plan that there should be an uprising of Uitlanders in Johannesburg, coinciding with an invasion from the British protectorate of Bechuanaland (now Botswana). The British high commissioner would then travel from the Cape Colony and proclaim British sovereignty over the Transvaal. Leander Starr Jameson was in charge of the raiding party.

The plan failed disastrously. Jameson decided to invade on 30 December 1895, even though he knew the "uprising" was postponed. The Boers heard of the invasion, and a commando under General Piet Cronjé forced Jameson's force to surrender at Doornkop on 2 January 1896.

Paul Kruger sent Jameson to be tried in England, where he was found guilty and sent to jail. Rhodes was forced to resign as prime minister, and left to spend his energies colonising the land that would be named after him, Rhodesia (now Zimbabwe).

The most surprising twist to this story was that, despite his experiences with Rhodes and Jameson, Hans Sauer was a member of the Reform Committee that was implicated in the conspiracy. However, there was no evidence that he had known about the planned raid or was in favour of an armed uprising. He was charged with treason with the other members of the committee, but pleaded guilty to a lesser charge and spent three months in jail.

The Jameson Raid damaged the relationship between the Transvaal Republic and Britain irreparably. On 11 October 1899 the Transvaal declared war against Britain, a war that raged for two years and nine months and changed the face of South Africa forever.

If only Rhodes and Jameson had been stopped in their tracks after the scandal of the pink slips.

11

Broedertwis

THE WORD *BROEDERTWIS* HAS LONG BEEN PART OF THE
South African political lexicon. It means a quarrel between
brothers, but is not usually used in the literal sense of biological
brothers in disagreement, but rather in the case of a fallout or
struggle between former partners, close associates or persons from
the same ethnic group.

This is the story of the mother of all *broedertwiste*, and this time
it is meant literally. It features one of the most famous Afrikaner
heroes of all time, who has been at the centre of glorious stories
told to children for more than a century, and his brother, whose
name hardly gets a mention in official Afrikaner history – or around
any self-respecting fire or kitchen table, for that matter. (A bit like
Coenraad de Buys.)

It is the story of Generals Christiaan and Piet de Wet.

Christiaan Rudolf and Pieter Daniël de Wet's parents were
young Voortrekkers, participants in the great migration of Eastern
Cape trekboers into the interior after 1838, later called the Great
Trek. The De Wets farmed in the Orange Free State, which became
a Boer republic in 1854, ten years after the Transvaal Republic
was declared. Christiaan, also called Krisjan, was born in 1854, and
Pieter, known to all as Piet, in 1861.

Christiaan and Piet grew up together on Nieuwejaarsfontein,
their father's farm in the district of the present-day town of
Dewetsdorp – so named, of course, after Christiaan. In 1879, Piet
joined Christiaan on his farm near Heidelberg in the Transvaal.
But they soon shared a lot more than a farm.

Towards the end of the nineteenth century, Britain started to show greater interest in the Boer republics, after diamonds were discovered in Kimberley and gold in Johannesburg. On 8 December 1880, the two brothers rode on horseback to Paardekraal outside Krugersdorp to attend a *volksvergadering*, a gathering of the people, where burghers of the Transvaal decided to resist the annexure of their republic by the British.

Later that year Christiaan and Piet joined the same commando fighting the British in what the Boers called the First War of Freedom. Together they took part in the glorious victory over the British forces of General George Colley at Majuba on 27 February 1881.

After the end of the war in 1881, both brothers returned to the Free State: Christiaan to a farm in the Heilbron district, and Piet to the neighbouring Lindley district. Both were elected members of the Free State parliament, the Volksraad. Piet spent 1898 in Pretoria, where he became a friend of President Paul Kruger. Christiaan also knew the president, because he had served on the Transvaal Volksraad in the year 1885.

When full-scale war between the British Empire and the Transvaal began in October 1899, the Anglo-Boer War or Second War of Freedom, the two brothers were in enthusiastic agreement that the Free State should join its sister republic in arms. They rode into battle, Piet as veldkornet of the Lindley commando, Christiaan as an ordinary burgher in the Heilbron commando.

Heilbron's commandant, Lucas Steenkamp, became ill right at the beginning of the war and appointed Christiaan as acting commandant. Together with other Free State commandos, including Piet's, they confronted the British troops at Nicholsonsnek on the Natal border on 30 October. The 300 Boer soldiers quickly forced the surrender of 850 British troops. It was the beginning of Christiaan's illustrious military career: Free State president MT Steyn was so impressed that he appointed Christiaan as field-general under General Piet Cronjé in December 1899.

Piet also led his men with distinction, first at Nicholsonsnek, then at the siege of Ladismith in November. On 16 December, a force under Piet's command liberated the British stronghold at Vaalkop. A few days after his brother, he was also appointed as general by President Steyn: he became the chief commandant in charge of the southern front. He was only thirty-eight.

Piet became quite famous as a fighting general during the first stages of the war. He opposed the passive policies of Generals ER Grobler and JH Schoeman, and in joint operations with another famous Boer general, Koos de la Rey, he became more and more aggressive towards the enemy.

In February 1900, his old friend President Kruger requested President Steyn to send Piet and his men to the western front to bolster the forces under General Cronjé. En route he was told that Cronjé had surrendered with four thousand men at Paardeberg. It was a massive blow. Piet and his men then joined Christiaan and his units in successful battles at Abrahamskraal, Sannaspost and Dewetsdorp in March and April 1900.

The first indication of a difference of opinion between the two brothers came towards the end of April 1900. Piet was in favour of using all resources and energy to stop the British head-on, but Christiaan believed the enemy should be attacked and disrupted from the rear. Albert Grundlingh says in his book *Die 'Hensoppers' en 'Joiners'* that Piet de Wet believed in a more conventional method of warfare than his brother. Christiaan's irregular, unconventional methods became a hallmark of his strategy, and he is still regarded as one of the early tacticians of guerrilla warfare.

Conventional or not, Piet de Wet remained a very successful and respected military commander. In May 1900, two days after General Roberts had annexed the Free State, Piet and his forces captured the 468 men of the 13th Battalion Imperial Yeomanry near his hometown of Lindley. There were many members of the

British aristocracy among the prisoners. It was a heavy blow to the British and a solid boost for the Boer morale.

Christiaan continued to develop his tactics of guerrilla warfare, making his fighting units more mobile, attacking the British from the rear and destroying their lines of supply and communication. On 31 March 1900, he defeated Brigadier-General RG Broadwood at Sannaspos, east of Bloemfontein, and captured 116 wagons of ammunition and supplies. The British lost 159 soldiers, the Boers only 13. This was the stuff that grew Christiaan into a legend, and he remained the main thorn in the British side right up to the end of the war.

(When I was a child, my own grandmother, Alberta du Preez, the survivor of a concentration camp, told me a story about Christiaan de Wet. In fact, she told the same story many times over. It has the feeling of an urban legend, if they existed during the Boer War, but she told it as if it had happened to her. She was on the family farm in the Free State when some British soldiers came by. Her mother (or aunt, I can't remember) offered them coffee, and they accepted. She asked them if they preferred their coffee black or white, and at that moment they jumped up and raced off. The Afrikaans for white is "wit", which sounded to them much like De Wet ... Anyway, that was my grandmother's story.)

Christiaan, by the way, strongly objected to being called a guerrilla. In his memoirs of the war, *Die Stryd tussen Boer en Brit,* he says the British first called the Boers "rebels", then "sniping bands" and "brigands", and "now the Boers were given the abusive name of guerrillas and their leaders are called guerrilla leaders. I cannot see how England can be so arrogant to make us out to be guerrillas ... [I]f England's capital were occupied by another country, England would be seen as having been annexed by that country, while its government was still standing: would the enemy have called the English guerrillas? Surely not!"

But by mid-1900 Piet started to realise that the war could not be won. The British Empire's army was vastly superior in numbers, armaments and supplies. By March the British had taken the capital, Bloemfontein, and soon thereafter the other temporary seats of government. General Michael Prinsloo, fighting with Christiaan, surrendered with three thousand men in July.

The first indication that Piet was considering giving himself up came in May, when he discussed the possibility in a letter to the British general Ian Hamilton. In June he agreed to a six-day ceasefire with Lord Methuen. Christiaan convened a meeting of top officers a few days later to discuss this ceasefire, and the two brothers had an angry and public disagreement. Piet accused Christiaan and the other leaders of misleading the people by saying that the Boers were going to get help from Europe.

According to one of the officers present, HG de Wet, the exchange between the brothers went like this: "General Piet de Wet told them that he considers it time to stop this fight; that the talk of the intervention of other Powers was manufactured to mislead the Burghers to keep them in the veld, and that the European Powers could not come to the assistance of the Republics if they wished, and that he refused to be a party to this deliberate false-hood. It will only end in the complete ruination of the country and innocent women and children will be the sufferers. General Christian de Wet, great fighter as he was, was well known to be very hotheaded and could not tolerate views that did not tally with his sentiments. He lost his temper and insulted his brother Piet. General Piet de Wet then said: 'I wash my hands, I will not order another man into a fight to be killed in a hopeless cause. I will not be a party to the complete ruin of my country.'"

Still, Piet continued to fight, and in late June he even made himself available for election as the supreme commander of the Free State forces. But the election was cut short by President Steyn, who bypassed the process and appointed Christiaan directly. Piet was very unhappy about this, and blamed the president for causing dissension.

The last straw for Piet came on 19 July, when he and the legendary Danie Theron were forced to retreat by the superior force of General RG Broadwood.

The next day Piet met Christiaan in the Lindley district and asked him if it wasn't time to consider peace. An incensed Christiaan shouted, "Are you mad?" Four days later Piet and some of his senior officers went to Lindley to negotiate a surrender with the British forces. On 26 July 1900, he gave himself up to the British officer at Kroonstad.

When Christiaan was told of his brother's surrender, he said to General CCJ Badenhorst: "If only I had shot him dead."

In August Piet warned that he would give the leaders of the two republics a chance "to get their foreign intervention or to produce their party that has guaranteed our independence, and if they don't do so in six months, I will take any action that is necessary to stop the war". He then left for Durban, where he stayed until mid-December.

On his way back he went to see Christiaan's wife, Cornelia, to plead with her to influence her husband to stop the war. She called his visit "a source of unpleasantness", and asked the local police commissioner to tell Piet that she didn't want him to visit again. But his own wife, Susanna, was apparently very supportive of his views. When General JBM Hertzog and Oscar Hintrager went to visit Piet on his farm in June, only to find her there alone, according to them, she "couldn't stop talking" of how many farms the British had set on fire and how much property they had confiscated.

Back home Piet formed the Burgher Peace Committee of the Free State. True to his statement that he was abandoning the war in the interest of the ordinary civilians in the Free State, he repeatedly registered his protest with the British forces at the way they were treating women and children. He even went to see General Kelly-Kenny to complain about the British "methods of carrying on the war with reference to the Boer women".

On 11 January 1901, Piet wrote an open letter to his brother, which was published in the *Bloemfontein Post*. It was published as a booklet by the Argus Company the same year, an original copy of which I found in the National Library in Cape Town. It has the cumbersome title *Broeder tot Broeder. Een prijzenswaardige Brief. Een smeekstem tot De Wet. De Wet's verantwoordelikheid.* [Brother to Brother. A praiseworthy letter. A voice pleading to De Wet. De Wet's responsibility.]

The letter was written in Dutch, and starts (my translation): "Dear Brother. I heard that you were very angry with me and that, if you found me, you would kill me. God forbid that you would have the opportunity to spill more innocent blood. Enough has already been spilled. I am informed that you are accusing me of high treason; but grant me a moment to present the case in the correct light, and to request that you read it in an unbiased manner and with the common sense God has given you.

"Did I not, from the beginning of the war, do my duty towards my government? And although not one of the bravest soldiers, I fought as well as I could. Judge me fairly. What did I do when I eventually saw that we were conquered by the English troops and that it was a lost hope to regain what we had lost? Did I lay down my arms in a reckless manner? No, I wrote a letter to the President requesting him to consider peace, to hand over the country rather than to ruin it and let the population die."

Stating that to continue the war against Britain was not only against God's word but also bad politics, Piet continues: "I beseech you again, put all your inflamed emotion to one side and use your common sense for one moment, then you will agree with me that the best the people of our country can do is to give in, to be loyal to the new government, to try to get a representative government, as soon as it is financially possible, also for the Cape Colony and Natal, and so rule our country ourselves, to see our children educated and to rescue our volk as a volk for the future of South Africa.

"On the other hand: if the war continues for another few months our people will be so poor – as a huge section of them already are – that we will be reduced to the working class of this country and in any case will disappear as a nation."

He concludes: "Are you blind? Can you not see that you are being deceived by the Transvaal generals and burghers? What are you doing? They are not fighting against one tenth of what we're fighting against and their country is not as ruined as the Free State. They are prepared to lay down arms; they are just waiting to see what you are going to do. The moment you fall, give over or are captured, they will surrender." He signed it "Expecting the best, I remain, Your Brother, PD de Wet."

In June 1901, Piet de Wet went from *hensopper* [hands-upper] to *joiner*. About ten months after he warned the Boer leaders to stop the war or else he would himself "take action" to stop it, he and members of his peace committee started acting as scouts and guides for the British forces. He also proposed to the British high command that an organised corps of burgher scouts be formed, which led to the formation of the Orange River Colony Volunteers in 1902. (Field Marshall Lord Roberts had formally annexed the Free State on 28 May 1900 and renamed it the Orange River Colony.) Piet's co-commander was another distinguished former Boer commander, Stephanus Vilonel. Vilonel had surrendered only two weeks after the Free State officers promoted him to general, a promotion he declined.

In the Transvaal, a similar organisation to the Orange River Colony Volunteers, the National Scouts, was established, with *joiners* as members. (The Volunteers were also often called the National Scouts.) One of the leaders of the National Scouts was General Andries Cronjé, brother of General Piet Cronjé. Now there were two Boer generals, both brothers of famous Boer generals, who had turned against their own people and joined the enemy.

Like Piet de Wet, Andries Cronjé had a distinguished record as a military commander. In January 1902, he explained his reasons for "joining" at a meeting in Potchefstroom: "We know perfectly well that we have no chance against the British forces, so in consideration of the prisoners of war, the families who are in Burgher camps, for our own sakes we must do our best to stop the war without bloodshed if possible, but stop it, and that right early."

In February 1902, Piet de Wet told a public meeting in Kroonstad: "I love my people with the same love wherewith I loved them before the war, and ever strived to procure their best interests, and we can thank God that, having lost our independence, it has been taken from us by a government that treats us as well as can be wished. We will go on hoping to have peace soon and that the day will soon dawn when we all in Africa, as Afrikaners that have one interest, will live together as brothers and will faithfully support our government."

The *joiners* were hated for a long time after the war ended in 1902 and the republics lost their independence. The Afrikaans writer Eugéne Marais wrote: "The hatred is there, as deep as the sea and as wide as God's earth ... We hate these people from the depths of our hearts because they brought dishonour throughout the whole world to our honest name. It is not possible to forgive, much less to forget."

After the war Christiaan de Wet told a meeting in Kroonstad that the *joiners* and *hensoppers* were "murderers of their own people" and that they belonged in a pig sty. Later that year Piet was having a drink at the Grand Hotel in Kroonstad when Christiaan walked in. According to an eyewitness account quoted by Albert Grundlingh, "On seeing each other they fell to and had an awful row, which would have undoubtedly led to a free fight had they not been separated. Christiaan then turned away and said he would not remain under the same roof with so black a traitor."

In his memoirs, Christiaan came close to blaming the *joiners* for the Boers losing the war. He writes that the British were terrible at scouting and intelligence, until they were joined by the "handsuppers, or better put: Boere-deserters". The night attacks on the Boers in the later stages of the war were devastating, but would not have been possible if they hadn't been led "by our own flesh and blood: the National Scouts".

"What calamity these defectors caused us! I call them by the real name later [he meant traitor]: the name they have to carry to the perpetual abhorrence not only of the Afrikaans people, but of every nation in the world who could possibly land in the difficulty the two Boer republics were pushed in, mainly by our unfaithful burghers." Not once in the book's many references to Piet de Wet does he call him his brother – in the first part he refers to him as General De Wet, and in the latter part simply as "Piet de Wet of the National Scouts".

For years after the war the hatred of the National Scouts led to schisms in Afrikaner society. Fights often broke out between *bittereinders*, those who were determined to fight to the bitter end, and *joiners*.

Former Scouts could not find jobs and were not elected onto church councils. The Nederduits Hervormde Kerk even demanded that former Scouts confess their guilt before they were allowed holy communion. This led to the formation of a breakaway Scout's Church with seven congregations in 1904, but the church did not last long.

Albert Grundlingh points out in his book about the *joiners* that there was a class difference: most of the members of the National Scouts were *bywoners*, tenant farmers, who did not believe they had something to fight for. (When I was a child in Kroonstad in the late 1950s and early 1960s, I knew who the families of the former *joiners* were. We didn't regard them as good Afrikaners.)

Christiaan de Wet remained a *bittereinder* until long after the war. He was a leader of the 1914 Rebellion and was captured in November that year. He was sentenced to six years in jail, but was freed after just six months. He died on 23 February 1922, and is buried at the foot of the Women's Memorial in Bloemfontein.

Piet died seven years later in a small house in the town of Lindley. His estate was worth only 500 pounds. The two brothers were never reconciled.

Most Afrikaners still regard Piet de Wet as a traitor and a shameful chapter in Afrikaner history. Few considered the validity of his arguments in mid-1900: the war against the mighty British Empire was indeed impossible to win, and if the Boer republics had surrendered then, the terrible scorched-earth policy of the British would not have devastated the Afrikaners (and South Africa) to the extent it did. In the end, 26 251 Boer women and children, and possibly even more black South Africans (the official figure is 14 154), died in the awful concentration camps; more than 30 000 Boer farmhouses and several towns were destroyed; many hundreds of thousands of sheep, cattle and horses were killed; many thousands of men, some of them boys as young as nine, were sent to prisoner-of-war camps in Ceylon, Bermuda, St Helena and the Cape. My paternal grandfather spent two years in Ceylon.

Afrikaners would later say they lost the war but won the peace. On 31 May 1910, the Cape, Natal, Transvaal and Orange Free State became the self-governing Union of South Africa, with a whites-only government. Fifty-one years later the Afrikaners again realised their republican dreams when they declared South Africa a republic. It lasted exactly thirty-three years. Afrikaner dissidents again played a significant role in its demise and transformation into a proper democracy in 1994.

12

That Bloody Coolie

PERHAPS IT HAD SOMETHING TO DO WITH THE UNIQUE confluence of peoples and cultures in South Africa during a particular time in history. Or maybe it was something in the water. Whatever the explanation, the southern tip of Africa is the place where two of the world's most prominent latter-day saints emerged: Mahatma Gandhi and Nelson Mandela.

Both men's greatness was first stirred by racism and oppression in South Africa. Yet one can hardly imagine two men more different: Gandhi a small, austere, self-effacing and soft-spoken man in a homespun cotton dhoti and shawl; Mandela a tall, forceful, proud man, wearing flamboyant shirts, whose inherent power dominates all he meets.

But they also shared much. Both were rural boys who became lawyers in Johannesburg. Both spent time in South African jails. Both were taken from their jail cells for personal meetings with the South African head of state: Gandhi with Prime Minister Jan Smuts on 30 January 1908, Mandela with State President PW Botha on 5 July 1989. Both were affectionately called names other than their own: Mohandas Karamchand was called Mahatma, the Great Soul, and Nelson Rolihlahla was called Madiba, his Xhosa clan name. Both were driven by a love of human freedom and dignity; both were blessed with patience and perseverance. Mahatma was the international icon of non-violent resistance to colonial oppression

133

and injustice, Madiba went on to become the father of South African democracy and the symbol of the African Renaissance.

Gandhi's relentless commitment to truth, peace, unity and dignity made him a major inspiration to the greatest libertarian spirits of our time, such as Mandela himself, Martin Luther King and Aung San Suu Kyi.

If only the petty racists who physically attacked this "uppity coolie" on several occasions on the streets of South Africa knew what his contribution to humanity was going to be.

Mohan Gandhi, also called Monya or Manu by his family, was born in Porbander in India on 2 October 1869. He trained as a lawyer in London, and at the age of twenty-four he came to South Africa at the invitation of an Indian law firm that was engaged in a large commercial court case. The first Indians were brought to South Africa from 1860 onwards as indentured labourers destined for the sugar plantations, and later some Indian traders and professional people also immigrated to South Africa.

He arrived by ship in Durban on 23 May 1893. His first impression as he disembarked to be met by his host, Abdulla Sheth, was that "Indians were not held in much respect". He soon had personal experience of this: two days later, when he was taken to the Durban court, the magistrate ordered him to take off his turban. He promptly refused and left the court. He wrote a letter to the local newspaper about the incident and it was hotly debated, Gandhi often being referred to as an "unwelcome visitor". Gandhi's struggle with racism had begun.

A week later he set off for Pretoria, where the court case was supposed to be held. He booked a first class ticket on the train and all went well as far as Pietermaritzburg, when a white passenger joined him in his compartment. When he saw the colour of Gandhi's skin, he fetched two officials, who told "the coolie" to move to the guard compartment. (The whites also sometimes called the Indians "samis", -*sami* being a suffix to most Tamil names.)

Gandhi related the incident in his autobiography.

"But I have a first class ticket," said I.

"That doesn't matter," rejoined the other. "I tell you,
you must go to the van compartment."

"I tell you, I was permitted to travel in this compartment
at Durban, and I insist on going on it."

"No you won't," said the official. "You must leave this
compartment, or else I shall call a police constable to push
you out."

"Yes, you may. I refuse to go voluntarily."

The constable came. He took me by the hand
and pushed me out. My luggage was also taken out.
I refused to go to the other compartment and the train
steamed away.

Gandhi spent a cold night on the platform, and the next day sent
a telegram to the general manager of the railway. The manager
defended the behaviour of his officials, but nevertheless gave orders
that Gandhi should be allowed on the train. He travelled without
incident to Charlestown, where the rail line ended, and tried to
get on the stagecoach to Johannesburg.

The white man in charge of the coach at first refused, but when
confronted with a paid-up ticket, he told Gandhi to sit on the seat
outside the coach box, because he thought it would be improper to
seat a "coolie" with the other white passengers. Gandhi was
seething, but wanted to get to Johannesburg without further delay
and took the seat.

But by the time the coach reached Paardekop, the coach master
wanted to have a smoke outside the coach box and reclaimed
his usual seat. He spread a dirty cloth on the footboard and told
Gandhi: "Sami, you sit on this, I want to sit near the driver."

Gandhi's indignation boiled over. "It was you who seated me
here, though I should have been accommodated inside," he said to

the white man. "I put up with the insult. Now that you want to sit outside and smoke, you would have me sit at your feet. I will not do so, but I am prepared to sit inside."

The man attacked Gandhi, hitting him on the ears and trying to throw him on the floor. Gandhi, a short and skinny man, simply clung to the brass rails of the coach while he was assaulted and sworn at. Eventually some of the white passengers intervened and Gandhi could take his seat once more.

In Johannesburg, Gandhi tried to book into a hotel, but the manager just looked at him and then declared that the hotel was full. Gandhi related his experiences to his new Indian friends in Johannesburg. They laughed, recounting many of their own experiences of racial discrimination. One, Abdul Gani Sheth, told him: "Only we can live in a land like this, because, for making money, we do not mind pocketing insults, and here we are. This country is not for men like you."

Gandhi rejected the advice of his friends and again insisted on travelling first class in the train to Pretoria. The guard tried to kick him off, but the only white passenger in the compartment said he didn't mind travelling with him. "If you want to travel with a coolie, what do I care?" muttered the guard and left.

These experiences made a deep impression on the young Gandhi and stirred him to perform his first political act. He called a meeting of all Indians in Pretoria and gave the first public speech of his life, discussing the social and political position of Indians in South Africa. They had to pay a poll tax to enter the old Transvaal, while they were allowed into the Orange Free State only if they worked as waiters. Indians were not allowed to use public footpaths and had to have a permit to be outside after 9 p.m.

Gandhi liked to walk the streets of Pretoria, especially along President Street towards a public square. This meant he walked past the simple house of President Paul Kruger every day. The police guarding the president never bothered him, until one day when a new policeman was on duty. Without warning the policeman pushed and kicked him off the sidewalk into the street. A white friend of Gandhi's noticed this and intervened, offering to be a witness if Gandhi wanted to have his attacker prosecuted. Gandhi responded: "What does the poor man know? All coloured people are the same to him. He no doubt treats Negroes just as he treated me. I have made it a rule not to go to court in respect of any personal grievance." But the incident deepened Gandhi's resolve to fight for a better deal for South African Indians.

After he had settled the legal case which brought him to South Africa, Gandhi returned to Durban. At a farewell party in his honour, he read in a newspaper of the Natal Legislative Assembly's plans to take away the Indians' right to elect members of that assembly. His hosts weren't even aware of the issue. When he explained it to them, they pleaded with him to stay and help them fight the Bill.

Gandhi stayed and applied for admission to practise as an advocate of the Supreme Court of Natal. The Law Society had never allowed men other than whites to practise law, so they opposed his application on several technical grounds. Eventually, these were overruled by the Supreme Court and he was admitted, but he was forbidden to wear his turban in court. Gandhi was unhappy, but decided to "reserve my strength for fighting bigger battles" and conceded. He remarked at the time that "all my life through, the very insistence on truth has taught me to appreciate the beauty of compromise".

Gandhi thought a formal organisation was needed to fight for Indians' rights, and in May 1894, exactly a year after he arrived in South Africa, he formed the Natal Indian Congress and was elected as the first secretary. This movement remained at the forefront of Indian political resistance for decades and eventually played a key role in the South African liberation movement, the African National Congress. The Congress's first victory was to have a new tax of £25 on indentured Indian labourers lowered to £3. Gandhi published two pamphlets, *An Appeal to Every Briton in South Africa* and *The Indian Franchise: An Appeal,* and both were distributed widely. Gandhi was fast becoming a household name in Natal and Transvaal politics.

After three years in South Africa, Gandhi returned home for six months in 1896, but continued to campaign for South African Indian rights through pamphlets and newspaper articles. He returned on the steamship *Courland,* which sailed from India with the *Naderi.* In Durban harbour the two ships were put under quarantine on the pretext that there had been a contagious epidemic in Bombay when they sailed. But the real reason was that the white people of Durban didn't want the ships full of Indian immigrants to dock. During the time that the ships waited outside the harbour, white pressure groups held protest meetings, issued threats against the ship owners and even offered to pay all the fares if the ships were sent back to India.

Gandhi was the real target of the protests. The whites, supported by the Natal colonial government, accused him of slandering them while in India and of bringing shiploads full of Indians to Natal to "swamp" the province. But under Gandhi's leadership, the passengers refused to budge and twenty-three days later the ships were allowed into the harbour.

The port authorities, fearing violence, advised Gandhi to disembark after dark. But it was decided that it would send a negative message if he were to return to South Africa like a thief in the night. He sent his wife and three children ahead by car, and stepped off the ship in daylight, walking to his lodgings a few kilometres away.

He hadn't even left the harbour grounds when he was recognised by some whites. When they started shouting at him, Gandhi and his companion got into a rickshaw to move faster. But the crowd became bigger and more aggressive, and eventually the rickshaw couldn't move any further. The whites pelted Gandhi with stones, rotten eggs and other missiles. Someone ripped off his turban, and then the crowd started hitting and kicking him. "I fainted and caught hold of the front railings of a house and stood there to get my breath. But it was impossible. They came upon me boxing and battering," he wrote later.

Gandhi was saved by Mrs Alexander, the wife of the local police superintendent, who knew him. She stood between him and the crowd and opened her parasol as protection, so that the crowd couldn't hurt him without hurting her first. Then the police arrived and escorted him to the house where he was due to stay.

But the crowd quickly surrounded the house, chanting: "We must have Gandhi!" The police superintendent advised Gandhi to leave the house if he wanted to save his family and his friend's property. He was dressed in an Indian police constable's uniform and escorted by a white policeman, his face painted dark and dressed as an Indian merchant, to a waiting carriage which took him to the local police station. While this was going on, the enterprising police superintendent, Alexander, entertained the crowd outside the house by singing the tune "Hang old Gandhi on the sour apple tree". When he was informed that Gandhi had successfully escaped, he allowed representatives of the crowd to inspect the house to verify that Gandhi wasn't there, and the crowd dispersed. Gandhi refused an offer by the colonial authorities to prosecute his attackers, saying that the white political leadership was to blame for their fury.

The odd thing about Gandhi at the time was his loyalty to Britain and his belief that the British Empire was a benign one. He had the British national anthem sung at all his meetings and often publicly defended Britain. "The colour prejudice that I saw in South Africa was, I thought, quite contrary to British traditions, and believed that it was only temporary and local. I therefore vied with Englishmen in loyalty to the throne," he wrote in his autobiography.

This would explain why, in 1899, he volunteered to establish an ambulance corps of 1 100 men to serve the British forces during the Anglo-Boer War – despite his personal sympathies being "all with the Boers". He explained: "I felt that, if I demanded rights as a British citizen, it was also my duty, as such, to participate in the defence of the British Empire." He did the same in 1906, when he raised an ambulance corps of Indian volunteers to serve the British forces acting to suppress a Zulu rebellion against a poll tax during which Chief Bambatha was killed. This time Gandhi was even appointed a temporary sergeant major in the British army. More than three thousand black people and only twenty-four British soldiers were killed.

Gandhi started a communal settlement on a farm north of Durban, called Phoenix, and with friends he launched a newspaper, the *Indian Opinion*. But when a new law was promulgated in 1906 forcing Indians in South Africa to carry registration papers documenting their fingerprints, he moved to Johannesburg to help organise a passive resistance campaign. The movement was called *Satyagraha*, which can be translated as soul force; its philosophy was honest and non-violent defiance of the offending law, the endurance of imprisonment if necessary, but always showing respect to those who made the law or enforced it.

Gandhi was one of the leaders jailed for failing to comply, and this was when he was taken to Prime Minister Smuts's office to negotiate. He accepted a compromise proposed by Smuts and tried to sell it to his followers, but some were upset that he had "sold out" and a number of them physically attacked Gandhi. In the end Smuts didn't stick to his end of the bargain, and Gandhi and many others publicly burnt their documents, which landed him back in jail.

In the following years the resistance grew, and Gandhi spent time in jails in Johannesburg, Bloemfontein, Volksrust, Balfour and Durban. Many Indian workers and coal miners joined the *Satyagrahis*, and many took part in a great protest march Gandhi led from Natal to the Transvaal. Only after further meetings between

Smuts and Gandhi in 1914, four years after the Union of South Africa came into being, did the government make some compromises and the resistance campaign was ended.

When Gandhi left for India in July 1914, General Smuts declared: "The saint has left our shores, I sincerely hope forever!"

Gandhi did indeed not return to South Africa, but his spirit of non-violent resistance lived on and served as an inspiration to the African National Congress's resistance of the apartheid laws – a resistance that remained passive until 1961, when a limited strategy of armed struggle was agreed to.

Gandhi's days in jail cells were not over: for the next three decades he devoted himself to peaceful resistance against British rule in India, spending more than two thousand days in prison. India gained its independence in August 1947. One year later Gandhi was assassinated.

13

The Boer
Nostradamus

SEVEN DAYS AFTER THE DEATH OF NELSON MANDELA, large numbers of black people will descend on the suburbs of Johannesburg and massacre all whites. This is referred to as the Night of the Long Knives or the Night of Johannesburg, and will signal the beginning of a nationwide effort to exterminate all white South Africans.

This apocalyptic prediction of the future, right-wing extremists believe, is a true interpretation of a prophecy made by a semi-literate Boer prophet who lived from 1864 to 1926. His name was Nicholaas Pieter Johannes Janse van Rensburg, known to all as Siener [Seer] van Rensburg.

Siener's prophecies have been the inspiration for most of the right-wing fanatics who have surfaced in South Africa in recent years, who see him almost as an equal to John the Baptist. In 2003, evidence was led in the Bloemfontein High Court that Hercules Viljoen and Leon Peacock had planned to blow up the Vaal Dam, thereby causing their own "Night of Terror" to pre-empt Siener's prediction of the slaughter of whites. That same year a group of militant fundamentalists called the Boeremag appeared in the Pretoria High Court, accused of planning a coup and nationwide terror. Evidence was led that they believed Siener's prophecy of a massacre of whites and planned to "bring that event forward" with their own terror and large-scale killing of blacks.

They even showed a video feauturing Siener at their recruitment meetings.

Right-wing South African websites (there is even a www.siener.co.za) feature regular discussions about Siener's prophecies. In August 2004, for example, Tanya du Preez wrote on the Freedom Front website that she had done an in-depth study of Siener's prophecies and that the Holy Spirit had convinced her that Siener was a real prophet of God. She wrote that Siener had predicted almost a century ago that the National Party would change its name and that a "clean-cut young man" would eventually destroy the party (a reference to New National Party leader Marthinus van Schalkwyk joining the ANC in August 2004). She also believed in the recent interpretation of Siener's prophecy of a massacre of whites, the Night of the Long Knives, and said she had received proof from members of the Police Service, the National Defence Force and the National Intelligence Service that blacks were already well advanced in the planning of this event.

Siener van Rensburg made hundreds of predictions during his lifetime, but the one that brought him the most fame and credibility as an authentic seer took place in July 1914, when out of the blue he warned Boer War general Koos de la Rey that he was going to die on the fifteenth day of one of the coming months. De la Rey was shot and killed in a case of mistaken identity on 15 September that year.

Nicolaas van Rensburg, known as Klasie as a child, was born on 30 August 1864 on a farm near Wolmaransstad, and grew up on the farm Rietkuil outside Ottosdal. He went to school at the age of seven, but his father needed him on the farm and brought him home after three weeks. Klasie never went to school again, but with the help of his mother he could read the words of the Dutch Bible one by one. He never read anything else, not even newspapers, but could recite large parts of the Bible from memory.

Klasie was a fragile, timid and intense child. He was a farm boy, yet he couldn't stand the slaughtering of chickens or sheep. His mother, Annie, herself a quiet and sensitive woman, became very protective of her son, with whom she had a close bond. And Klasie had strange blue eyes – described as *"verskriklik droewig"* [frighteningly sad], *"asof hy vanuit 'n grenslose diepte na jou kyk"* [as if he were looking at you from unfathomable depths], and with a *"heimlike verdriet"* [secret melancholy]. His hair and beard turned grey when he was only twenty, and throughout his adult life much older men addressed him as "Oom Niklaas".

His father, Willem, was a hard and difficult man, popularly known as Kortkoos. He was bitterly disappointed that his son was such a "sissy" and really wanted a hardened *boerseun* who would one day take his place on the farm. He declared that Klasie was worthless and incapable of anything other than looking after the sheep. So, early every morning, Klasie took his Bible and some food and went to the veld, where he painstakingly deciphered the Bible. He was a terribly lonely little boy.

Klasie had his first vision when he was only seven. His father was away on a long trip when the Van Rensburgs' farmworker, one Moos, came to warn Annie that a Koranna gang leader named Skeelkoos was planning to attack their homestead that night. She started to make arrangements to flee, but Klasie told her that God had come to him in a dream and told him that He would protect them, but that they had to stay right there on the farm that night. When Klasie refused to leave, his mother decided to remain there, with her three other children. Klasie stayed awake with her all night. In the first morning light they saw Skeelkoos and his henchmen near the house, but they never attacked. For no apparent reason the men suddenly ran away. Nobody ever knew why Skeelkoos and his gang didn't attack that night, or what scared them off.

Siener wasn't only very religious, he was also deeply nationalistic, or, as he would have seen it, patriotic. During most of the Anglo-Boer

War he served under General Koos de la Rey. According to some versions of history, he often served on the frontline, but never even carried a gun. Other versions insist he had a rifle, but never used it.

It was right at the beginning of the war, in October 1899, that Siener had one of his most famous visions. He was on commando with De la Rey near Kimberley when he woke his brother around midnight. He was very upset and said he had a foreboding that the British were burning the Boers' houses and farms and capturing their women and children. His brother told him to go back to sleep.

Late the next morning Siener was found under a bush on a nearby hill. He was in a terrible state. His eyes were red from crying all night, his hair and beard were wild, his fingernails torn and bloody from digging in the earth. His face was distorted, as if he had experienced extreme trauma. He later told friends that he had struggled with the devil and nearly lost his mind.

He explained his terrible vision once more. He saw the Boers fleeing over a blackened earth. Then he saw the Boer women and children in one large crowd, the children crying bitterly. The women were desperate as the British soldiers pushed them on. Siener saw them surrounded by burning farmsteads and fields, the whole country in flames and smoke.

It was only two years later that the British began their scorched-earth policy, burning most of the Boer farmsteads, killing all the cattle and sheep, and driving the women and children into concentration camps where eventually some 27 000 of them died. (Two of his own daughters later died in the concentration camp at Mafeking. He had a vision of them climbing a ladder weeks before their death and knew that they were going to die.)

Siener's vision made him very unpopular with some Boers, because it implied that the Boers were going to lose the war. He was often mocked and once even manhandled by Boers who thought he was a coward and a weirdo. Some Boer soldiers told stories of how Siener asked for tobacco in return for telling them his visions.

There are differing interpretations of Siener's role in the war and his influence on one of its greatest heroes, Koos de la Rey. De la Rey's biographer, Johannes Meintjies, writes: "The Siener was brought to him, a man with such simplicity and invincible faith that De la Rey was won over and ever treated whatever Niklaas van Rensburg had to say with deference. De la Rey might also have decided that the Siener had not come into his life without reason. Thousands of people discussed the Siener's visions as the war went on, and it may be because of his hold on De la Rey that many also gave credence to them."

Professor AWG Raath, who wrote a book on Siener's role in the 1914 Rebellion, believes that Siener held "an important influence" over De la Rey. Siener was no militarist, he says, and it was unlikely that the general would have accepted any military advice from him. "Still, Siener's visions brought important information to light which De la Rey could consider in his planning of war. In this sense Siener could indirectly have played an important role in De la Rey's military plans."

Another Siener biographer, Adriaan Snyman, says De la Rey had a special gift of recognising a fraud or an opportunist. If Siener was a charlatan, says Snyman, De la Rey would never have referred to him as a "messenger of his volk" and "the instrument of a power that I recognise and respect".

Raath states as a fact that some of the commandos threw all caution to the wind when Siener was with them. If he said that there weren't any British soldiers in the vicinity, they regarded it as a waste of energy to put out guards for the night. There are many stories of how Siener's predictions about British troop movements proved to be correct.

An elder in the Hervormde Kerk in Lichtenburg once asked the church council to act against his brother, because this brother thought Siener to be a prophet and believed every word he said. The council decided to investigate whether Siener was a man of

God or a false prophet, and appointed General De la Rey and one Dominee Du Toit to conduct the investigation. En route to Siener's farm, one of De la Rey's horses, Bokkie, developed a problem, so he borrowed another to pull his cart. When they arrived at the farm, Siener immediately asked De la Rey where his "old friend" was. What friend, the general asked, and Siener replied: "Old Bokkie. I saw that he was pulling the cart when you left Lichtenburg." De la Rey and Du Toit reported to the church council that Siener was unquestionably "a man of God".

In April 1901, Siener told De la Rey that there would soon be a comet visible in the skies and that its tail would be in the shape of a "V". A few weeks later the Boers saw the V-shaped comet, but there is confusion as to whether Siener had said the "V" stood for *vrede* [peace] or *vlug* [flee].

Siener had several forebodings about the First World War. Shortly after the end of the Anglo-Boer War, he had visions of red and blue bulls (symbolising Britain and Germany) fighting in Europe, of herds of springbok trekking over scorched earth in Eastern Europe, of a black curtain falling over Russia, of pigs becoming human beings, and locusts with lion heads. He created the impression that Britain was going to lose that war, which greatly raised the hopes among his own people. On another occasion, in 1911, he told people that he saw a huge thundercloud over Europe, and when it started to rain, the drops were made of blood. At the same time he saw five bulls engaged in a fierce fight.

General De la Rey himself told the story of a vision of the impending war and a devastating epidemic Siener had told him about in 1914. Siener said he saw many nations moving into a deep darkness, and millions being killed in battle. But after the war he saw a black cloth enveloping the earth, with millions more dying of a terrible disease. This was explained as the great influenza epidemic of 1918.

Siener was active in the Rebellion of 1914, when Afrikaner leaders rose in armed resistance against the South African government's decision to fight on the side of Britain and to seize the German colony of South West Africa, now Namibia. In his monumental work on Afrikaner history, Hermann Giliomee states that De la Rey, who was one of the leaders of the Rebellion, "was under the influence of Nicholaas ('Siener') van Rensburg, a religious mystic from Lichtenburg. De la Rey summoned armed burghers to a meeting, apparently to discuss Siener van Rensburg's vision of a call from God 'for the release of the Boer people'."

The Rebellion was not a success. Many of the leaders, including Siener, were caught and jailed. (Siener served his time in the Fort in Johannesburg, where Mohandas Gandhi had also served time a few years earlier. Today this jail is part of the new Constitutional Court.) Several witnesses testified that Siener's visions had contributed to the fervour that had fuelled the Rebellion. Because of his influence, he was held in solitary confinement for at least two weeks.

But there was also testimony that Siener never carried a gun. At his trial, the magistrate told Siener: "You eat too much meat at night. That's why you see visions and dream dreams. But I tell you to keep your dreams and visions to yourself, else I will put you in jail for the rest of the war."

Siener responded that he could not help it, that he was seeing something that very moment. "What do you see?" the magistrate asked. "I see my son has died," Siener replied. According to several versions of the story, a court orderly went up to the magistrate while this discussion was taking place and gave him a note. The magistrate opened it and told Siener: "Your son is dead." Siener had told friends earlier that day that he saw his wife in black clothes, and then a funeral cortège passing. He knew that it meant his son was going to die.

While in jail in 1914, Siener told his fellow prisoners that they should not lose hope, that all was not lost for the Afrikaner. In a vision he saw a black pig with a few white hairs in England. This meant that black nations were going to rise up against Britain – a foreboding of the Uhuru period in Africa some five decades later, some say. The few white hairs on the pig meant that some whites would also resist Britain, a vision later interpreted as Ian Smith's unilateral declaration of independence in Rhodesia, now Zimbabwe. Then Siener saw the same pig, scraped clean, hanging in Bloemfontein. This meant, he said, that the Afrikaners would again have a republic with its own flag. (South Africa became a republic with a white Afrikaner government in 1961.)

Siener always predicted which of the prisoners in the Fort would be released, and when. Once he even wrote down the names of 115 men who he said would be released on a certain date, and it happened exactly like that.

Siener had a powerful vision of three little girls lying in a pram: one with long, dark hair, one with a dark skin, and one with golden curls. The girl with the long hair grew up the fastest and got up, followed by the dark-skinned girl and then the one with the curls. His own interpretation was that this signified the emancipation from Britain first of Ireland, then India and then South Africa. He had several other visions about the south of Ireland becoming an independent republic.

Of all Siener's visions, his prediction about the death of his great friend and hero Koos de la Rey is best documented, although there are many variations of the story. On Saturday 11 July 1914, Siener arrived unannounced and unexpected at De la Rey's farm just outside Lichtenburg. Siener lived some ninety kilometres away, and had never before visited De la Rey on his farm. (The two men called each other Oom Koos and Oom Niklaas.) When De la Rey saw his old friend, he immediately knew that he had brought distressing news, but told him to withhold it until the next morning, so that he could have a proper night's rest.

De la Rey's daughter Polly was a witness to the early morning conversation between the two men. She said Siener had tears in his eyes most of the time "because he loved my father very much". Siener said: "Oom Koos, this is serious. Something is going to happen to you. Every time I see you, your head is bare and I know it is serious."

Siener said he saw a white piece of paper with the figures 1 and 5 on it hanging over Lichtenburg. He also saw an important South African leader who was abroad, wearing smart clothes, with gold braid on his hat, and carrying a sword. (De la Rey whispered to Polly that he had to be talking about General CF Beyers, who was in Germany at the time.) He saw the black number 15 again, said Siener, and the important man returning to South Africa, taking off his sword and declaring that he didn't want to wear it any longer. And again he saw De la Rey without a hat.

With tears streaming down his face, Siener continued to recount his vision. He saw a train carrying De la Rey's wife, Nonnie, and his children. There were many beautiful flowers and lots of food, but they did not eat. De la Rey was also there, but he was without his hat (De la Rey was never without a hat). The man wearing the smart clothes was also there. The train stopped at many places, and people came to visit it. They were all very sad, Siener said.

He saw the train arriving in Lichtenburg, a black cloth hanging over the town, and the flags flying half mast. He saw a commando on horseback arriving from Schweizer-Reneke, and many trains. Polly said that when he had finished his explanation, Siener was silent for a long while, looking at her father. Then he said: "Oom Koos, you must be careful."

Three weeks later, the First World War broke out. By this time Siener's vision had become widely known, but distorted to such an extent that the "15" was interpreted as the day that the Afrikaners would be "liberated" again. A big "volksvergadering" was organised for 15 September at Potchefstroom. The organisers sent a car to fetch Siener, so he could be present on the big day, but he refused to go. That day, General Beyers (the man in the smart clothes with the braid on his cap who refused to carry his sword again) returned from Europe, and resigned as commandant-general of the Union Defence Force.

De la Rey went by train to Johannesburg, and late on the afternoon of 15 September he left with General Beyers in a car for Potchefstroom. They got as far as Langlaagte (some versions say Orange Grove), where they were stopped at a police roadblock. At first sight, the two generals immediately thought that the police were looking for De la Rey. What they did not know was that the police were trying to capture the dangerous Foster criminal gang, which had been terrorising parts of Johannesburg. The generals instructed their driver to proceed through the roadblock, and the police fired on them. De la Rey was fatally wounded and died on the spot. When he died, he was without his hat – it had apparently blown away in the wind after the car came to a stop. (Other versions say that De la Rey was indeed the policemen's target, while others believed they had wanted to kill Beyers.)

More than forty special trains carried the mourners to the general's funeral, and the Schweizer-Reneke commando travelled on horseback. Siener van Rensburg had seen these events in detail more than two months before. His vision was also mentioned in the Union government's report on an investigation into the Rebellion.

Siener once described to a friend the physical experience of a vision. He felt pressure in the back of his head and became dizzy. Then he lay on his back with his eyes closed and his hands behind his head. He sensed a blurriness in front of his closed eyes, which became denser until it felt like storm clouds milling about, and then he started to see things. Everything appeared in the form of symbols, and, uneducated man that he was, these symbols all related to his tiny world: animals, farm implements, scenes from nature. And all in colour.

He had to decipher these symbols himself, but often he didn't, and that's where dozens of "Siener experts" come in: they took his original vision and interpreted the symbols according to their own views and prejudices. In recent years this has become a cottage industry among right-wing Afrikaners – to think up new explanations for some of Siener's dreams.

But the meaning of some of his symbols became clear while he was still alive: a red bull meant Britain, and a blue one, Germany; a Boer leader or a friend without a hat was going to die; a statue indicated incarceration; a thatched-roof house referred to the Afrikaner government or a political leader; cork tops on water symbolised ships; and so on. The self-styled Siener expert Adriaan Snyman has actually compiled a list of symbols and their meanings, although he doesn't offer a source for his explanations. Thus, he says, peaches mean gold or wealth; dogs symbolise civil servants; burnt porridge means a nation that is suffering; a big pot on a fire indicates rebellion against the government; a new hat is a new government; a yellow dog with a white collar represents an Englishman with an Afrikaans name or a "Boer with English loyalties"; a yellow wheel is Islam; and overripe corn signals trouble.

Professor Raath points out that Siener himself often didn't know what all the symbols meant and that his own interpretations were sometimes wrong. Some visions involved such complex symbolism, says Raath, that they could be interpreted in numerous ways.

Siener also had visions that were not political and didn't involve symbols. He predicted, for example, that diamonds would be discovered in the Lydenburg district where he lived, and this happened seven years later. His son became a diamond miner, and Siener predicted when he was going to find a large diamond and when his workers would steal his diamonds.

But his most famous diamond prediction, still discussed among diamond diggers today, referred to a diamond as big as a sheep's head that was lying under the ground in the Western Transvaal. It is not clear what information came from his vision and what grew out of popular legend, but it was said that this diamond would weigh 9 318 carats, three times bigger than the famous Cullinan diamond.

The story spread that Siener had stated that the "Skaapkop-diamant" would be found by a very poor man wearing only a tattered pair of trousers. From then on, many a miner worked without a shirt and in his oldest trousers. Another rumour had it that the diamond would be found in a poplar grove near Pretoria. Within days all the trees had been uprooted by eager miners, but nothing was found. Thirty years later, when new diamond diggings were opened near Bloemhof, hundreds of diggers arrived in the hope that the Skaapkop was going to be found there.

Adriaan Snyman, author of several books on Siener and – judged by the language he uses – also a right-winger, documents a long list of other Siener predictions. He writes that the old prophet had correctly predicted the Second World War, the division of Germany, the rise of communism, the assassination of Prime Minister Hendrik Verwoerd, the Cuban presence in Angola, the independence of Zimbabwe and Namibia, the Chernobyl nuclear disaster, the "betrayal" of the Afrikaner cause by PW Botha and FW de Klerk, the fall of the Berlin Wall, the release of Nelson Mandela and the negotiated settlement with the ANC. Siener, says Snyman, even predicted the AIDS pandemic. But most of the visions Snyman quotes could be interpreted in many other ways.

One of Siener's visions that is popular with right-wing extremists today goes like this: he saw an old wagon wheel rolling from the Eastern Cape; after a few wobbles it stabilised and rolled across the country, first losing a spoke and then its rim, until it slowly became a new wheel. The wheel came to a stop at Vereeniging. A snake came slithering through the long grass from further north in Africa and also settled in Vereeniging, where it curled itself up.

Many bizarre explanations have been given for this vision, but the following version is particularly popular. The Eastern

Cape is the strongest base of the African National Congress and the birthplace of Nelson Mandela and Thabo Mbeki, the first and second presidents of a democratic South Africa. The snake is a symbol of treachery and of the communist threat. Vereeniging was former state president FW de Klerk's parliamentary constituency, the place where he practised law and where he gave his first speech after becoming state president. It was De Klerk and Mandela who negotiated an end to apartheid and white rule in 1994. Say no more ...

On 4 April 1915, Siener told of a vision he had about the funeral of a very prominent leader. Suddenly there was a great fire, and naked people appeared. It became very dark, but then silver letters appeared on a shiny plate. Shortly before his death, Siener said he saw that the Afrikaner volk would one day "take matters into their own hands" and kill those who didn't want to leave. There would be a great silence before a vicious storm. A pail of blood would tipple over, and the Afrikaners' flag would be dipped in the blood. This "blood flag" would then fly over a free Afrikanerdom.

These visions, and others, even more obscure, are now the basis of many a right-wing extremist's belief that there will be a great slaughter of whites after Mandela's death. The silver letters on the shiny plate, they say, symbolise the crucible through which the Afrikaner will have to journey. Those "impure" Afrikaners will be burnt to death. The "true" Afrikaners will then rise up, and after a bloody revolution establish a new, whites-only Afrikaner republic in South Africa.

If it were not for the fact that there are some crazies out there who take this seriously, it would actually be hilarious.

My guess is that poor old Siener is turning in his grave.

14

The Black Jews of Africa

THE MORAL OF THIS STORY: DO NOT DARE DISMISS THE authenticity of oral histories and stories of origin of the people of Africa, even when these refer to events that took place more than a thousand years ago.

Ever since people can remember, there were groups of black people in southern Africa who told all who would listen that they had come from Israel more than a thousand years ago. Those who live in the northern parts of South Africa call themselves the Lemba, those in Zimbabwe are known as the Vamwenye or Varemba, and those in Mozambique, the Basena. Four hundred years ago there were reports in Europe of black Africans descended from the Moors who were great builders and medicine men and lived near the Mberengwa mountain in Zimbabwe. President Paul Kruger apparently believed them, because he called them the black Jews.

But in the past century or so, few people have believed the Lemba story, despite the fact that these people were very different from other African groups on the subcontinent and upheld many typically Jewish customs and rituals. Not even other Jews, in South Africa, Israel and elsewhere, took them seriously.

Even now, the intriguing story of this ancient Semitic tribe who have been living, like the descendants of Coenraad de Buys, among the Venda in northern South Africa, is not generally known among South Africans.

Scientists were cynical when confronted with the Lemba's fantastical story of where they originated and how they came to southern Africa. But when geneticists, anthropologists and historians meticulously studied their story, they found it to be substantially true, although its truth had been preserved for more than a millennium only by parents telling it to their children.

Twenty years ago, the director of the Centre for Jewish Studies at the School of Oriental and African Studies in London, Dr Tudor Parfitt, visited South Africa to give a talk about his book on the exodus of the Falashas, the black Jews of Ethiopia, to Israel. Among the sea of white faces, sitting in the back, he noticed a few black people wearing the Jewish skullcap, the yarmulke.

Curious, he asked them after the lecture where they were from. He found their answer "rather intriguing but difficult to believe": they were Jews, they said, whose ancestors had come from the Middle East to Africa more than a thousand years ago.

The men, seeing that Parfitt didn't believe them, invited him to spend a weekend with them in Limpopo Province to introduce him to the Lemba elders and to show him their culture. Parfitt accepted, and was astonished. "I could see that it was almost certain that they must have some kind of Semitic connection," he said later, "because all their pre-modern religious and social practices seemed to me imbued with a quality that was essentially Middle Eastern." Their culture and customs were different from the black groups of southern Africa. They were against marrying outside the Lemba group: "They had a good Semitic disdain for all other people that they referred to as vhasendzhi, the gentiles," Parfitt says.

Their ritual slaughtering of animals also seemed un-African and very much Middle Eastern. Each boy was given a knife for use in this ritual, which he would keep all his life and be buried with after his death.

Parfitt became so fascinated that the Lemba story became the focus of a research project that involved many months living among them. He followed their story and gathered clues across Africa, but when he reached the Indian Ocean the clues stopped dead.

This is the story the Lemba elders were told by their elders, and they by theirs. About 2 500 years ago, a group of Jews under the leadership of a man named Buba left Judea and settled in Yemen, probably for reasons of trade. They built a city and called it Sena. Sena still plays an important part in Lemba culture as a place of origin, but it also has a spiritual meaning – "We'll meet one day in Sena," one Lemba elder would say to another.

About a thousand years ago, something happened that forced them to leave. According to oral history, they "crossed Pusela" and went to Africa. The Lemba don't have a clear idea what Pusela was, but that's how the story has been told. Buba is now the name of one of the Lemba clans.

When they arrived on the African east coast, they built a new settlement and called it Sena. Then they moved inland, where, according to the story, they helped construct the stone city of Great Zimbabwe. During that time they broke the law of God – some say by eating mice, and the Lemba were not allowed to eat rodents – and they were scattered among several nations in Africa. In South Africa they settled in the areas of Louis Trichardt, Polokwane, Tzaneen and Thohoyandou in Limpopo Province.

As far back as 1908, a Lemba told the writer HA Junod (author of *The Balemba of the Zoutpansberg*): "We have come from a very remote place, on the other side of the Phusela. We were on a big boat (some say on the back of a tree). A terrible storm nearly destroyed us all. The boat was broken in two pieces. One half of us reached the shores of this country, the others were taken away with the second half of the boat and we do not know where they are now. We climbed the mountains and arrived among the Banayi. There we settled, and after a time we moved southwards to the Transvaal; but we are not Banayi."

Some believe that the group that left Yemen was made up of

men only. Unisa theologian Dr Magdel le Roux, who wrote her PhD on the Lemba, was told by the Lemba's relatives on the east coast that a war had broken out in their home country. This meant that they could not go home to marry, so they took brides from local Bantu-speaking groups.

The Lemba of southern Africa circumcise all young boys. They do not eat pork, warthog or hippo, or fish without scales such as barbel. They play musical instruments not found elsewhere in Africa. Those who follow the old traditions obey eating prescriptions pretty close to the rules of kosher: animals are slaughtered by designated individuals and bled properly, and milk and meat are never mixed. If a Lemba man wants to marry a non-Lemba, she has to "convert" by undergoing complex and exhausting ceremonies.

A Lemba woman told Dr Parfitt: "We came from the Israelites, we came from Sena, we crossed the sea. We were so beautiful with beautiful long, Jewish noses and so proud of our facial structure." The Lemba sing a song at festivals and funerals with the words "We came from Sena, we crossed Pusela, we rebuilt Sena. In Sena they died like flies. We came from Hudji to Chilimani. From Chilimani to Wedza. The tribes went to Zimbabwe. They built the walls and lived on the hill. Mwali [God] sent the star. From Zimbabwe to Mberengwe. From Mberengwe to Dumghe. We carried the drum. We came to Venda, Solomon led us."

Le Roux says the sacred drum referred to plays a similar role among the Lemba to the Ark of the Covenant among the ancient tribes of Israel. "Once we had a drum because we were a holy people and once we had a book because we were a wise people," they say. Some believe that the original sacred drum is still hidden in the caves on Dumghe Mountain in Zimbabwe. The priest at Mberengwa said he wasn't allowed to tell her about it, because "we are only allowed to reveal to people who have been circumcised". An informant told Parfitt about the "book", saying that it had been in their possession long ago, "but the Arabs were jealous and destroyed the book. Ours was the book of the Mwenye. Theirs was the book of Allah." Other Lemba say that their grandfathers told them that the Lemba had a Bible made of skin very long ago, but lost it.

Professor Matshaya Mathiva, spiritual leader of the Lemba and president of the Lemba Cultural Society until his death in 2002, asked Parfitt during his stay in South Africa to go and find this place called Sena in Yemen. Yemeni imams quickly directed Parfitt to a town with that name in a remote valley in the south of the country.

What he found complied with the Lemba's story. To get to the sea from Sena, one has to cross the Masilah River, which sounds very much like the Lemba's "Pusela". The port town of Sayhut on the southern coast of Arabia would have been the ideal place to launch ships to Africa – Ethiopia, Djibouti and Somalia are on the opposite side of the narrow strait of water. The ships of the time were very capable of reaching Kenya, Tanzania or even Mozambique, and therefore could have reached Mombasa, Zanzibar or even Sofala within a few days.

Parfitt uncovered other tantalising snippets of information that appear to confirm the Lemba's oral version of their origins. In the Hadramawt valley where Sena is situated, many of the tribes have exactly the same names as used by the Lemba, like the Sadiki and the Hamisi. And why did they leave Sena for Africa? Parfitt found out that about a thousand years ago, a huge stone-built dam supporting agriculture around the substantial city of Sena broke. The people of Sena told Parfitt that many residents were forced to leave because the area could not sustain that many people without the dam's water.

Dr Parfitt has recently published a book about his work titled *Journey to the Vanished City.*

The Lemba were overjoyed with this confirmation of their oral traditions and saw it as final proof that they were indeed Jews from the Middle East. But while they regarded this new information as proof, some cynical scientists maintained that it could all be due to amazing coincidence. Here enter the geneticists.

The genetics story does not begin with the Lemba. It begins when a Jewish priest (as opposed to a rabbi), Dr Karl Skorecki, wondered if genetic comparisons would confirm the general Jewish belief that the priests, the Conahim, are the descendants of Aaron, brother of Moses. He contacted an expert on the genetics of human populations working with the Y or male chromosome, Dr Michael Hammer of Arizona.

Unlike other chromosomes, the genetic material of the Y chromosome does not change with every generation. These Y chromosomes are passed down unchanged, apart from possible mutations that occasionally occur, from father to son. This means that such research is an accurate tool to reconstruct the history of a population, as each lineage's mutation patterns are different.

Skorecki's expectation was proven valid. The geneticists identified the "Cohen genetic signature", a DNA pattern prevalent among the Jewish priestly caste, wherever they live in the world, rare among other Jewish populations and virtually absent from non-Jewish groups. They found that 45 per cent of Ashkenazi priests and 56 per cent of Sephardic priests have this Cohen signature, compared to between 3 and 5 per cent of general Jewish populations.

An Oxford population geneticist, David Goldstein, developed this discovery by calculating how long ago those with the Cohen signature shared a common ancestor. He concluded that this was somewhere between 2 600 and 3 100 years ago – close enough to the Jewish belief that their exodus from Egypt took place 3 000 years ago, after which Moses assigned the priesthood to the male descendants of his brother Aaron.

Goldstein then tested DNA samples collected from the Lemba by Tudor Parfitt and his associate, Neil Bradman of the Centre for

Genetic Anthropology at London's University College. The results stunned geneticists.

Nine per cent of Lemba men living in South Africa were found to carry the Cohen genetic signature, further proof of their Jewish ancestry. But among those males belonging to the Lemba clan named after the leader who led their ancestors from Judea, Buba, it was as high or higher than the known Jewish priestly castes: 53 per cent. The Buba are recognised as the oldest and most senior of the twelve Lemba clans.

Parfitt and Bradman also collected DNA samples from the people of the Hadramawt in Yemen and compared these to the Lemba DNA. They found close similarities between the Lemba Y chromosome and the Hadramawt Y chromosome.

A South African scientist, Professor Trevor Jenkins of the University of the Witwatersrand, also did comparative DNA testing on the Lemba, finding that they were genetically significantly different from the Venda people among whom they lived. "There can be no doubt that more than a thousand years ago males from the Middle East came into the area. What they contributed to the local populace via marriage and procreation was a characteristic Y-chromosome which has remained unaltered in the men all these years. We have, in a sense, confirmed their oral tradition," he says.

The Lemba and Dr Parfitt were excited by all these results of confirmation. If twenty-five years is seen as a generation average and one accepts the premise that the Lemba left Yemen a thousand years ago, it means that the Lemba came to Africa more or less forty generations ago. The story of these Jews leaving Judea and building the city of Sena is essentially correct and accurate.

Parfitt told the *New York Times* at the time: "I was strongly criticised by a number of colleagues for listening to this nonsense because they assumed the sense of a different origin had been imposed on the Lemba by missionaries. As an anthropologist, I had a sense one should listen to what people say about themselves and shouldn't be too arrogant. It turned out that what they are saying about themselves is substantially correct."

The Lemba so appreciated Parfitt's work that they made him an honorary Lemba. This was a special honour, because Lemba tradition forbids outside males from becoming Lembas. This exclusion explains why the Cohen genetic signature has been preserved among them for more than ten centuries.

Many modern Lemba are now Christians, and this has led to some Jews being reluctant to accept the Lemba. One of the senior Lemba cultural leaders, Rabson Wuriga, explains that the first colonial governments his people came into contact with in South Africa and Zimbabwe were Christians. "Lembas could not live in isolation in the wake of modernisation and urbanisation ... With passage of time and new generations coming, also isolated from the fatherland, many of us became Christians because that was the only route available to skills and academic development."

But, says Wuriga, "our answers to those who questioned our identity were never intended to prove our religion, but our identity and origins. We believe that the person is a Lemba because his father is a Lemba. The whole idea was simply to reclaim our historical, religious and cultural heritage that some people wanted to rob us of." He reminds sceptical Jews that the Lemba do not practise Rabbinic Judaism, because "we came out of Israel before Rabbinical Judaism".

Over the centuries that the Lemba have been in Africa, they have lived among the Bantu-speaking peoples and gradually lost their own language, adopting the language of the group among whom they lived in South Africa, Venda. Through the inevitable inter-marrying over the generations, their skins have become darker and they have been influenced by African traditions and customs.

Many of their practices remain essentially Judaic, but with a strong African feel. The purification ritual followed when a non-Lemba woman wants to marry a Lemba is an example. The woman has to crawl over anthills so that the ants can bite off her "pig skin", fire is used on her body to burn off her non-Lemba impurities, and she is forced to eat raw meat so that she can vomit out her gentile soul. She then puts her head through a hole in a hut, and when her hair has been shaved, she crawls through the hole, thereby becoming a Lemba.

Dr Le Roux points out that circumcision is central to Lemba culture and beliefs. Zvinowanda Zvinowanda, the high priest at Mberengwa, told her that their circumcision rites are very similar to those of the Old Testament. Le Roux says most ethnographic accounts of Lemba life agree that it was the Lemba who brought circumcision to South Africa centuries ago, and passed it to the Venda, the Sotho and the Tsonga. The Lemba insist that their ancestors performed all the circumcisions at Great Zimbabwe, which grew into the most powerful metropolis in the region between 1250 and 1450.

Since 1999 many Jews from Israel, the United States and elsewhere have visited the Lemba in South Africa, and some of the Lemba leaders have visited Israel by invitation. There are now programmes in place to build synagogues and inform the Lemba of contemporary Judaism.

The next time you hear a story about the origins or events of African people from ancient times, think twice before you dismiss it as an old wives' tale. These wives may have a thing or two to teach us.

15

The Nazi
Assassin

Berlin, 1936. SOUTH AFRICA'S GREATEST HOPE AT THE Olympic Games, twenty-three-year-old light-heavyweight boxer Sidney Robey Leibbrandt, leads the South African sports team in their march past the podium where German leader, Adolf Hitler, stands in his brown uniform with his arm outstretched in the Nazi salute. "Eyes right!" shouts Leibbrandt, and all the South Africans turn their heads to look at the Führer.

It was a moment that changed the young athlete's life – and very nearly the whole course of history in southern Africa.

"I looked straight at him," Leibbrandt wrote later in his autobiography. "Suddenly I was seized by a strange sensation. I still don't know if it was his humble uniform or his magnetic personality that fascinated me, but it was as if I was taken over by a hypnotic force. I stopped hearing the march music and marched on mechanically."

Leibbrandt's commands of "Eyes front!" and "Hats on!" led to some confusion, because he spoke Afrikaans instead of the agreed English, and some athletes didn't understand him. "It was all my fault," wrote Leibbrandt. "At the sight of Hitler the German-Irish blood pumped turbulently through my Afrikaner heart and I gave the orders in my mother tongue. Perhaps I wanted to impress the Führer. I wanted to tell him in the language of General De Wet that the descendants of a heroic people were marching in front of him. I knew that Adolf Hitler held General De Wet and the Boer people in very high esteem."

The German newspapers declared Leibbrandt the "most interesting" athlete at the games. He was rather eccentric: a fitness fanatic who refused to sleep on a bed, a dedicated vegetarian who regularly fasted to enhance his self-discipline. Oh, and he spoke German and had a German surname. His main motivation for driving himself so hard, Leibbrandt said, was to be the first Afrikaner to win a medal so that he could then insist that the wording on the official Springbok jackets should also be in Afrikaans.

But he had other reasons to work hard. He had been the South African champion since the age of nineteen, but couldn't take part in the 1932 Olympics because he broke his thumb shortly before the games. At the Empire Games in 1934 he knocked out British champion George Brennan in the opening seconds, but was disqualified for a low blow. He regarded it as an "anti-Boer" decision and it made him hate the British even more passionately.

In Berlin, Leibbrandt won his first two matches easily. His quarterfinal bout was against a boxer from Czechoslovakia. At the end of the second round Leibbrandt hit his opponent so hard on the side of the head that he broke a bone in his hand. Despite the extreme pain, he continued and was declared the winner. The team doctor ordered him to withdraw from the competition, but Leibbrandt simply ignored him and decided to fight Frenchman Roger Michelot. His hand was so swollen before the match that the glove had to be cut open in order to fit.

It was a remarkable fight, with the large crowd mostly on Leibbrandt's side. He fought the French and European champion with only his left hand. At the end of the fight, Leibbrandt, his corner and the crowd were convinced that he had won. But the fight was given to the Frenchman, and the judges were booed by most in the crowd. Frank Rostron, the South African sports journalist reporting for the *Star*, wrote the next day that Leibbrandt's use of his left hand was extraordinary and that he agreed with most present that Leibbrandt had won. Leibbrandt was without a doubt the winner in the last round, he said, but when he checked the judges' scorecards, he discovered that one judge had given Michelot four points for that round, which resulted in the Frenchman winning on points. Michelot went on to win the gold medal at the games.

Leibbrandt attracted more than just the attention of the media and the public at the Berlin Olympic Games.

Nazi Germany was preparing for war. South West Africa was a prized German colony, and a sympathetic South Africa lying south, with all its mineral riches, could be helpful. There were already a large number of Germans living in South West Africa who were sympathetic to the Nazis, and in South Africa the hard-core Afrikaner nationalists were known for their hatred of Britain and their love of Germany. It would be a good idea to start recruiting agents to play a role in Germany's plans, the men in the German Abwehr decided. Already the Nazis had a shortwave radio station, Radio Zeesen, broadcasting to South Africa.

It so happened that there was a senior Nazi leader who had the same name as the young South African boxer: Dr Georg Leibbrandt, assistant to the Philosopher of the Reich, Dr Alfred Rosenberg. Dr Leibbrandt was given the task of befriending Robey at the Berlin Games, and made sure he was among the thirty athletes from around the world who were invited to meet Hitler together with the German team. Hitler remembered reading about the young man with the strange habits, greeted him with a smile and even had a short chat. It was a moment Robey would cherish for decades. (He later compared Hitler to Jesus Christ.)

Robey claimed in his autobiography that Dr Georg Leibbrandt was related to him, but this was apparently not true. Robey's father, Meyder, was an Afrikaner whose family had been in South Africa for generations. Robey's mother, interestingly enough, was Susan Marguerite Joyce, cousin of William Joyce. He was the notorious Lord Haw-Haw who produced radio propaganda for the Nazis and was executed for high treason after the war by Britain.

After the Olympics, Robey was admitted to the Reich's Academy of Physical Education in Berlin. Dr Leibbrandt facilitated invitations (and an SS bodyguard) for Robey to attend top party functions. But at the end of 1936, Robey rushed back to Pretoria to write an officer's exam in the Railway Police, his employers prior to the Olympic Games. When he didn't get the commission, he resigned and became a professional boxer. Within six months he had become South Africa's heavyweight champion.

Robey went to London to fight professionally, but lost interest after a few fights and went to study at the London College of Physical Education. After completing the diploma, he went on to complete courses in Denmark, Finland, Poland and Hungary before returning to Germany, where he rejoined the Reich's Academy.

Robey was in love with the Führer, with Germany and with National Socialism. "The closer my affinity to the National Socialism grew, the greater my love of my volk and fatherland became," he wrote. "This growth process later reached full maturity; I was not only a convinced and committed National Socialist, but a fanatic."

At the end of August 1938, Germany invaded Poland, and on 3 September 1939, Britain and France declared war against Germany. Robey's role in the Nazis' plans suddenly became more pressing. Two men devised the plan: Ernst Bohle, head of the German Auslands Organisation responsible for nurturing pro-Nazi movements in foreign countries (he was born in Cape Town, where his father was a professor at the university); and Rudolf Karlowa, the former consul-general in South West Africa. Both men knew the politics of South Africa and both spoke a little Afrikaans. (Robey later called Karlowa "the Afrikaners' German father".)

But even before the Nazi command informed Robey of their

plans for him, he asked Karlowa's permission to return to South Africa. Robey said that he wanted to organise an armed uprising in South Africa and establish a pro-German government. It was exactly what the Germans had in mind.

The plan, code-named Operation Weissdorn, was simple. Robey had to liaise with and further radicalise the militant anti-war, pro-German Afrikaner organisation, the Ossewa Brandwag [Oxwagon Sentinel]. A campaign of sabotage would be launched to destabilise the country, and then Robey was to assassinate Prime Minister Jan Smuts, who was also a member of Winston Churchill's war cabinet. The entire cabinet and leading politicians such as Oswald Pirow and DF Malan had to be detained. Sir Ernest Oppenheimer, the man who controlled most of the minerals in South Africa (which Germany would need if the war lasted a long time) had to be assassinated as well. Other prominent Jewish leaders also had to be eliminated, which would mean that most Jews would leave the country, the planning documents stated.

The details of Operation Weissdorn were proposed to Hitler by the chief of the Abwehr, Admiral Wilhelm Canaris, and his head of the sabotage division, Major-General Erwin von Lahousen de Vivremont. Hitler approved the plan and was quite pleased that the young boxer he had met was to be in charge.

Karlowa organised German citizenship for Robey, had him join the German army and sent him to the Führer Leadership School to be educated in political organisation and propaganda. He was also trained as a glider pilot, a parachutist and a saboteur. Robey was an excellent and enthusiastic student and trainee, although he often clashed with individuals who he thought were "soft" or didn't show him enough respect. His sabotage teacher wrote in his report that Robey was a "fanatic, incapable of organising or making deliberate decisions. His intolerance of other people makes him unsuitable for working in partnership with anyone. But his inexhaustible energy and complete fearlessness makes him the ideal lone sabotage agent." This assessment later proved to be entirely correct.

Robey was given the alias of Walter Kempf. He was introduced to Christiaan Nissen, an experienced yachtsman who at that stage was running Nazi agents to Wales. Nissen was to take Robey by yacht to South Africa's west coast. Robey was also introduced to the radio operator who was to accompany them, a Frenchman called Emil Dorner, who had joined the German army. Robey was immediately put off by Dorner's soft handshake and asked Karlowa to replace Dorner. Karlowa refused.

On 2 April 1941, Leibbrandt, Nissen, Dorner and four German sailors departed aboard the yacht *Kyloe*. On board, Leibbrandt had fourteen thousand US dollars, a radio transmitter, a suitcase of clothing, a pistol and a rubber dinghy.

It was an acrimonious trip, the seasick Leibbrandt in almost constant conflict with Nissen and Dorner. After two weeks, Leibbrandt told Nissen that he refused to take Dorner onto land with him, because he suspected the radio operator of being an enemy agent. He was equally suspicious of the German agent they were to meet at Lambert's Bay. He wasn't going to land at Lambert's Bay, Leibbrandt told Nissen, but at Mitchells Bay further north. When Nissen threatened to sail back to Germany, Leibbrandt pointed his pistol at the skipper and said he would kill him if he didn't do exactly as he was told.

Some five weeks later, on 10 June 1941, they caught sight of the Namaqualand coast. Leibbrandt covered his body in vaseline to keep out the cold in case his dinghy capsized. He then looked at the German crew, kicked his heels, raised his right arm and greeted them with the peculiar greeting he had been using for months: "Sieg heil! Die Vierkleur hoog!" (The Vierkleur was the flag of the old Transvaal Republic.) Then he rowed the dinghy to the coast, capsizing only a few metres from the beach.

Leibbrandt cut up the dinghy and buried it. He was making

sure that if he were captured, the men on the yacht would have enough time to depart for Germany. He decided there and then to cook up the story, if it became necessary, that he had been dropped by a German submarine. He would use this story on several occasions. Much later, when he was in court, the police brought fishermen to testify that they had seen a submarine on the Namaqualand coast. The judges in his case found that he had indeed arrived by submarine. One gets the impression that Leibbrandt stuck with his submarine story long after it became necessary because it appealed to his sense of drama and self-importance.

Leibbrandt staggered around without water for days, eventually burying his radio transmitter. Just before collapsing, he came upon a shepherd named Hendrik Rietjie, who showed him the way to the nearest farm. At the farm Leibbrandt told the owner, Joos Engelbrecht, that he was a Pretoria student called Jan Smit and that he was lost. Engelbrecht was very suspicious, not only because there were holes in Leibbrandt's story, but because he had just walked through a forbidden diamond mining area.

Engelbrecht wanted to trace Leibbrandt's steps to check his story, but Leibbrandt stopped him and confessed that he had arrived by submarine and was on a mission from Germany. Fortunately for Leibbrandt, Engelbrecht also resented Jan Smuts and his decision to join Britain in war, so he kept his secret and even went to fetch the radio where Leibbrandt had buried it. Leibbrandt buried the radio again, this time on Engelbrecht's farm. Engelbrecht arranged for neighbours to take "Mr Smit" to Cape Town.

Leibbrandt's next task was to get in touch with and co-opt the Ossewa Brandwag, especially its paramilitary wing, the Stormjaers [Storm Chasers]. His first contact, through an old girlfriend, was with the assistant commandant-general of the OB in the Cape, General JA "Sambok" Smith. It was a disastrous meeting. Leibbrandt blamed the OB leadership for meekly allowing Jan Smuts to disarm the Afrikaners and for being soft, paranoid and scared – bloated tin soldiers, he called them. Leibbrandt demanded that the OB take his lead and "be faithful to his leadership".

Smith, who called Leibbrandt an "arrogant upstart", passed the buck to his equivalent in the Free State, General Chris de Jager, who didn't believe Leibbrandt and sent him and one Hendrik Erasmus to fetch the radio transmitter in Namaqualand in order to prove his story. Erasmus became one of Leibbrandt's close confidantes.

General De Jager was impressed once he saw the German radio transmitter, and decided it was time Leibbrandt met the leader of the OB, Commandant-General Dr Hans van Rensburg. This was an important step in Operation Weissdorn.

The meeting took place in great secrecy under a karee tree in the veld between Pretoria and Silverton. Guards armed to the teeth surrounded Van Rensburg's car, and Leibbrandt was told to get in. The two men immediately disliked each other. Van Rensburg's first question, according to Leibbrandt, was whether Adolf Hitler had sent him a message. Leibbrandt, who was sure Hitler had never even heard of Van Rensburg, lied. Yes, he said, the Führer said that if the OB were to become a proper National Socialist movement and align itself with Nazi Germany, he would order Radio Zeesen to produce propaganda for them. The OB general offered Leibbrandt a training position in the Stormjaers, which Leibbrandt declined, and warned the younger man that he would not condone a reckless sabotage campaign.

Leibbrandt claimed in his autobiography that it was due to his intervention with the OB that the organisation declared itself a National Socialist movement soon after this meeting.

A few days after the meeting, Leibbrandt heard nasty rumours about himself circulating in OB circles. He promptly got into his car with Erasmus and, without an appointment, drove to Van Rensburg's house.

Van Rensburg apparently accused Leibbrandt of being a German agent. The volatile Leibbrandt stormed across the room, grabbed the OB leader, called him a lackey of Jan Smuts and threatened to do him serious harm. The two men were pried apart by the others present, and Van Rensburg apologised.

Van Rensburg wrote later that Leibbrandt was "brimful of self-confidence, impervious and not inclined to accept any views but his own. To me he hardly seemed able to form a picture of the South African scene at the time." Leibbrandt wrote that Van Rensburg was "unsuitable" as a leader of Afrikaners and that he had a suspect past, as he had apparently served in the military units which had hunted down the 1914 Rebellion leaders. He described Van Rensburg as his "bitterest enemy".

Leibbrandt's recruitment of a body of fanatics was more successful than he had hoped. ("I was looking for men of courage and action, not political lavender johnnies (*laventeljônnies*).") The mercurial Leibbrandt mesmerised them at small recruitment meetings with stories of Germany and his meetings with Hitler, and with a bizarre mix of Nazism, Afrikaner nationalism, anti-communism and religious fanaticism. Most of those present were members of the OB or the Stormjaers, but now they were obliged to pledge a new allegiance. He called his mission Operation Karlowa, and his movement, the National Socialist Rebels.

Hendrik Erasmus and his brother Doors were very close to Leibbrandt. Hendrik introduced him to the reckless but innovative Karel Theron. When the government ordered that all weapons in private hands be handed over to the police, he stole police invoice books and collected a huge arsenal of rifles. He also stole a large quantity of dynamite and detonators from Iscor in Pretoria. Karel became the National Socialist Rebel leader in the Transvaal.

Robey went to visit his parents in Potchefstroom for the first time in years, but he was actually in town to meet up with an old friend he had met in London. Dr Louis le Roux, a chemistry lecturer at the university, was to train the rebels in bomb-making.

All the recruits had to swear a "Blood Oath" drawn up by

Leibbrandt and signed with each recruit's blood. "I will strive and struggle for the freedom and independence of the Afrikaner volk in South Africa and the building of a National Socialist state with the ideas of Adolf Hitler as basis, adapted to the character of the Afrikaner volk," it stated. "I act before God and I swear with this sacred oath that I, as an Afrikaner, will faithfully serve my volk and fatherland with my whole heart, soul, body and mind in the direction I shall be given by the leader of the National Socialist Rebels in the person of Robey Leibbrandt and nobody else, from now until death." It ended with the words: "I am nothing, my volk is everything! God be with us. The Vierkleur high!"

Robey and the senior members of his movement would be clad in gowns and masks in a darkened room when recruits were asked to enter and take the oath. They would hand the recruit a loaded gun, bring an unknown person into the room and order the recruit to shoot him in the head. After the second click of the mechanism they would take the gun away and welcome the recruit into their midst. If he hesitated or refused to shoot, he was out.

Hans van Rensburg now found himself in an impossible position. The moderates in the OB wanted to avoid a civil war in South Africa, but under the agitation of Robey Leibbrandt, the militants were pushing harder for more military action. These elements, egged on by Leibbrandt's open disdain for Van Rensburg, increasingly gossiped that he was a "Smuts lackey". Leibbrandt was growing in stature as leader as he spread his revolutionary gospel. People were aware that he had indeed met Hitler more than once, and that he was indeed a German army parachutist and trained saboteur.

But the South African police had no idea that Leibbrandt was back in South Africa and had formed the National Socialist Rebels. Blame for Karel Theron's sensational raid on Iscor and the Leibbrandt gang's escalating sabotage campaign was being placed at the door of the OB and Van Rensburg.

So Van Rensburg decided to inform the government that Leibbrandt was back and organising a rebellion. He ordered the Transvaal leader of the OB, advocate Pat Jerling, to inform the Acting Minister of Justice, Harry Lawrence. Jerling had a secret meeting with Lawrence and told him about Leibbrandt's return (by submarine) and his plans to assassinate the prime minister. But when Lawrence relayed the information to his police commissioner, the police declared that it could not be true – they knew about his views and his studies in Germany, and they would certainly have known if he had been back for four months. After all, the man was one of the most famous Afrikaners of the time.

When nothing happened to Leibbrandt, Van Rensburg decided that he had to be eliminated. He ordered one of his trusted followers, police sergeant Dirk van Jaarsveld, to kill Leibbrandt. But unbeknown to him, Van Jaarsveld had already taken Robey Leibbrandt's Blood Oath and was in the heart of the National Socialist Rebels.

Johannes van der Walt was probably slightly more famous than Robey Leibbrandt during the 1930s and 1940s. He was a huge, handsome man with piercing blue eyes, and he was the world wrestling champion. He stirred the imaginations of millions when he fought the world's best as the "Masked Marvel", but when he eventually lost a fight he abandoned his mask to reveal himself as Johannes van der Walt. He was a national hero, and the Stormjaer general.

But Van der Walt was also a man of integrity. As a member of the inner circle of the OB, he was present in November 1941 when Jerling instructed someone in the organisation to betray Robey Leibbrandt. Shortly afterwards, Jerling ordered Van der Walt to assassinate another senior officer in the OB, advocate Joe Ludorf (later Mr Justice Ludorf).

Van der Walt then made a sworn affidavit with this and other damning evidence of financial improprieties against Jerling and

Van Rensburg. It was given to the new Minister of Justice, Colin Steyn, who read out the charges in Parliament. In December 1941 Van der Walt, now on the run from the OB and the police, had an emotional reunion with Robey Leibbrandt and took the Blood Oath.

Two key elements in Leibbrandt's mission failed him: he could not exchange his big stash of American dollars for South African currency without getting caught; and he could not contact his masters in Berlin because he couldn't get the radio transmitter to work, not even after he recruited a post office technician. And, all of a sudden, he had become the most wanted man in South Africa.

Leibbrandt went into hiding on the farm Ontmoet in the mountains outside Louis Trichardt (now Makhado), but he must have been careless, because someone reported to the police that he had seen strange men with weapons moving around the mountain. Sergeant Christiaan Pauley and two of his men went to investigate, and discovered Leibbrandt and his party. But two of Pauley's men not only knew Leibbrandt, they also supported his cause. After a short standoff, Pauley left, asking Leibbrandt to report to the police station. Leibbrandt ignored this, well knowing that the policemen would protect him, and stayed on the farm for some time thereafter.

A few days later, one of Robey's men told him that the whole district was gossiping about a German agent in the mountains of Ontmoet farm. Leibbrandt identified the rumourmongers as two farmers, Dirk Coetzee and Edward Dames, and went to their farms. He beat them up badly with a sjambok, and called them traitors of the Afrikaner and agents of Jan Smuts.

In early October 1941, Leibbrandt moved to the Brits district, where he hid on the farm belonging to his uncle, Dominee Robey Joyce. But it turned out that Sergeant Pauley had submitted a report about Leibbrandt, his transmitter and his illegal arms after all, and not long after his arrival in Brits, two police cars arrived on the Joyce farm. After his assaults on the two farmers, little about Leibbrandt remained a secret.

Leibbrandt saw the police cars pull up and immediately came out, pistol in hand. The policemen shot at him, but missed. The reverend was pleading for the shooting to stop – Karel Theron was inside the house and he was going to kill them all, he told the police. Leibbrandt walked up to the police and said, famously: "Shoot this Afrikaner heart. It is big enough. You can take my corpse, but you can never take me." Leibbrandt wrote in his autobiography that the policemen were cowards and ran into the bushes. But they gave a different version.

The policemen told Leibbrandt that they were under strict orders to take him in for questioning, and that they couldn't leave without him. Leibbrandt wrote a letter to their commander, Colonel Verster, there and then and asked the policeman to deliver it to him before doing anything else. He wrote: "Dear Colonel Verster, I understand your position and also that of my fellow Afrikaners you sent to arrest me. But I ask you to recognise me as the carrier of the true will of Young South Africa and as such I refuse before God and my nation to ever surrender. My dead body may fall into the hands of the government, but I as freedom fighter, never! You ask for blood, Colonel, but remember I as Afrikaner have not robbed, murdered or committed sabotage. I stand as an honest citizen for right and justice. I will fight and fall like I am, an Afrikaner through and through. The Vierkleur high!"

Chief Constable De Kock ordered his men to stay there, and took the letter to his commander in Brits. Leibbrandt went into the house and the police stood outside, waiting. About an hour later De Kock returned with a Major Orsmond, who ordered a search of the house. There was no one there. Leibbrandt and Theron had escaped.

A few days later, two of Leibbrandt's lieutenants, Andries and Frederik van der Walt, were captured at a police roadblock just outside Buysdorp, the town where Coenraad de Buys's descendants live. The police took the two men to the farm Ontmoet, where they confiscated Leibbrandt's German radio transmitter.

Leibbrandt's escape and the discovery of his German radio transmitter sent shock waves through the Union government and its security establishment. Prime Minister Jan Smuts's security was virtually non-existent, and his farm and official residence were difficult to protect. It was also clear that a large section of the South African police was sympathetic to Leibbrandt and could not be trusted to apprehend him. The intelligence services were clearly useless: even after they were told by Pat Jerling that Leibbrandt was back in South Africa and planned to overthrow the government, they had insisted that he could not be in the country.

There was only one option: Leibbrandt's organisation had to be infiltrated by someone he would trust. There was one such a man: police captain Jan Taillard. In 1939 he had been sent to gather intelligence in South West Africa after rumours suggested there was a group of Germans and Afrikaners who were militant followers of Adolf Hitler and planned to take over the administration in the territory. Taillard's evidence led to the arrest of more than two thousand Nazi supporters.

Louis Esselen, special adviser to Smuts, had the foresight to tell Taillard to refuse to sign the oath of allegiance the government demanded of police officers and to resign from the force. Esselen had sensed even before Leibbrandt's return to South Africa that an undercover man with a right-wing image could one day be useful. Taillard sat on his farm and waited, and now his time had come. Esselen gave him the task of capturing Robey Leibbrandt, and the policeman, posing as an anti-Smuts militant, started making overtures to people he thought would know Leibbrandt. His luck was in: one of his neighbours was Erna Eggert, a German woman who was close to Leibbrandt. She recommended Taillard to Leibbrandt.

Close to midnight on 10 December 1941, Robey Leibbrandt, Johannes van der Walt and other senior Nazi rebels arrived unannounced at Taillard's farm. Leibbrandt had done his homework and knew how Taillard had "sacrificed" his career as a senior officer for his principles.

Leibbrandt trusted Taillard completely and told him about all his plans. He had two thousand committed men and more than enough guns, ammunition and explosives, he told Taillard. He said the signal for the takeover of the country would come when he assassinated Smuts. Then his rebels would hit hard: arrest or kill all the white political leaders; kill Ernest Oppenheimer and "other top Jews"; blow up power stations, dams, railway stations, bridges and telephone exchanges. The country would be paralysed, and on its ashes a new National Socialist South Africa would be built.

Taillard later testified that listening to Leibbrandt was almost like watching a film clip of Adolf Hitler – the same gestures, the same fanatical glow in the eyes. He would speak about Hitler and the wonders of Nazism, adding that he had been personally chosen by the Führer to liberate the Afrikaner from Smuts and the Jews. He asked Taillard to spy on the police for them, even hinting that Taillard would be his commissioner of police when he took over South Africa.

But not everything was going Leibbrandt's way. At the end of November, his lieutenant Hendrik Erasmus was killed by the police after being trapped on a farm in the Waterberg. On 14 December, Karel Theron and Doors Erasmus tried to blow up two passenger trains carrying soldiers, but the bomb exploded in their faces and they were both killed. The next day the police arrested Johannes van der Walt at his home in Westdene, Johannesburg. The top leadership of Leibbrandt's rebels was in disarray and had to reorganise. Leibbrandt decided that it was crucial to his plans for Van der Walt to escape.

The senior officers at Marshall Square, the police headquarters in Johannesburg where Van der Walt was being held, knew there was a real danger that some of their policemen would want to help their national hero escape. So they put an English-speaking officer, Ron Shelver, in charge of Van der Walt's cell – not realising that Shelver was a very senior leader of the Stormjaers. With the help of Shelver and Constable Fred van 'Onselen, Van der Walt escaped on 21 December.

Taillard's break came at the same time. Through Erna Eggert, he was asked to set up a meeting between Leibbrandt and a wealthy Afrikaans industrialist, Danie Malan. Taillard knew that this was his chance to nab Leibbrandt – he had just discovered that Leibbrandt was planning to assassinate Smuts on 20 January, the eighth birthday of Hitler's Third Reich – which left him less than a month. Taillard needed the police for this operation, and so decided to come clean with the police commissioner and his staff and explain that his resignation and refusal to sign the oath had merely been a front.

On Christmas Eve 1941, Robey Leibbrandt joined Jan Taillard in his car in Johannesburg to drive to Rosslyn, where the meeting was planned to take place. Only, there wasn't going to be a meeting: Taillard had instructed the police to set up a roadblock just north-west of Johannesburg. At the roadblock Taillard hit the brakes hard and when the car came to a stop, it was swarmed by policemen, who arrested both men.

Operation Weissdorn was over. And South Africa remained intact.

Jan Taillard received eighteen stitches to his head after being hit with a truncheon by a policeman who didn't know he was an undercover cop. He was kept in a cell with other rebels for two days in order to gather more information before he was released.

During the follow-up investigations, substantial quantities of arms and ammunition, explosives, detonators, pipe bombs, hand grenades and even bomb factories were discovered. A large number of Leibbrandt's followers were members of the police, railway police and prisons service.

On 20 January 1942 a special parade was held at Marshall Square, without the policemen being told the reason for it. At the parade, dozens of policemen who were members of Leibbrandt's rebels were arrested. In the end, 349 policemen – 60 non-commissioned officers and 289 constables – were arrested, and 52 of this group were charged with treason. But not all the police rebels were caught: on 2 February a couple of them tried to blow up the storeroom at police headquarters in Pretoria, where all the evidence against Leibbrandt was being kept. Part of the room was burnt, but the 150 sticks of dynamite didn't explode.

But rebel leader Johannes van der Walt was still on the loose. He was on the run until early 1942, when the police trapped him on the farm Rietfontein outside Krugersdorp. As Van der Walt tried to escape, he was shot in the back. Johannes van der Walt, world champion wrestler and national hero, was paralysed for the remainder of his life. In February 1942, the leader of the National Party, Dr DF Malan, made a rousing speech in Parliament protesting the shooting of an "Afrikaner hero". The Afrikaner was not afraid of government terrorism, he said; the more Afrikaner blood spilt, the stronger the Afrikaner would become.

On 16 November 1942, Robey Leibbrandt and six senior members of his organisation were charged with high treason in the Pretoria Supreme Court. Nearly two hundred witnesses were called, the most crucial being a German prisoner of war who testified that Leibbrandt was a German soldier and that they were in the same unit.

Leibbrandt didn't testify in his own defence, but did make a stirring speech before he was sentenced. The Afrikaner's salvation does not lie in the senseless making of crosses on ballot papers, he said, but in action and sacrifice and on the ideas of "he who was sent by the Almighty to save the peoples of this planet from the morass of oppression and suffering, Adolf Hitler!" He ended, with many tears among his followers in the courtroom: "To hell with mercy, I demand justice. Long live the Afrikaner volk! Long live National Socialist South Africa! God be with my comrades! The Vierkleur high!"

Leibbrandt was sentenced to death on 11 March 1943. When the judge finished reading the sentence, Leibbrandt gave a Nazi salute and shouted: "I greet death! The Vierkleur high!"

But Leibbrandt wasn't hanged. The day before Christmas 1943, Prime Minister Jan Smuts mitigated his sentence to life imprisonment – he could not hang the son of such a brave soldier who had fought with him in the Anglo-Boer War, he said.

Leibbrandt's views of General Smuts are interesting. In one of his diatribes about true leadership in his autobiography, he wrote that there was only one leader in South African history who was worth that title, and that was Smuts. "General Smuts was not only the greatest leader South Africa had ever seen, he was also my biggest wartime enemy. He wanted to crush me and I wanted to annihilate him." In 1950, when Smuts was lying on his deathbed, Leibbrandt sent him a telegram: "I respect you as a great leader, a courageous fighter and a brave enemy. Get well soon, General."

Leibbrandt served only five years of his life sentence. A few weeks after the National Party, led by Dr DF Malan, won the white elections in May 1948 on an apartheid ticket, they released Leibbrandt. He opened a butcher's shop in Springbok – the joke in the area was that nobody ever complained about the meat he sold them. Because they didn't dare.

Leibbrandt married and had five children, one named Izan – Nazi spelled backwards. He gradually disappeared from public life and died in 1966.

If Robey Leibbrandt had not been such a megalomaniac hothead and had planned his little revolution a bit better, South Africa would have looked a lot different today.

16

The Men in the
Dry-Cleaner's Van

To MOST YOUNGER SOUTH AFRICANS THE NAME
Rivonia merely refers to the posh suburb adjacent to
Sandton, north of Johannesburg. Few of them realise the name's
association with political intrigue and the struggle for liberation
from apartheid rule.

In 1963 Rivonia wasn't yet a built-up suburb; it was a network
of farms and smallholdings connected with tree-lined dirt roads.
One of these farms was called Lilliesleaf, and the official occupants
were a prominent architect and artist, Arthur Goldreich, and his
family. This is the story of what happened on the twenty-eight-acre
Lilliesleaf farm, Rivonia, on the afternoon of 11 July 1963.

The early 1960s was a turbulent time in Africa, with many African
states pushing for independence, and several achieving it. In South
Africa, the African National Congress and the movement which in
1959 had split from it, the Pan-Africanist Congress, were stepping
up their resistance to apartheid and particularly the laws forcing
all black South Africans to carry pass books. On 21 March 1960,
police shot and killed 69 protestors at an anti-pass demonstration
in Sharpeville near Vereeniging, and wounded 180. Later the same
day three protestors were killed at a demonstration in Langa outside
Cape Town, and 47 injured. The white government of Dr Hendrik
Verwoerd was unmoved: they outlawed the ANC, the South
African Communist Party (SACP) and the PAC, and on 31 May

1961 they transformed the country into a republic in which only whites had the vote.

It was against this background that the ANC leadership decided in June 1961 to abandon its long tradition of non-violent resistance and to embark on a limited sabotage campaign. The ANC and the SACP immediately set up sabotage units, which were merged later that year into Umkhonto we Sizwe (MK), the Spear of the Nation. One of the driving forces behind MK was Johannesburg lawyer Nelson Mandela. MK's first act of sabotage took place on 16 December 1961, the day Afrikaners celebrated as the Day of the Covenant, or Dingane's Day.

Early in 1961 the Communist Party financed the purchase of Lilliesleaf farm as headquarters, safe house, sanctuary and meeting place for members of the MK High Command. It was perfect – who would look for a viper's nest of communists and terrorists in such a neighbourhood? The transaction was handled by the editor of the left-wing journal *Liberation* and Communist Party theorist, Michael Harmel, lawyer Harold Wolpe set up the bogus company to buy it, and it was registered in the name of Vivian Ezra, a communist not suspected by the security police.

Lilliesleaf's first occupant was Mandela, who by now had gone underground, who moved there in October 1961. The house had to be fixed up and more rooms added, so Mandela acted as what he called "the houseboy", wearing the customary blue overalls of a black servant. He called himself David Motsamayi, the name of one of his former clients. He made breakfast and tea for the black builders and painters from Alexandra township who worked on the farm. They called him "boy" or "waiter" and ordered him around. "To those men," Mandela wrote in his autobiography, "I was an inferior, a servant, a person without trade, and therefore to be treated with disdain. I played the role so well that none of them suspected I was anything other than what I seemed."

Once the buildings had been repaired, Arthur Goldreich, his

wife Hazel and their children moved into the main house, with Mandela staying in the domestic worker's cottage. Twenty years earlier Goldreich had fought with the Jewish military movement Palmach in Palestine, and he now shared his knowledge of guerrilla warfare with Mandela during long discussions on the farm.

Ironically, his undercover stay at Lilliesleaf was the best times in the marriage between Mandela and the woman he had married in 1958, Winnie Madikizela. She and their daughters Zindzi and Zenani often visited on weekends from their home in Soweto. Winnie remembered later that this was the first time she was able to cook meals for her husband and children "and retain something of a family life". It was also the only time Mandela had to really bond with his children. "So Zeni imagined that to be her home, because it was the only place where her father had played with her," Winnie wrote in *Part of My Soul Went with Him*. "For years later, she dreamt of this home and asked me, 'Mummy, when are we going home to see Daddy?'"

Mandela described the visits by his wife and daughters as "the loveliest times" and an "idyllic bubble". During these weekends "time would sometimes seem to stop as we pretended that these stolen moments together were the rule, not the exception of our lives".

Elaborate security precautions were taken every time Winnie went to visit Lilliesleaf, but several times she was stopped at a police roadblock on her way. She said her "robustness" helped her many times, but once she had to feign labour pains. "I was huge, my face has always been round and I did look pregnant all the time." Winnie's acting was more convincing because they were travelling in a Red Cross ambulance, complete with a legitimate medical doctor, stethoscope around the neck. The police allowed the "gasping and sweating" Winnie through without asking questions.

In his various disguises, Mandela attended meetings virtually every night. In fact, he was quite bold for the most wanted political "criminal" in the country – he wasn't dubbed the "Black Pimpernel"

for nothing. On one occasion Winnie's old car broke down. Someone went to her office, telling her to drive to a particular corner. "When I got there, a tall man in blue overalls and a chauffeur's white coat and peaked cap opened the door, ordered me to shift from the driver's seat and took over and drove. That was him. He had a lot of disguises and he looked so different that for a moment, when he walked towards the car, I didn't recognise him myself." He drove her to a car dealer, traded the car in on a new one and drove it to the Johannesburg city centre. In busy Sauer Street he stopped at a stop sign, "got out, bade me goodbye and disappeared. So that was the kind of life we led."

Mandela told of the day he shot a sparrow with an old air rifle in the Lilliesleaf garden. He was about to boast about his marksmanship when Goldreich's five-year-old son Paul turned to him with tears in his eyes, saying, "David, why did you kill that bird? Its mother will be sad." Mandela was shamed. "I felt that this small boy had far more humanity than I did. It was an odd sensation for a man who was the leader of a nascent guerrilla army."

Zindzi and Zenani were too young to know that their father was in hiding, but Mandela's son from his previous marriage, Makgatho, was older and he knew. The Goldreich's children obviously had no idea. One day Makgatho and young Nicholas Goldreich were paging through a copy of *Drum* magazine and saw a picture of Mandela taken before he had gone underground. Makgatho recognised his father, but Nicholas said it could not be, because the person in the picture's name was Nelson, and Makgatho's father's name was David. Mandela realised it was time to leave, and a short time later left for Africa. It was January 1962.

Despite tight security at all border posts, Mandela slipped out and lobbied several African heads of state and liberation movements, even undergoing military training in Algeria. He returned safely six months later and arrived back at Lilliesleaf with a special gift for Winnie: the national dress of each of the countries he had visited. Nelson and Winnie spent one last night together. When they parted, Winnie had a strong sense that they would not see each other for a long time. The image of her tear-filled eyes when they parted stayed with him for years.

It was indeed their last private moment for almost three decades. Mandela went to Durban the next day, and after discussions with ANC president Chief Albert Luthuli and a party with comrades at Ismail and Fatima Meer's home, he travelled back to Johannesburg. Someone betrayed him, because the police knew his route and his car registration number. On 5 August 1962, he was captured at a police roadblock. He only regained his freedom on 11 February 1990.

Senior ANC officials had for a while suggested that Mandela had perhaps become too blasé about security, and now also started worrying about the safety of Lilliesleaf. Ahmed Kathrada and Lionel "Rusty" Bernstein were among those who felt that too many people knew about Lilliesleaf – Bernstein later wrote that there was "a gung-ho spirit of recklessness" in the top MK echelons. It was decided to stop using the farm.

The ANC leadership, meanwhile, was disappointed with the progress made by MK's sabotage units. A document called "Operation Mayibuye" was therefore drawn up by Joe Slovo and Govan Mbeki of the High Command, suggesting more vigorous military action than just sabotage. Bernstein and Walter Sisulu were among those who had serious reservations about the plan. Kathrada called it "a far-fetched strategy for guerrilla warfare" that was "causing much debate and consternation among some of us". Senior Communist Party leader Bram Fischer also fought against it. At his own trial three years later, he called it "an entirely unrealistic brainchild of some youthful and adventurous imagination. If ever there was a plan which a Marxist could not approve in the prevailing circumstances, this was such a one … if any part of it at all could be put into operation, it could achieve nothing but disaster."

Mandela's official biographer, veteran journalist Anthony Sampson, described it as a "reckless and ambitious scheme".

The senior leadership could not agree on Operation Mayibuye, and decided to use Lilliesleaf one more time as a meeting place where their differences could be sorted out. So, on 11 July 1963, all the top men gathered at Lilliesleaf: National High Command members Walter Sisulu, Govan Mbeki, Raymond Mhlaba, Ahmed Kathrada, Rusty Bernstein and Denis Goldberg, as well as Johannesburg advocate Bob Hepple.

Just before 3 p.m., when the meeting was to start, a dentist arrived at the farm. He had been asked to make a false plate for Walter Sisulu's mouth to make his disguise more convincing. He made Kathrada suspicious, because he seemed nervous and unduly curious. He asked Kathrada if there was going to be "much bloodshed" in South Africa.

Then the meeting got under way. At the same time, a delivery van bearing the name of a well-known Johannesburg dry-cleaning company turned into the road that led to the Lilliesleaf homestead. Two men in white dustcoats were sitting in front and a rug screened the back of the van. A black worker stopped them and told them to turn back. The driver said they were merely calling to see if they couldn't pick up new customers in the area.

The guard insisted that they leave the property, and the van reversed as if to turn around. Suddenly an Afrikaans voice shouted from behind the driver: "Slaan toe!" [pounce]. It was the voice of Lieutenant WPJ van Wyk of the South African Police. Ten policemen poured out of the van, one with a police dog on a leash.

Kathrada writes that they saw the van approaching. "Although we notice a closed delivery vehicle bearing the name of a dry-cleaning firm drive up to the main house, we ignore it. It's not unusual for merchants to deliver meat, groceries and other items to the Goldreichs, who are living on the farm as a front for the underground Communist Party, and our attention is focused on the merits and demerits of the grand plans we are contemplating." But when they saw the policemen jumping out, he says, they were "electrified with shock".

Mbeki quickly stuffed the documents relating to Operation Mayibuye into an unlit coal stove. Kathrada and Sisulu jumped through a window, but were confronted by policemen. The police didn't know who Kathrada was, because he'd dyed his hair red and grown a moustache to disguise himself as a Portuguese man (calling himself Pedro Perreira). "Who is this white man?" one of the policemen asked. But when Kathrada spoke, Lieutenant Van Wyk and Warrant Officer CJ Dirker recognised the man they knew so well. More police arrived at the farm within minutes.

The other Rivonia men also looked very different from the way the police knew them. Sisulu had straightened hair and a Hitler moustache, Mbeki looked like a farm labourer, the once clean-shaven Goldreich had a full black beard and moustache.

The police were totally surprised at their catch: six of the most wanted men in South Africa all in one house; almost the entire High Command of Umkhonto we Sizwe. It was the biggest single blow the security police had ever struck against the liberation movement. It set the ANC's military and political struggle back many years.

Arthur Goldreich, who was away at the time of the raid, now arrived back at Lilliesleaf. The moment he saw the police cars, he tried to turn back, but was stopped at gunpoint. Within days, four other MK leaders, incriminated by evidence found on the scene, were also arrested: James Kantor, Harold Wolpe, Elias Motsoaledi and Andrew Mlangeni. Two other MK properties, the farm Travallyn in the Krugersdorp district and the Mountain View cottage where Kathrada had stayed, were also raided within days, although by then everyone who stayed there had fled. The police confiscated stacks of important documents, including the blue-print for Operation Mayibuye.

Two of the "big fish" who often visited Lilliesleaf but were not there on the fateful day got away: Communist Party leaders Joe Slovo and Bram Fischer. Slovo left the country and later became the commander of MK, but Fischer, an advocate, stayed and defended the Rivonia trialists in court. He was arrested on separate charges and sent to jail for life in 1966.

Exactly a month after the arrests, Arthur Goldreich and Harold Wolpe made a dramatic escape from Marshall Square police station in Johannesburg after bribing a young warder who was in financial trouble. Disguised as priests, they fled to Swaziland and from there flew to Botswana, then still a British colony. The aeroplane sent to fetch them from Francistown was blown up by South African agents, but eventually they succeeded in flying to Dar es Salaam via Katanga.

Mandela had by now already served nine months of his initial five-year prison sentence for leaving the country illegally and for incitement to strike. A few days after the Rivonia raid he was taken to the prison office, where all his captured comrades sat. They were informed that they were going to be charged with sabotage the next day.

How did the police find out about Lilliesleaf? To this day this is not clear. The police leaked a story about an anonymous informant who took them to the farm, but didn't say who he was. At the time the police claimed they had had the farm under surveillance for hours. Kathrada disputes this. Why did they not arrest the dentist who visited Lilliesleaf less than half an hour before the police swooped, and why did they allow him to emigrate?

A former Judge President of the Eastern Cape Division of the Supreme Court, HHW de Villiers, wrote a book on the Rivonia raid and trial in 1964, *Rivonia – Operation Mayibuye*. He suggests that the policemen in the dry-cleaner's van were not sure what Lilliesleaf was. He mentions the guard who stopped the van and says, "This was time for decision – whether to withdraw on the employee's peremptory instructions to leave because the master was not at home and tradesmen were not permitted to call there, or openly and immediately to test the police suspicion that there was more to Lilliesleaf than met the eye." He adds that "from the police point of view, this raid provided unexpected results".

Another version, proposed by Stephen Clingman in his biography of Bram Fischer, is that the police had "turned" one of the MK members in detention and that he then spilled the beans.

The trial of the ten accused in what became world famous as the Rivonia Trial got under way at the Palace of Justice in Pretoria in October 1963. Nelson Mandela was Accused Number One. Then followed Walter Sisulu, Denis Goldberg, Govan Mbeki, Ahmed Kathrada, Lionel Bernstein, Raymond Mhlaba, James Kantor, Elias Motsoaledi and Andrew Mlangeni. They were charged under the Sabotage Act, specifically with recruiting and training people for sabotage acts and guerrilla warfare, and under the Suppression of Communism Act.

The accused followed the lead of Mandela when asked to plead: "My Lord, it is not I, but the Government that should be in the dock today. I plead not guilty."

The State's case was led by Dr Percy Yutar, SC. In one of the ANC's publications detailing the history of their struggle, it is stated that Yutar was "a Jew whose intense emotional involvement in the case was said to be due, in part, to his animus towards Jews who were communists" (most of the leading whites in the ANC and the SACP at the time were Jewish).

In opening the State's case, Yutar stated: "The planned purpose was to bring about in the Republic of South Africa chaos, disorder and turmoil, which would be aggravated, according to their plan, by the operation of thousands of trained guerrilla warfare units deployed throughout the country at various vantage points." These operations, he said, "were planned to lead to confusion, violent insurrection and rebellion, followed at the appropriate juncture by an armed invasion of the country by military units of foreign powers".

What Yutar was giving was a summary of Operation Mayibuye, of which the draft plan was found at Lilliesleaf – the very plan so many High Command members had opposed that it had to be discussed again on that fateful day in June.

In his closing address, Yutar said that the evidence led disclosed "a classical case of high treason par excellence". In his judgment, Judge Quartus de Wet agreed that the accused were guilty of treason. And yet the ten men were not accused of high treason, only sabotage and conspiracy. Judge de Villiers writes that Yutar had explained to him that this decision was made after the abortive marathon Treason Trial of 1956 to 1961, in which all the accused were acquitted, and the stricter proof required by law for treason.

The State's star witness was called Mr X, later revealed as Bruno Mtolo, one of the MK saboteurs and someone who had once visited Lilliesleaf. He volunteered an enormous amount of information and implicated people never before suspected by police. Many suspected that it was Mtolo who had betrayed Mandela, leading to his arrest.

But the star of the trial, which lasted until June 1964, was not Yutar or Mtolo. It was the tall, charismatic figure of Nelson Mandela. His address to the court reverberated around South Africa and the world. He made it clear that he was "an African patriot" and not a communist, although he welcomed the SACP's assistance. He concluded with these words: "During my lifetime I have dedicated myself to this struggle of the African people. I have fought against white domination, and I have fought against black domination. I have cherished the ideal of a democratic and free society in which all persons live together in harmony and with equal opportunities. It is an ideal which I hope to live for and to achieve. But if needs be, it is an ideal for which I am prepared to die."

He did not have to die for this ideal. The accused, their families, friends and supporters were fearing the worst: that they would be sentenced to death. But on 12 June 1964, Judge De Wet, after finding them guilty, passed sentence: "The crime of which the accused have been convicted, that is the main crime, the crime of conspiracy, is in essence one of high treason. The State has decided not to impose the supreme penalty, which in a case like this, would usually be the proper penalty for the crime. But consistent with my duty, that is the only leniency I can show. The sentence in the case of all the accused will be one of life imprisonment."

Within days, seven of the original accused were taken to Robben Island – Kantor had earlier been released on condition he turned state witness, and then fled the country; Rusty Bernstein was found not guilty; and Denis Goldberg was sent to serve his sentence in Pretoria Central Prison, because white and black prisoners were not held together. Goldberg was later joined in Pretoria Central by his counsel, Bram Fischer, who was released a very ill man three months before his death in May 1975.

Goldberg was released after serving sixteen years of his sentence. The Robben Island men were released a few months before Mandela walked free on 11 February 1990.

(In 2001, Nick Wolpe, son of Harold and nephew of James Kantor, set up the Lilliesleaf Trust to restore and preserve the historic buildings "and to ensure that the beliefs, aspirations, spirit and soul that Lilliesleaf personifies and embodies are preserved for current and future generations". Surrounding properties have been bought out, and a Learning Centre and a "Camp Lekgotla Retreat" are to be developed with a boutique hotel and conference facilities.)

17

A Stranger on
the Phone

MENTION THE NAME WINNIE MADIKIZELA-MANDELA, and the name Stompie Seipei immediately comes to many a South African mind. The death of this child activist in 1989 will hang around Nelson Mandela's former wife's neck for the rest of her life.

Stompie's murder was a very public story – at the time it took place, when Madikizela-Mandela was criminally charged with his kidnapping and assault, and again when she appeared before the Truth and Reconciliation Commission eight years later. To many, especially white South Africans, the death of fourteen-year-old Stompie defined Winnie Madikizela-Mandela. The media had a field day and declared that the Mother of the Nation had become the Mugger of the Nation.

Journalists and political analysts struggled to understand that ordinary people still loved and adored Winnie despite this dark stain on her record. All available information indicated that she was an irresponsible, power-hungry, selfish and cruel woman. How could people still call her the Mother of the Nation?

There is a story, a story too insignificant ever to make newspaper headlines, that perhaps helps to answer this question. It does not involve politics or the liberation struggle. But it does offer a private and very telling insight into another side of Winnie Madikizela-Mandela.

First, the story of Stompie and how it came about. Winnie's

history is a dramatic tale of a spectacular rise to fame – and an even more spectacular fall from grace.

Nomzamo Winifred Madikizela was born in 1936 in the Eastern Cape. She studied in Johannesburg and became South Africa's first qualified black social worker. She became involved in resistance politics in the late 1950s, which was how she met the charismatic lawyer Nelson Mandela, whom she married in 1958. It was also the first of many times she was detained by the apartheid police. The couple had two daughters, but not much of a marriage because Mandela's political activism took up much of his time. She became a single mother when he was imprisoned in 1962.

Between 1962 and 1975 she was banned and jailed several times, which included a lengthy term in solitary confinement. The burden of being called Mandela while the real Mandela was locked up on an island far away was a heavy one. During the 1976 youth uprising in Soweto, she became the de facto leader of the ANC in the township, and a comrade, mother and inspiration to most of the student leaders. Her fearlessness became legendary: she was the only black leader who took no nonsense from white policemen.

She paid dearly for her obstinacy: in 1977 she was banished to the rural, conservative backwater town of Brandfort. She was harassed, isolated and traumatised. Most of her friends point to these years as the time when Winnie became unstable.

Once again defying the police, she returned to Soweto during the turbulent mid-1980s. This was the period of the most violent, lawless repression by the security forces. She surrounded herself with a number of undisciplined youths, called the Mandela United Football Club, "coached" by an unstable man of dubious character, Jerry Richardson. Winnie's behaviour became more and more erratic, and that of the young thugs (who didn't actually play much football) more unruly and unpopular.

It was during this time that the fourteen-year-old Stompie Seipei entered her life. Despite his youth, he was a prominent figure among radical youngsters in Soweto, respected for his bravery and his ability to organise and inspire. But he was really only a child, a fact that didn't escape the security police. Winnie believed that he had been recruited by the police, and she and her football club became paranoid that he would spill the beans on the underground activities at the Mandela household.

The boy was caught, taken to Mandela's house and told to confess. He didn't, and was savagely tortured, beaten and thrown against the wall – in Winnie's presence, according to Richardson's testimony. Stompie was subsequently killed by Richardson. Winnie was charged and found guilty of the boy's kidnapping and of being an accomplice to assault. She received a suspended sentence and a fine. Richardson was sent to prison for Stompie's murder.

During 1997 the Truth Commission held a special hearing on Winnie, her football club's activities, and the death of Stompie and others. She again vehemently denied involvement in Stompie's death. TRC chairperson Desmond Tutu praised her role in the struggle, but added that something "had gone horribly wrong" in her life. He pleaded with her to apologise to Stompie's mother and the families of other victims, which she did – some said reluctantly.

Nelson Mandela publicly supported his wife through all this, but in 1995, when he was president, he fired her from her job as deputy minister and divorced her a year later. Thabo Mbeki, Mandela's successor as president, clearly disliked her. At the twenty-fifth anniversary of the Soweto uprising in 2001, he shoved her away from him – on national television – when she approached to greet him on the stage. It was the most public of humiliations of a once proud symbol of the struggle. Her political career faded after that.

And yet many township dwellers, unemployed mothers and youngsters continued to adore her, to still call her the Mother of the Nation. Why?

Because there has always been another side to this turbulent, enigmatic woman. This is one story that gives a glimpse of that.

It involves an old friend and colleague of mine, a newspaper reporter named Herman Joubert. I got to know Manie, as I called him, as a highly intelligent but complex man when we both worked at the Afrikaans newspaper *Beeld* in the late 1970s. I liked Herman, his sharp mind and his quirky sense of humour.

The incident happened before Stompie's murder. We only got to know about it because Herman wrote a short column in *Beeld* many years later, on 7 March 1995. Before that, nobody knew about the story.

Herman was a sub-editor at the time, which meant that he worked from late afternoon until early morning, *Beeld* being a morning paper. But on this particular night he had the day off. Perhaps that was why he was overcome by a "bitter loneliness" that night. Herman wrote that by one o'clock he could still not fall asleep. "My children were far away from me, my marriage in pieces and I was on the edge of the precipice."

He drank a beer and paged through his contact book looking at the telephone numbers. He had nobody to call. Then he noticed a number without a name next to it; probably a number he had been given by a reporter in the newsroom, but he had no idea whose it was. What the hell, he thought, he was going to phone a nameless telephone number.

A courteous young woman answered the phone and simply said: "She is not here, she'll call you later. It sounds as if you need help." He gave her his number, then fell asleep "in a world of horrible nightmares".

Around 3 a.m. his phone rang. Herman had forgotten about his earlier call and wasn't in a good mood when he answered the phone. A voice asked him if he had phoned earlier. He realised it was a black woman's voice and was so irritated he slammed down the phone. But she phoned again. "Are you Herman?" she asked. Then she identified herself as Winnie Mandela.

Herman was in such a state that he responded aggressively,

telling her that he didn't need her help and she should leave him alone. But Winnie insisted: Why was he so lonely and depressed? What was going on in his life? Did he have children?

Herman ended up telling her his whole life's story and all his sadnesses. Winnie listened and listened, occasionally asking a question. "For the first time in many months someone really cared and listened to what I had to say," Herman wrote.

At the end of a long conversation Winnie told him to make himself a sandwich, to drink a glass of hot milk and to go back to sleep. She added: "Remember, you have to look after yourself. You are not alone in the world. There are people who care about you. We care about you." She wished him a peaceful night and put the phone down.

"I followed her advice and for the first time in months I slept peacefully. I almost had the feeling that the angels were guarding over me," Herman recalled. His life got back on track after that and he never needed to talk to her again, although he was tempted sometimes.

Herman ended his column wishing Winnie well in the difficult time she was going through (1995), and reminded her that not only bad things revisit one, but also the good one has done.

If this was Winnie's attitude towards a total stranger, and a white Afrikaner male to boot during the most hectic time of white oppression, I can begin to understand why so many people love her and are ready forgive her mistakes.

18

The Breastfeeding
Warrior

PHILA PORTIA NDWANDWE WAS WELL ON HER WAY TO becoming a legend like the great female warrior Manthathisi, the formidable chief and general of the Batlokoa during the early 1800s. Phila was destined to become the most senior woman commander ever of Umkhonto we Sizwe, the ANC's liberation army. But fate had other plans for her.

Phila was arrested for her political activities shortly after she left school in KwaZulu-Natal. It did not deter her: she skipped the border to Swaziland, and in 1985 she was taken with a group of KwaZulu-Natal students to do her basic military training as an MK soldier in Angola. She was an exemplary recruit, intelligent, deeply committed and hardworking, says Bheki Mabuza, one of her seniors at the time. He knew her as Zandi or Zandile, because none of the MK guerrillas used their own names – "I never even bothered to find out her real name," he says.

After her training Phila was despatched to Swaziland, where Mabuza had been stationed for some time. It did not take long for her to make an impression on the military structures of MK responsible for KwaZulu-Natal, and she was quickly given more responsibilities. "She never acted like a woman, she did everything the men did," says Mabuza. "She was seen as a tomboy." She had a taste for men's clothing, he says, and was always among the men in the forefront of any operation. Unlike most of her female comrades, she was very independent and stubborn – and she liked "deep jazz, the music mostly preferred by men at that time".

Richard Jones was a member of Phila's unit. He describes her as "a strong person, with a powerful personality, and she had a strong and powerful body too". He also remembers that she had a soft, motherly side and a well-developed sense of humour.

Phila didn't make friends easily, partly because she was so committed to her work as a freedom fighter. Bheki Mabuza became her closest friend, and in the late 1980s they also became lovers and lived together in Manzini, Swaziland. Their baby was born in June 1988.

Not long after she became MK commander for Natal Operations did the security police in Durban start taking notice of her unit's efficiency. The security police informers placed in Swaziland started telling them about this capable commander: a beautiful young woman. With her successes in directing acts of sabotage and attacks on police stations and policemen, as well as infiltrating MK operatives into South Africa, she was given more responsibilities and access to top MK personnel. She handled large amounts of money and arms and knew the entire MK network intimately.

Then in October 1988 she disappeared without a trace. She had a meeting with some of her comrades, got into their car afterwards and was never seen again. Her friends knew immediately that something was wrong, because she was still breastfeeding her baby and simply didn't return home. Her disappearance caused consternation among the MK High Command: she was a key person in the entire operation in Swaziland and KwaZulu-Natal, knew everybody involved and had knowledge of all MK's secret plans and places.

The rumours started flying, and a lot of stories reached Phila's family. Someone had seen her in Cape Town, disguised as a coloured person, they were told. Someone else saw her in Pretoria with a strange man, they heard. None of the stories led anywhere.

Phila's father, Nathan, treasured the last reminder he had of his daughter: a handwritten letter she sent him in December 1987. It read:

> My dearest Dad,
> I know a letter from me is least expected by you at this point in time. As your daughter this is really my fault for not writing to you. I miss you all. I am always with you in all respects, hoping it's the same with you.
> With tons of love, from your loving daughter
> Phila.
> PS It is not advisable to keep my letters.

Inevitably, the longer Phila didn't reappear, the more the speculation started: had she become an askari, the name given to former guerrillas who were "turned" by the police and were fighting against the ANC? Speculation became truth, and many of her former friends and colleagues thought this could be the only explanation for her bizarre disappearance. Several other former MK operatives were stationed at the police death squad camp at Vlakplaas outside Pretoria and were used to kill anti-apartheid activists. Was Phila now at Vlakplaas, fighting her own people with apartheid killers like Eugene de Kock?

Phila's family had no answer to the rumour, and suffered in silence. The father of her son, Bheki Mabuza, had no answers either, and quietly brought up their son, Thabang.

In 1990, State President FW de Klerk unbanned the ANC and other organisations, and soon afterwards MK ceased hostilities. Exiles and guerrillas started going back home. Still no Phila.

The ruling National Party, the ANC and other political parties reached a political settlement after long negotiations, and on 27 April 1994 South Africa had its first proper democratic elections.

An integral part of the political settlement was that there would be no Nuremberg-style trials as happened in Germany after the Second World War, but there would also not be general amnesty for all political crimes. The Commission for Truth and Reconciliation was created to deal with human rights abuses of the past. It would have two legs: hearings where victims of human rights abuses could tell their stories; and an Amnesty Committee where those who were guilty of politically motivated abuses could confess to their crimes and be granted full indemnity – if they made a full disclosure of all the facts and proved that they had a political rather than personal motivation.

In 1997, investigators of the Truth Commission visited Nathan Ndwandwe at his home with bad news and good news. Phila was dead. But she didn't die as an askari, she was killed by the police. Six security policemen who were responsible had just disclosed the circumstances of her death in their applications for amnesty: Andy Taylor, Lawrence Wasserman, Johannes Steyn, Hendrik Botha, Salmon du Preez and Jacobus Vorster.

The full story gradually unfolded before the Amnesty Committee's hearing in Durban. The security police had become more and more concerned at the successes of Phila Ndwande's unit in Swaziland. In October 1988, Captain Andy Taylor, Colonel Johannes Steyn and Major Hendrik (Hentie) Botha decided that Phila had to be neutralised. First prize to them would be if they could persuade or force her into turning sides and working with the police, because she would have been of immense value. It was thus decided that she should first be abducted from Swaziland in an effort to recruit her, failing which she should be killed.

Captain Taylor, Colonel Steyn, Colonel Vorster and Major Botha left in Taylor's car for the Onverwacht border post between KwaZulu-Natal and Swaziland. Steyn waited at a police house, while the others crossed into Swaziland using false passports. Warrant Officer Wasserman and Major Du Preez travelled in a Toyota minibus and an Isuzu bakkie. They were accompanied by two former MK operatives who had switched sides and were now working with the police. They also went up the Onverwacht border post, where the two askaris crept through a hole in the border fence and met up with Wasserman and Du Preez on the other side.

The two askaris then took the bakkie and travelled to Manzini, where they made contact and set up a meeting with Phila Ndwandwe. Phila's comrade, Richard Jones, drove her to the meeting at the George Hotel. "She was really pleased to see the comrades," he recalls. "I remember her talking to them in an animated fashion. She came back to my car to fetch her purse from the dashboard. I had no petrol in the car and asked her for money. She opened her purse and gave me R10. I will never forget the sight: Phila looking at me through the passenger window, giving me R10 and saying, see you later. That picture is burned into my memory." It was the last time Jones saw Phila.

While this was going on, the other policemen were monitoring the meeting from Taylor's car while keeping in radio contact with the minibus. Phila got into the bakkie with the two men and drove off. When they reached the minibus, Phila's hands were tied with tape and she was transferred to the minibus. They drove to Hlubi, where Phila was put on the back of the bakkie with Major Botha. Near Onverwacht border post, Botha forced Phila to creep through the border fence with him, while the others went through the border post.

Back in South Africa, Phila was held in a house belonging to the police, and Botha started interrogating her. Botha testified before the TRC that she was reluctant to talk to him at first, but later responded freely. He stressed that he did not touch her. Botha said he was particularly looking for signs that she might cooperate as a police informer, and he even made a direct offer to her. But she showed no such signs, he said, not in her body language nor in what she said. She did not raise the issue of her safety, as he would have expected, or ask who else would know or how communications would work.

The next morning Botha and his colleagues took Phila to a

police safe house on the farm Elandskop near Pietermaritzburg. The pressure on Phila to change sides continued, but she gave no indication that she was going to crack. Botha and Wasserman repeatedly denied to the Amnesty Committee that they assaulted her, despite TRC evidence leader Paddy Prior's apparent incredulity. The TRC commissioner responsible for KwaZulu-Natal, Richard Lyster, had no qualms to declare afterwards that she was kept naked in a small concrete room and tortured.

The men also testified that they'd had no intention of prosecuting Phila: not only had her kidnapping been illegal, but a court case would also have identified the two askaris who had lured Phila into the bakkie. (Captain Andy Taylor did not testify before the TRC: he had died of brain cancer shortly after completing his amnesty application.)

Phila was also interrogated by security policemen of the Eastern Transvaal branch, and then by Colonel Steyn, to make sure for himself that she would not switch sides. Phila told him that she would not cooperate with them, whatever they did, and that she would continue with her MK activities should she be released. The policemen concluded that Phila Ndwandwe was "too tough a nut to crack", that she was brave and that she would never betray her colleagues in MK.

Steyn then ordered Taylor, Wasserman, Du Preez and Vorster to kill Phila, and left the farm.

Wasserman and Du Preez went outside and dug a grave near the farmhouse, with Taylor and Vorster continuing the interrogation – Taylor now spoke to Phila in Zulu.

Wasserman and Du Preez came back, and told Phila that she was going to be transferred to another police house. They blindfolded her and took her outside.

Wasserman: "Du Preez and I took her outside to where a
grave had been dug previously. The grave was about

sixty metres from the verandah. Once outside I
rendered her unconscious with a heavy blow."

Prior: "Using?"

Wasserman: "A wooden police riot baton. She was
immediately unconscious and Du Preez and I then
carried her to the grave that was dug among the trees.
We then placed Miss Ndwandwe in the grave, sort of
half-way in. I then fired a single shot into her head."

Prior: "Yes?"

Wasserman: "From here she was dead. We then undressed
her."

Prior: "Why was that done?"

Wasserman: "Clothing and identification purposes.
Clothing could be identified at a later stage."

Adv Louis Visser (Wasserman's counsel): "And did you
then place her in the bottom of the grave?"

Wasserman: "We then placed her in the bottom of the
grave and began to fill it in."

Phila's father, stepmother and sister were in the room when this
evidence was led. Nathan Ndwandwe, his eyes filling with tears,
just slowly shook his head from side to side when he heard how his
daughter had died.

But another relative jumped up and angrily shouted from the
public gallery: "We want to know all the killers, black and white.
Where are those informants you talk about? We want to see them
all like we see these men here. Why did you kill our people? We
need to know why. Why don't you kill me too?"

Richard Jones was also in the public gallery and was deeply
moved to find out how brave his former commander had been.
"Now everybody knows Phila was one of the bravest comrades," he
said afterwards. "Even these policemen begrudgingly admit that
she was a brave woman."

The amnesty applicants took the TRC to the banks of the Tugela River, where they had killed several other activists and thrown the bodies into the river. And then they took the investigators to Phila's grave on Elandskop. When her skeleton was laid bare, it showed a round hole on the top of her skull where Wasserman's bullet had entered her head.

When her body was uncovered, a blue plastic bag was found around Phila's waist. Truth Commissioner Richard Lyster asked the policemen what it was. "They said she had put this plastic bag over her to try and maintain some sense of female dignity while she was being interrogated and tortured," Lyster wrote later. He called Phila's exhumation "the most enduring moment, the one that will stay with me for the rest of my life".

A few weeks after the exhumation, the ANC gave Phila a hero's funeral. President Nelson Mandela attended personally, as did cabinet minister Ronnie Kasrils, who was one of Phila's commanders, and other senior MK leaders.

Bheki Mabuza also went to the funeral, and brought his and Phila's son, Thabang, with him. Thabang was then nine years old. The ANC awarded Phila a medal for bravery, and asked Thabang to accept it. Nelson Mandela himself had tears in his eyes.

Mabuza says when Thabang is a bit older, he will tell him the whole story of his mother's proud life and brave death.

The Amnesty Committee of the TRC decided that the policemen were telling the truth and had been acting under orders as police officers, and granted them full indemnity from criminal as well as civil prosecution. The Committee also decided not to force the policemen to divulge the names of the two askaris who had betrayed Phila, as they were not directly linked to her murder.

19

The Sleeping Gorilla

"Where does the gorilla sleep? Well, it sleeps where it wants."
— a senior military commander explaining apartheid
South Africa's rationale for developing nuclear bombs

SUNDAY 7 AUGUST 1977. VASTRAP, SOMEWHERE IN THE Kalahari region of the remote Northern Cape. An unmarked light aircraft, flying low, passes over a site in the middle of absolutely nowhere, with peculiar structures on it. Men in white coats and soldiers in camouflage uniforms scurry about in panic. Who are these intruders, and why does their aircraft not have any of the compulsory markings on it? Frantic calls are made to find out where the aeroplane took off and where it is destined to land. But all in vain, because the mysterious aeroplane doesn't have a scheduled flight plan. Within days, much of the equipment at the site is buried in the sand or carted away. Most of the staff depart in great hurry, leaving only a few soldiers behind.

The South African government had been caught red-handed. The men in the white coats were nuclear scientists and technicians. The peculiar towers on the site stood over immense boreholes drilled deep into the earth. The men were about to explode a nuclear device deep underground – a nuclear device they vehemently denied ever possessing. The government denied for sixteen more years that it had manufactured nuclear bombs.

Actually, the unmarked aeroplane did not uncover South Africa's secret. The Soviet Union's Cosmos satellite had taken a series of photographs of the Vastrap site when it passed over the area on successive days from 21 to 25 July 1977. On 6 August, USSR president Leonid Brezhnev informed US president Jimmy Carter that the photographs revealed that South Africa was preparing to detonate a nuclear device in the Kalahari. The Americans confirmed these findings by way of satellite photos and those taken by the unmarked aircraft, and asked South Africa for an explanation.

On 23 August 1977, President Carter announced that Prime Minister John Vorster had assured him that South Africa wasn't developing nuclear weapons and that the structures in the Kalahari had not been intended for a nuclear test. A month later, Vorster told the ABC television network that he had given no such assurances, but stated that South Africa was only interested in peaceful applications of nuclear technology.

In 2003, three key men in South Africa's nuclear weapons programme, former general manager of the Atomic Energy Corporation Richard van der Walt, former senior manager of Armscor Hannes Steyn and former South African Air Force chief Jan van Loggerenberg, confirmed the Russian and American findings of what Vastrap really was. They write in their limited-edition book *Armament and Disarmament* that the Vastrap area had been selected for the nuclear test because so few people lived in the area, because it had almost no underground rivers and because there were deep underground rock formations with hardly any geological faults. The nuclear devices would have been exploded so deep below the surface that ground-level radioactive releases would have been kept to undetectable levels.

The obvious drilling process and the heavy equipment used were camouflaged as a military underground munitions depot. To "camouflage" the increased activity in the area by people and vehicles preparing for the test, it was arranged that the National

Institute for Defence Research would test their version of the Soviet-made Stalin Organ multiple rocket launcher at the same place at the same time. It didn't fool the Russians or the Americans.

These governments were not exactly surprised to discover that South Africa was developing a military nuclear capacity. It was known that South Africa and its "colony", Namibia, had rich uranium deposits. A commodore in the South African Navy, Dieter Gerhardt, had been leaking some highly secret military information to the Soviets, some of it indicating that Pretoria was engaged in nuclear research for military purposes. Documents concerning top secret military transactions involving uranium enrichment technology had been stolen from the South African embassy in West Germany and handed to the African National Congress. Renfrew Christie, a Cape Town academic, passed on sensitive nuclear information to the ANC, and was jailed for it. Right through the 1970s, foreign intelligence agencies registered the acquisition of sophisticated components that could be used in nuclear development, and on several occasions noticed contact between Israeli, American, French and German nuclear scientists and engineers and their counterparts in South Africa.

We will probably never know if the suspicion is valid that the United States government and the CIA knew all about South Africa's nuclear plans by the mid-1970s but played the game because they thought they could control the Pretoria government. It is almost certain, for instance, that US satellites had picked up signs of the Vastrap site before the Soviet satellite, but nothing was said or done. The Vastrap installation was dismantled in 1978.

Hysterical indignation broke out in white South Africa in April 1979 when the government revealed that the American ambassador's aeroplane had been used to take clandestine photographs of the Valindaba nuclear plant. South Africa expelled three military attachés serving at the US embassy. And the US expelled all but one of the South African attachés in Washington. (The Atomic Energy Board's research reactor was based at Pelindaba, a name that means the debate (or problem) is finished. The later uranium enrichment programme was based at Valindaba, which means the debate (or problem) is closed.)

The government line, swallowed as gospel by all South African newspapers, was that the Americans were jealous of the "unique and revolutionary" method developed by South African scientists to enrich uranium. The US had falsely accused South Africa of developing nuclear weapons, so the line went, in order to protect its own lucrative trade in processed uranium.

We now know exactly what happened at Vastrap in August 1977. But the people who developed South Africa's nuclear bombs, and their political bosses, still seem to deny the second incident that alerted the world that apartheid South Africa had become a rogue nuclear state.

On 22 September 1979, an American Vela satellite detected a double flash over the southern oceans in the vicinity of Prince Edward and Marion Islands – the telltale double flash of a nuclear explosion. The US authorities had no doubt what it was, and announced on 25 October, after all the data had been analysed, that it was indeed a nuclear explosion. They didn't want to make the announcement, but scientists deeply unhappy with the US administration's softly-softly approach towards South Africa had leaked the story to ABC television news and the network was about to break it.

The CIA added to the picture by establishing that the South African Navy had been conducting secret exercises in the same area at the end of September 1979. The US Air Force Technical Applications Center reported finding acoustic soundings from listening posts, which confirmed the suspicions.

On 13 November, the New Zealand Institute of Nuclear Science at Gracefield reported that they had detected an increase in the measurement of radioactive fallout, also in rainwater, possibly from a nuclear explosion with the force of between two and four kilotons. Two months later the Arecibo Ionospheric Observatory in Puerto Rico reported that its scientists had observed a ripple or wave in the ionosphere moving from south to north at the time of the suspected explosion.

The suspicions were further confirmed by the findings of Dr L van Middlesworth of the Department of Physiology and Biophysics at the University of Tennessee College of Medicine. He reported that he had examined the sheep and cattle thyroids from Australia on a routine basis, and his samples for 12 and 13 November contained six times the normal levels of radium. A major cyclone had moved over the Marion Island area on 22 September and reached Australia six days later. The explanation was given that a radioactive cloud had probably been caught by this storm and carried eastwards.

Early in 1980, CBS News reported they had evidence that South Africa had exploded a nuclear bomb over the southern oceans in September 1979. The *Washington Post* reported that South Africa had offered to help Israel test a nuclear bomb since 1966, but the offer was only accepted in 1979. The newspaper stated that Israel and Taiwan were cooperating with South Africa in the development of missile delivery systems.

On 14 July 1980, the US Defense Intelligence Agency, after an extensive analysis of the Vela satellite's recording of an optical flash, declared its conviction that the flash was "probably a clandestine nuclear explosion".

The *Sunday Times*, then under the editorship of Tertius Myburgh, who had a very close relationship with the South African intelligence community, published an angry editorial on 28 October 1979. The American government "has inflicted grave damage on South Africa's international relationships by suggesting that this country might have carried out a nuclear test explosion somewhere between Australia and Argentina", the editorial said, suggesting that the Vela light flash was "possibly of natural origin".

The *Sunday Times* said the Americans' false allegation that South Africa had become a nuclear power fell into "a pattern that began with South Africa's announcement that it had discovered a means of enriching uranium, a discovery that might pose a new threat to America's crumbling, but still immensely lucrative, monopoly over enrichment services in the Free World".

The 22 September incident and the wide-ranging scientific findings created great consternation in the US and Britain. President Jimmy Carter was fighting for re-election in 1980 and was already battling with the storm around the Iranian hostage crisis – he didn't need other tricky problems and accusations that his nuclear nonproliferation policies had failed. (The Carter administration had passed the Nuclear Non-Proliferation Act earlier that year, establishing new criteria for American exports of special nuclear materials.) And, of course, if it was proved that Israel had something to do with the September explosion, it could complicate the already volatile situation in the Middle East and perhaps spur Arab states on to start developing nuclear capabilities themselves. In short, it wasn't in Jimmy Carter's interest that proof was found that South Africa and/or Israel had exploded a nuclear bomb.

But, more importantly, the Rhodesia/Zimbabwe problem was at a critical stage in 1979. In fact, the Lancaster House conference between Britain and the Zimbabwean liberation movements had convened exactly ten days before the suspected nuclear explosion. White-controlled Rhodesia was about to become black-ruled Zimbabwe. It was very important for the West that this violent hot spot in Africa be settled once and for all, and confirmation that its aggressive white neighbour to the south was exploding nuclear bombs could upset the delicate negotiations.

So the Carter administration quickly established a panel of experts under Dr Frank Press, the White House science advisor, to review all the evidence relating to the 22 September "double flash". The panel set out to systematically undermine all the various findings that indicated a nuclear explosion. Eventually it declared that, because of "the lack of persuasive corroborative evidence" and "discrepancies in the September 22 signal", the panel "considers it more likely that the signal was probably not from a nuclear explosion", although they could not rule out that possibility.

The panel's findings were met with incredulity by most of the scientific community, and were seen as a rather crude damage control attempt motivated by foreign policy and internal political considerations. For example, Ronald W Walters, one of the more astute researchers into South Africa's nuclear programme, raised serious questions about the panel's bizarre finding in his book *South Africa and the Bomb*. "These questions and many others point to the strong conclusion that there was political interference from the White House in the conduct of this investigation, with the intention of preventing any clear and conclusive evidence from emerging that suggested that there had, in fact, been a nuclear explosion in the Indian Ocean–Antarctic region by either South Africa, Israel, or both of them working together."

Naturally, the South African government vehemently denied exploding a nuclear bomb. But they felt they had to offer some explanation for the double flash in the southern oceans. Their first attempt was to state that a Soviet submarine in the area had exploded. Then Professor Raul Smit of Durban University came up with the suggestion that a Soviet nuclear-armed missile fired in August 1963 had suddenly exploded after lying dormant for sixteen years. Both explanations were quickly dismissed by experts – for one thing, such explosions would have produced very different flashes than the one observed.

In their 2003 book, Steyn, Van der Walt and Van Loggerenberg list the Vela flash among "a series of disclosures" used to subtly communicate South Africa's "nuclear posture", but then proceed to deny that they ever detonated a nuclear bomb. The bomb completed in 1977, they say, was placed in a casing 60 centimetres in diameter and 2 metres long, weighing about a ton. "As such it was much too large and heavy to be delivered to a point in the atmosphere above the South Atlantic Ocean, or in fact anywhere else, by the means available at the time. The South African Air Force only became involved in the Nuclear Weapons Programme in the 1980s and was, simply, not ready for such delivery in 1979."

Experts believe this explanation is too simplistic to be taken as proof that there was no South African testing in September 1979. They also point out that the three men made no other mention of or offered no explanation for the incident that had occupied international nuclear arms scientists for years.

On 24 March 1993, just thirteen months before South Africa's first non-racial elections, President FW de Klerk finally admitted that South Africa had indeed manufactured six nuclear bombs similar to the one used on Hiroshima at the end of the Second World War. He also insisted that these bombs were "never tested – despite persistent reports of a mysterious event over the South Atlantic Ocean towards the end of the 1970s".

There still seems to be a broad consensus in the international scientific community that the September 1979 event was most likely a nuclear explosion, despite the White House panel's report and South Africa's denials. If it was indeed a nuclear bomb, then there are two possibilities: either the South African officials are lying and they did indeed test one of their bombs, or it was an Israeli bomb, tested in cooperation with South Africa.

It is quite possible that the South Africans feel they should stick to their lies of the time to protect or not embarrass those in the US, Israel and possibly France and Germany who had cooperated with them or helped conceal the 1979 test. We now know that South Africa did have a nuclear device ready for testing at the time. It is also not a secret how paranoid the apartheid government was at the prospect of the black liberation movement taking over government in Zimbabwe in 1980, and a nuclear explosion could have been meant as a serious warning to that new government (it turned out to be Robert Mugabe's ZANU) not to mess around with South Africa.

But it has subsequently also been proved beyond a doubt that Israel has an arsenal of nuclear devices, and it is therefore possible that it was they rather than South Africa who exploded a device in 1979. If this is the case, then there can be absolutely no doubt that the South African government knew and cooperated with this test, which would strengthen speculation that Israel had helped South Africa in developing its nuclear capacity. This, of course, is still denied by all concerned, including De Klerk when he owned up in 1993. He said the bombs were developed "without the cooperation of any other country".

Why did the South African government of the time decide to spend such a vast amount of money (in the end it cost close to R30 billion) to develop nuclear bombs?

Most of the explanations coming from the former government, their defence force and nuclear engineers point to the big Cuban military presence in Angola as the main motivation for starting to develop nuclear bombs – they did so, in other words, out of fear of "Soviet expansionism". But according to FW de Klerk's auto-biography, the decision to launch a nuclear weapons programme was already made in 1974. The Cubans only arrived in Angola in mid-1975 – and they maintain they only came because South Africa had invaded Angola on behalf of UNITA and the MPLA.

De Klerk says apart from the "threat of Soviet expansionism", the National Party government also regarded a nuclear capacity essential "because we knew that because of our international isolation we would not be able to rely on help from outside if we were attacked". But in his autobiography he suggests that he didn't believe in the programme, although he had full knowledge of it when he was Minister of Mineral and Energy Affairs. (The real driving force behind the nuclear arms programme was PW Botha, first as Minister of Defence under John Vorster and then as prime minister after September 1978.)

The authors of *Armament and Disarmament* also cite fear of communism: "With the USSR being on the (southbound) march to conquer Africa for communism, the white South African government saw itself as the last bastion of Western civilisation in Africa. South Africa considered itself, moreover, as left in the lurch by previous allies and besieged by the sanctions of the United Nations." Elsewhere they state: "There was a sense of terrible isolation, a sense of having to stand up against the whole world. This feeling of being alone and left in the lurch, soon turned into a bitter and pervasive determination."

One can't help but wonder why, rather than spend R30 billion on weapons of mass destruction, these men did not recognise the source of their alienation and instead start preparing for a settlement with the black majority, as happened from 1990 onwards. (Included in the R30-billion project was the design and manufacture of the RSA3 space launch vehicle and medium-range ballistic missiles.)

There's an anecdote that's a favourite among nuclear programme insiders. When PW Botha visited the nuclear warhead plant, a senior engineer said these words to him: "By placing these weapons in your hands, we are placing a terrible responsibility on your shoulders. We want you to know that we who understand the consequences of these systems regularly pray for you and your colleagues. We pray that you will have the wisdom and the necessary understanding of your accountability when you consider their use."

The architects of the programme realised that the nuclear bombs could never actually be used – who would they bomb? Steyn, Van der Walt and Van Loggerenberg agree: "The South African nuclear weapons were of no use and could not be employed against civilian or revolutionary targets; they were designed for credible deterrence."

But these weapons would serve as a deterrence only if others knew about their existence. In the case of apartheid South Africa, a public announcement or a public testing of a device would have caused an international uproar. "The least problematic option," say Steyn, Van der Walt and Van Loggerenberg, "was to inform a small number of very highly placed officials or politicians in the community of nations of either South Africa's intention or present to them the fact of an existing capability." A safe deduction would be that the US, Britain, Germany and France would have been so informed.

After De Klerk's announcement, all the nuclear devices and the facilities to manufacture more were dismantled under the close supervision of the International Atomic Energy Agency. It made South Africa the first country in the world that voluntarily relinquished its entire nuclear capability.

20

A Glimpse Over the Precipice

THEY SAY THE WORST NEVER HAPPENS IN SOUTH AFRICA. Few South Africans know how close they came, just a few months before the political settlement in 1994, for their worst nightmare to come true: more than 50 000 white conservatives armed, organised and ready for war; units of the South African Defence Force poised to join them.

For a few months in late 1993 and early 1994, the decision whether South Africa was going to be immersed in blood or make a lasting peace rested largely with one man: General Constand Viljoen, former head of the SADF. If he had buckled under the pressure of many of his followers, a civil war based on race would have erupted that would have made democratic rule impossible for a long, long time.

During the late 1980s, a time of great polarisation, violence and repression in South Africa, both the white National Party government and the main liberation movement, the African National Congress, came to realise that they were not going to win the war by military means and that negotiations were the only way forward. The first tentative contacts between the government and prisoner Nelson Mandela led to secret meetings between ANC leaders and members of the National Intelligence Service in Switzerland in September 1989.

Two unforeseen events boosted the climate of negotiation: in

January 1989, State President PW Botha had a stroke and was succeeded eight months later by the more pragmatic FW de Klerk; and in November 1989 the Berlin Wall fell and the Soviet Union started to crumble, removing white fears that the ANC would establish a communist regime in South Africa. On 2 February 1990, De Klerk unbanned the ANC, the Communist Party and the Pan-Africanist Congress, and on 11 February Nelson Mandela walked out of prison. Negotiations between the ANC and the government started in May that year. In a referendum held in March 1992, whites voted overwhelmingly for De Klerk's reform process, and the multiparty negotiations held at the World Trade Centre in Kempton Park got under way.

But the speed of developments was far too fast for conservative Afrikaner nationalists and right-wingers, and trouble was brewing. In March 1993, fifteen thousand Afrikaner farmers attended a rally to express their fear and anger at the direction the negotiations had taken. They appointed a "Directorate of Generals" to give them strategic leadership: Constand Viljoen and retired generals Tienie Groenewald, Kobus Visser and Dries Bischoff. Within two months, Viljoen and his generals organised and addressed 155 meetings countrywide. "We had to mobilise the Afrikaners psychologically, start our propaganda campaigns and stimulate thinking on alternatives for the ANC/NP model," Viljoen told me. "But, as importantly, we had to quickly build a massive military capability."

Viljoen and his fellow generals embarked on a hectic schedule of recruiting men with military experience, training farmers who had no or little training, and establishing military command structures.

Viljoen says during the course of 1993 he mobilised "between 50 000 and 60 000 men" countrywide, and organised in regions, towns and cities. "We had computers in all centres with the details of all the men we knew we could really rely on." Most of these men had weapons issued by the commandos, but Viljoen says he never used the commando system itself.

But he also bargained on getting a substantial number of permanent force officers and soldiers in the then SADF to join him when the moment came. "I didn't go from unit to unit recruiting them, but most officers had a special bond with me. I knew I wouldn't get the support of all the SADF units, but I knew which ones I would get. I had enough men and small arms, but I also needed armoured cars and heavier weapons. I knew I would have had to rely on certain units of the SADF to supply that."

In order to send a signal to the ANC and the National Party that they should be taken seriously, Viljoen's men engaged in the sabotage of infrastructure, such as electricity pylons, late in 1993. "We planned it carefully to avoid loss of life. And we got our message across."

Was he contemplating staging a coup with his formidable military machine?

"No, I said right from the start that even if someone wanted to give me the New South Africa as a gift, I wouldn't accept it. I never even had the idea to forcefully maintain the status quo of the Old South Africa. Even way back when I was the head of the Defence Force my advice to the government was that you can't win a revolutionary war by military means; it can only win you time and opportunity. No, a coup would have been stupid, and it would never have worked. Nelson Mandela was a figure who was highly regarded internationally; we could not have acted against him. It could even have led to foreign intervention.

"I had two strategies: I wanted enough military power to defend our people, and I wanted to enforce a volkstaat, if necessary. I had enough capacity to occupy the Northern Cape or Mpumalanga and then tell the ANC: We have the military might. We are prepared to talk about how we fit in with your New South Africa. If you want to talk, we'll talk. If you want to fight, we'll fight. That was the plan I had in my drawer.

"But, as importantly, our military power had to give scrumming power behind our negotiations. If a wolf and a lamb argue, the wolf will bite the lamb's head off. If you want to argue with a wolf, make sure you have a pistol in your hand."

When the Conservative Party and the Inkatha Freedom Party walked out of the World Trade Centre talks in 1993, the generals decided to talk directly to the ANC. Constand asked his identical twin brother Abraham, a progressive Afrikaner theologian who had a good relationship with ANC leaders, to help. "People were queuing up to introduce me to Mandela," says Viljoen, "but I chose Abraham. We are politically far apart, but he is an honest man and I trusted him."

Abraham Viljoen used his network of friends and associates, and shortly afterwards, on 12 August 1993, the first highly secret meeting between the three generals and Mandela, MK commander Joe Modise and ANC intelligence chief Joe Nhlanhla took place at Mandela's house in Houghton.

Patti Waldmeir, South African correspondent for the *Financial Times* and author of *Anatomy of a Miracle*, remarked about this meeting: "Ironically, Mandela and Viljoen – both nationalist leaders, both men of principle as well as politicians – almost immediately found the closeness that had always eluded Mandela and De Klerk … Mandela's aides put it simply. General Viljoen won the old man's heart; he was to become just about the only opposition politician who Mandela trusted."

Viljoen remembers it this way: "It was a good meeting. Mandela and I agreed that we should do everything in our power to prevent a conflict between Afrikaner and black African."

But the generals' most important constituency consisted of white farmers and rural Afrikaners. They had to be taken along this new path of talking rather than shooting. Enter one of South Africa's quiet political operators, stockbroker and entrepreneur Jürgen Kögl. His wife, Annemarie, is a distant relative of the firebrand leader of the Transvaal Agricultural Union, Dries Bruwer. Kögl had already organised a meeting between Bruwer, his Free State counterpart Piet Gouws, and former Opposition leader Frederik van Zyl Slabbert. The generals had wanted Slabbert's word that the ANC leaders "were people honourable enough to talk to". Now Kögl and Abraham Viljoen brought them and the ANC together.

Two weeks after the meeting between the generals and Mandela, Viljoen, Bruwer and Gouws met Thabo Mbeki and Jacob Zuma at a secret venue: the pigeon racing club in Lynnwood, Pretoria. Zuma told them: "We can't go for war – we are from war already! We thought we could destroy each other – we couldn't! Why can't we talk?"

Two weeks later a follow-up meeting, again with elaborate security arrangements to keep it secret, took place at a house in Waterkloof: present were Viljoen, Tienie Groenewald, Bruwer, Gouws, Mbeki, Zuma and Nhlanhla.

Kögl recalls: "The National Executive of the ANC already took notice of Viljoen's military capacity earlier that year. They took the discussions with the generals and the agricultural leaders very seriously. Viljoen was always upfront: they were going to defend themselves; they were not prepared to give up their land; they wanted self-determination to be recognised; they wanted to talk about a volkstaat. I remember Zuma saying after that first meeting: These are our people, they are people of the soil. We must work with them."

In May 1993, the head of the SADF, General George Meiring, gave the ANC and the NP government a confidential briefing on Viljoen's military potential and the ghastly consequences that would follow if he didn't take part in the election.

Viljoen says the Commissioner of Police, General Johan van der Merwe, and a senior colleague, General Basie Smit, came to see him during this time. Van der Merwe told Viljoen they had found out about his plans. "It's easy," he said to Viljoen. "Those colleagues of yours with the khaki clothes [a reference to Eugene

Terre'Blanche's Afrikaner Weerstandsbeweging] have a tendency to sit in bars, and after a few beers and brandies they spill all the beans. They have an unquenchable need to brag." Viljoen saw their visit as a warning.

But in October the talks started breaking down. The Afrikaner Volksfront, under whose banner Viljoen operated, joined forces with Mangosuthu Buthelezi's Inkatha Freedom Party, as well as the Bophuthatswana homeland leader Lucas Mangope and Ciskei leader Oupa Gcozo, in the Freedom Alliance. The black leaders were far more hardline about talks with the ANC. The multiparty talks in Kempton Park were in trouble, and KwaZulu-Natal and the East Rand townships were bathed in blood almost daily.

Viljoen decided to break the deadlock, and reopened his own channel of communication with the ANC. On 3 December, he and his delegation, which included the hardline Conservative Party leader, Ferdi Hartzenberg, and the brothers Pieter and Corné Mulder, had a meeting with Nelson Mandela and Thabo Mbeki in Kögl's house in Johannesburg.

Viljoen remembers: "At one stage Mbeki threw his hands up in the air and said: We are miles apart. I said: Yes, we are, let's do something about it. Then Mbeki said: If it's self-determination you want, then let's address it. I thought that was a breakthrough."

Kögl and Abraham Viljoen then facilitated the drawing up of a document to be signed by both sides. The idea was to incorporate the principle of self-determination into the Interim Constitution that had just been adopted by all the negotiating parties. The document was going to be signed on 18 December at the Carlton Hotel, with Mandela, Mbeki, Zuma, ANC Women's League leader Winnie Madikizela-Mandela and Youth League leader Peter Mokaba all in attendance. But the night before the signing, Hartzenberg told Viljoen that their Freedom Alliance partners didn't want him to sign the agreement, so Viljoen went to the ceremony without the mandate to sign. Zuma suggested they call it "The Unsigned

Agreement", because, he said, it remained an agreement between them and Viljoen.

In January 1994, Mandela made a statement that the ANC would never allow a volkstaat or allow the country to be balkanised. Viljoen says it appeared to him that the ANC had constituency problems about the idea, and they were not the only ones: "By January my own followers started pushing hard: they wanted an end to all talks, they wanted the war to start." (Mandela later apologised to Viljoen for the statement, saying it had been a mistake.)

At the end of January, Viljoen and Mbeki met at the home of the grandson of Jan Smuts in Irene. Mbeki suggested that the coming elections be used by Viljoen to prove "substantial support" for the volkstaat idea. Viljoen thought it was an excellent suggestion. A version of the "Unsigned Agreement" was eventually signed by Viljoen and Mbeki on 23 April 1994, called the "Accord on Afrikaner self-determination".

But Viljoen was becoming unpopular among his own constituency. At a huge meeting of right-wingers at the Skilpadsaal in Pretoria on 29 January 1994, people shouted him down and chanted: "We want war!" He told the leadership: "You don't know what war is like. You don't understand the implications of war. If I can't say to myself, my God and my volk that war is the last way out, I will not make war." But, he says, he kept on expanding his military capacity all the same.

Viljoen explains why he was so reluctant to use the military might he had assembled behind him: "I am a militarist. I have experience of war. I knew that if we went over to military action, it would lead to an enormous bloodbath in South Africa. MK didn't waste their time – they had huge amounts of weapons stashed inside the country. It would have been a battle between us and the elements of the SADF that joined us, and MK and the remaining elements of the SADF. It would have been a bloody war.

"I knew the price of war. It would have led to great suffering of my people and the other peoples in South Africa. It would have meant a disaster in the economy, and it would probably have led to international interference. I studied revolutionary warfare; I know you can't win a cold war with a hot war. The purpose of the hot war is only to stabilise and to support your political struggle. But we were ready, and if we believed there was no way out, we would have gone to war."

Then came the opportunity for Viljoen to test his military machine. In March 1994, Lucas Mangope told him that the ANC and MK were destabilising Bophuthatswana in order to overthrow him, and asked for help. "On the Tuesday I went to Mmabatho to do reconnaissance. We heard that MK was going to launch hard action that weekend. On Wednesday I started putting the plan in motion, and when we heard on Thursday that MK was going ahead, I ordered three thousand men to quietly start moving to Mmabatho. It was brilliant. It was a great operation. Our men came via different routes, and at no point did the intelligence services pick it up. Seven o'clock on Friday the first men were issued with firearms by the Bop Army, and we deployed them. They had an immediate stabilising effect.

"And then came the AWB *gemors* [mess]. Mangope specifically asked me not to include any AWB men, because his people wouldn't accept it. We ordered Eugene Terre'Blanche to pull out, but he ignored us. His men behaved very badly. They drove into Mmabatho hurling hand grenades and shooting people. The anger in Mmabatho led to a mutiny, and the arms the Bop Army had to issue to my forces were handed out to the public. When my forces asked for their firearms, they were told it had been stolen. I had to pull back all my men to the airport. It was a damn disaster. I told my men to go home."

On the evening of 11 March 1994, a remarkable scene played itself out on national television. Three men in the khaki dress of the AWB were lying next to an old grey Mercedes Benz on a dusty Bophuthatswana road. They were the last car in the AWB convoy to pull out of the homeland, and they were attacked by Bophuthatswana soldiers. Millions of South Africans watched as Alwyn Wolfaard and Fanie Uys pleaded for water and for help. Their friend Nick Fourie was already dead. Wolfaard and Uys were then executed by a black policeman. This shocking scene was the turning point in right-wing extremist violence, and the beginning of the end of the AWB.

The Bophuthatswana disaster also had a profound effect on Constand Viljoen. "I suddenly realised that I would find it very difficult to conduct a complicated military operation under these fluid circumstances without plunging the country into wholescale war. I wasn't prepared to do that. The AWB factor, and their indiscipline, meant that I would not have been able to absolutely control our forces. I knew for certain then that the political strategy was the only one left.

"I phoned the Mulder brothers from Mmabatho and said: We are going to register for the elections. Today. It was now the only way. In that sense Mmabatho was a very important turning point."

The registration of the Freedom Front as a party participating in the elections was the first sign that the process was going to be peaceful – the registration of the IFP was the other.

Was Viljoen naive to believe the ANC would actually contemplate a volkstaat? "No, I think we did extremely well with the Unsigned Agreement and the agreement of 23 April. But the ANC realised, especially after 1996, that most Afrikaners didn't experience the New South Africa that negatively. So they started thinking they could take chances and ignore these agreements. I don't think they were dishonest in the beginning: they were not just taking me for a ride. Also, we could never get consensus among our people about where the volkstaat should be. But I still think it is something we can and should achieve, but then over a period of twenty, fifty years. You can't buy a volkstaat off the shelf."

Constand Viljoen has since retired from politics, and Dr Pieter Mulder replaced him as leader of the Freedom Front. The Freedom Front is still playing an important role as the voice of conservative Afrikaners in mainstream politics. In 2004 it swallowed up the Conservative Party and other smaller right-wing groups, and renamed itself Freedom Front Plus.

During the early 1990s many analysts predicted a massive growth of white right-wing militancy in the period of black majority rule. It made sense: these people were white supremacists and would never accept the "communist", "terrorist" African National Congress as their government.

Yet the Bophuthatswana fiasco proved to be the demise of white extremist politics, now restricted to minute parties on the lunatic fringe, mocked by everyone but a handful of Afrikaners.

But it wasn't only because white military resistance was proved to be futile. Most white South Africans were surprised to find the leadership of Nelson Mandela a reassuring and reconciliatory one. Within a few months of his swearing in as the first democratic president, they found themselves admiring and loving Mandela more than they had his apartheid predecessors. They discovered that the new democratic order was actually in their own interest, and a process of redefining their identity started.

The story of confrontation between black and white that began in February 1488 had come a full circle.

A Last Word

FOR GENERATIONS, SOUTH AFRICAN HISTORY WAS USED to divide people. Our past was turned into a place inhabited, in one camp, by nasty characters who betrayed, stole from or killed people of other groups, and, in the other, noble heroes who defended their own. Many historical resentments still lurk under the surface of ethnic, racial and regional attitudes today.

At the same time, history is about not forgetting. We cannot properly understand who we are and why we are where we are today if we don't fully know how our ancestors interacted and what they did to and for each other over time.

So how do we remember in a way that doesn't paralyse us; a way that doesn't make us resentful of others and blindly glorify our own?

For me, it's about seeing the characters who populate our past as human beings first, and as members of racial, ethnic or class groups second. To try to understand what the actors of our past were like as people and to judge their actions in terms of ordinary human behaviour. Most of all, to read history with an open mind rather than with a view to justify our prejudices or narrow nationalism.

This doesn't mean that we should sweeten or sanitise the stories of our past. Ugly things happened and great injustices were done. We need to know the truth about all of it. Only then can we begin to understand the attitudes, fears, aspirations, frustrations and prejudices of the different communities in our country today.

Not even a hardened white conservative can fail to have deep sympathy with the slave woman Trijntje of Madagascar, or to feel proud of our own Socrates, Mohlomi, or admire the wise Mountain King, Moshoeshoe.

Show me the Black Consciousness disciple who would not be fascinated by the tale of that rogue trekboer Coenraad de Buys or the life of Boer prophet Siener van Rensburg.

To an open mind, the story of Shaka does not merely tell of a military killing machine, it is the intriguing story of a deeply traumatised young boy who grew up to do spectacular things that changed the course of history.

One doesn't need to have been in the struggle against apartheid to have deep admiration for the bravery and steadfastness of breast-feeding MK commander, Phila Ndwandwe.

These stories, along with those of kidnapped Khoikhoi chief Coree, Nazi firebrand Robey Leibbrandt, "traitor" Piet de Wet, Winnie Mandela's caring for a white man, and right-wing militarist Constand Viljoen who saved us from communal war, and many others, tell the story of how we became the South African nation we are today.

All these people were influenced by and reacted to their surroundings and prevailing attitudes at the time, and in turn influenced events and attitudes that affected those who came after them.

These people, oppressors and oppressed, heroes and villains, are all my ancestors. My DNA doesn't have to be scientifically linked to specific individuals in order for me to regard them as my ancestors. Just as a Mosotho with no family links to Mohlomi calls him his ancestor (or a Zulu from another family tree than that of Shaka calls him his ancestor, or an Afrikaner with primarily French Huguenot roots calls Christiaan de Wet an ancestor), so I regard all those South Africans who came before me and shaped my society as my ancestors. Autshomato and Shaka and Sandile and Moshoeshoe are my ancestors in the very real way that Paul Kruger is my ancestor, although, as far as I know, I only share a direct bloodline with Oom Paul.

Another South African has said all this in a much more beautiful and poetic way: Thabo Mbeki, when he was still deputy president, on the occasion of Parliament's adoption of South Africa's new Constitution on 8 May 1996. This is what he said:

I owe my being to the Khoi and the San whose desolate souls haunt the great expanses of the beautiful Cape – they who fell victim to the most merciless genocide our native land has ever seen, they who were the first to lose their lives in the struggle to defend our freedom and dependence and they who, as a people, perished in the result.

Today, as a country, we keep an audible silence about these ancestors of the generations that live, fearful to admit the horror of a former deed, seeking to obliterate from our memories a cruel occurrence which, in its remembering, should teach us not and never to be inhuman again.

I am formed of the migrants who left Europe to find a new home on our native land. Whatever their own actions, they remain still part of me.

In my veins courses the blood of the Malay slaves who came from the East. Their proud dignity informs my bearing, their culture a part of my essence. The stripes they bore on their bodies from the lash of the slave master are a reminder embossed on my consciousness of what should not be done.

I am the grandchild of the warrior men and women that Hintsa and Sekhukhune led, the patriots that Cetshwayo and Mphephu took to battle, the soldiers Moshoeshoe and Ngungunyane taught never to dishonour the cause of freedom.

My mind and my knowledge of myself is formed by the victories that are the jewels in our African crown, the victories we earned from Isandhlwana to Karthoum, as Ethiopians and as the Ashanti of Ghana, as the Berbers of the desert.

I am the grandchild who lays fresh flowers on the Boer

graves at St Helena and the Bahamas, who sees in the mind's eye and suffers the suffering of a simple peasant folk, death, concentration camps, destroyed homesteads, a dream in ruins.

I am the child of Nongqause. I am he who made it possible to trade in the world markets in diamonds, in gold, in the same food for which my stomach yearns.

I come from those who were transported from India and China, whose being resided in the fact, solely, that they were able to provide physical labour, who taught me that we could both be at home and be foreign, who taught me that human existence itself demanded that freedom was a necessary condition for that human existence.

Being part of all these people, and in the knowledge that none dare contest that assertion, I shall claim that – I am an African.

I am an African. A proud and powerful statement with many layers of meaning.

In a very literal sense, every human being on earth can stand up and declare: I am an African. This continent is where all humanity began. We who were born here are privileged to say: We are from the Mother Continent. Ours was the First Civilisation.

Just recently, scientists found proof in the Blombos Cave between Witsand and Stilbaai on the southern Cape coast that the people who lived there more than 77 000 years ago were the first of our species to make art and develop culture.

It wasn't long thereafter that Africans started to leave the continent, moving to the Middle East, Europe and Asia, eventually to populate the entire earth. Through diet, genetic isolation and climate some became much paler. Some of these pale ones rediscovered the southern tip of Africa five hundred years ago, and came home. They became Africans again.

Let's acknowledge our differences and enjoy the stories of how those who came before us struggled with each other at times. But let's never forget that we are all Africans.

And here, here in southern Africa where it all began and where the circle was closed with the magnificent peace of 1994, it is time for us to let go of the notion of separate histories. It is time to start thinking of our past as the time that forged all of us into the nation we are now at last becoming.

We all have only one history.

South African History at a Glance

100 000+ years ago:	Modern human beings, *Homo sapiens*, develop along the eastern side of Africa from the Cape to Ethiopia.
6 000+ years ago:	Nomadic herders of sheep and cattle called the Khoikhoi, who had developed in the northern parts of today's Botswana, move south into South Africa. There they join their close relatives, the aboriginal hunters called the San or Bushmen.
1 000 years ago:	Bantu-speaking farmers, who had gradually migrated south from the Great Lakes region over more than a millennium, form a rich, powerful kingdom at Mapungubwe in northern South Africa. During the next 500 years different groups move down the east coast and central areas of South Africa.
1488:	The Portuguese seafarer Bartholomeu Dias becomes the first European to set foot on South African soil when he lands at Mossel Bay. His party is met by Khoikhoi. Eleven years later, Dias's colleague Vasco da Gama lands at the same spot and plants a cross and a *padrão*. As he sails away, he sees the Khoikhoi defiantly push down the *padrão* and cross.
1510:	The Portuguese viscount Francisco d'Almeida lands in Table Bay harbour and he and his men get into a fight with the Khoikhoi. The viscount and fifty of his men are killed.
1613:	The men of the English ships *Hector* and *Thomas* kidnap Khoikhoi chief Coree from Table Bay and take him to London. They bring him back the next year.

1652: The representative of the Dutch East India Company, Jan van Riebeeck, establishes a refreshment station at the Cape. It is the first permanent settlement of Europeans in South Africa. Van Riebeeck plants a hedge of bitter almond on the outskirts of the settlement to keep settlers and Khoikhoi apart – the first act of apartheid.

1658: The first ships with slaves arrive at the Cape. The slaves came from Dahomey, Angola, Mozambique and Madagascar, and in larger numbers from India and the East Indies. Altogether about 60 000 slaves are brought to the Cape.

1688: The first French Huguenots arrive at the Cape. The Dutch, French and later German arrivals (with some slave and Khoikhoi blood on occasion) form a new group that later becomes known as the Afrikaners.

1703: Dutch beer brewer Willem Menssink and the slave Trijntje of Madagascar start their famous and fatal relationship.

1713: Large numbers of Khoikhoi die during a smallpox epidemic.

1720: The great philosopher of central South Africa, Mohlomi, is born. His grandfather was Monaheng, chief of the Bakoena, a black farmer people who settled in what is today the Free State and Lesotho.

1761: Coenraad de Buys is born. He becomes one of the first trekboers to move to the Eastern Cape, where the white settlers first clash with the Xhosa farmers. In 1789 he almost single-handedly causes a war between the two groups.

1766: The ship *Meermin*, hijacked by slaves from Madagascar, runs aground at Die Mond on the Cape south coast.

1786: Two great South Africans are born: Moshoeshoe, the founder and king of the Basotho, and Shaka, founder and king of the Zulu.

1795: Britain conquers the Cape Colony, gives it back to the Dutch in 1803, but recaptures it in 1806.

1820: The British settle some four thousand British subjects, mostly farmers and tradesmen, in the Eastern Cape.

1828: Shaka is assassinated by his half-brothers Dingane and Mhlangana.

1834: Xhosa king Hintsa is killed during a savage war with the British colonial forces. In 1850 some sixteen thousand Xhosa are killed in another war.

1836:   The Afrikaner trekboers in the Eastern Cape start their migration into the interior, later called the Great Trek, eventually clashing with black chiefdoms north of the Gariep River.

1843:   Britain annexes Natal, ending the Voortrekker Republic of Natalia. The Boers declare the South African Republic, with Pretoria as capital.

1854:   The Boer republic of the Orange Free State is proclaimed and conflict with the Basotho starts. Most parts of South Africa are now occupied by whites.

1856:   A young Xhosa woman called Nonqause has a vision that a great resurrection will occur if the people kill their cattle and stop planting crops. Tens of thousands die as a result.

1860:   The first shiploads of indentured labourers from India arrive in Natal to work on the sugar plantations.

1876:   Diamonds are discovered at Kimberley.

1886:   Gold is discovered at present-day Johannesburg.

1893:   Mohandas Gandhi arrives from India and inspires and organises resistance against discriminatory practices.

1899:   The South African Republic declares war against Britain and is joined by the Orange Free State.

1900:   Boer general Piet de Wet, brother of the famous General Christiaan de Wet, surrenders to the British forces and starts helping them in the war effort.

1902:   The two Boer republics surrender and sign the Peace of Vereeniging. Almost 30 000 Boer women and children, and a similar number of black people, die during the war.

1910:   The Union of South Africa, consisting of the two Boer republics and the two British colonies, comes into being. Black people are denied the vote.

1912:   The South African Native National Congress is formed in Bloemfontein to campaign for black rights. The name is later changed to the African National Congress.

1914:   The National Party is formed as primary political vehicle for Afrikaner nationalism, also in Bloemfontein.

1918:   The secret, all-powerful Afrikaner Broederbond is formed to further the cause of Afrikaner nationalism in business, education and culture.

1938: Afrikaner nationalism experiences a major upsurge with the national re-enactment of the Great Trek a century earlier.

1941: Nazi agent Robey Leibbrandt arrives at the west coast via yacht from Germany with plans to assassinate Prime Minister Jan Smuts.

1948: The National Party wins the white general election and starts putting its ideology of apartheid into practice.

1952: The ANC gains momentum as a resistance movement with the successful Defiance Campaign to protest racial laws.

1955: Delegates from all over South Africa adopt the Freedom Charter at Kliptown. It remains a crucial policy document for almost forty years.

1957: Africanists in the ANC break away because of the Freedom Charter's non-racial clauses and form the Pan-Africanist Congress, with Robert Sobukwe as first president.

1960: Policemen kill sixty-nine people at a protest meeting against the pass laws in Sharpeville, and three at a march at Langa, Cape Town, later the same day. The killings lead to an international outcry. The government outlaws the ANC, the PAC and the Communist Party.

1961: South Africa is declared a republic and leaves the Common-wealth. The ANC decide to launch an armed struggle, and Umkhonto we Sizwe is formed. A sabotage campaign is launched on 16 December.

1962: Nelson Mandela is arrested and sentenced to five years for leaving the country illegally.

1963: Walter Sisulu, Govan Mbeki, Ahmed Kathrada and other members of MK's High Command are arrested at Lilliesleaf farm, Rivonia. The first of several black bantustans, the Transkei, gets self-government. The policy is that black South Africans should exercise their political rights in these "homelands", of which four later become "independent".

1964: Mandela and the Rivonia detainees are sentenced to life imprison-ment under the Sabotage Act and taken to Robben Island.

1966: Prime Minister Hendrik Verwoerd is stabbed to death in

Parliament by a messenger, Dimitri Tsafendas. John Vorster becomes prime minister.

1967: District Six, a vibrant suburb of Cape Town with mostly coloured inhabitants, is declared a "white area", as were other suburbs. The people are forcibly removed to new townships miles away on the Cape Flats and Mitchells Plain.

1974: Government decides to launch a programme to manufacture nuclear weapons. A coup in Portugal leads to the independence of its colonies Angola and Mozambique.

1975: South African forces invade Angola to fight on the side of UNITA and the FNLA. Cuban forces arrive at the same time.

1976: Pupils in Soweto protest against Bantu Education and the use of Afrikaans as a language of instruction. The police kill some protestors, leading to a revolt in townships nationwide. Many black youngsters leave the country to join the ANC in neighbouring states.

1977: The charismatic Black Consciousness leader Steve Biko is assaulted by police, thrown naked in a police van and taken to Pretoria. He dies on the way. Justice Minister Jimmy Kruger says Biko's death leaves him cold. A Soviet satellite takes photographs of Vastrap, the base in the Kalahari where South Africa was about to explode a nuclear device underground. Winnie Mandela is banished to Brandfort.

1978: Prime Minister Vorster resigns after a scandal over the misuse of secret funds for the Department of Information. He is replaced by his Minister of Defence, PW Botha, who appoints his Defence Force chief, Magnus Malan, as Minister of Defence. The militarisation of South Africa starts, and a programme of military destabilisation of neighbouring states follows.

1979: An American Vela satellite registers the typical double flash of a nuclear explosion in the ocean south of South Africa. South Africa denies responsibility.

1980: Zimbabwe becomes independent, with ZANU leader Robert Mugabe as its first president.

1983: Prime Minister Botha wins a referendum on proposals to institute separate houses of parliament for Coloureds and Indians. Black South Africans remain excluded from political participation. The

"Tricameral Parliament" angers the majority of South Africans, leading to the formation of the United Democratic Front. It is ideologically aligned with the ANC, as is one of its major constituencies, the newly formed Congress of South African Trade Unions. A period of severe repression and resistance starts, with several states of emergency declared.

1984: South Africa and Mozambique sign the Nkomati Accord, a non-aggression treaty.

1988: MK commander for Natal, Phila Ndwandwe, is kidnapped from Swaziland by security policemen and killed near Pietermaritzburg when she refuses to become an informer.

1989: PW Botha suffers a stroke and is succeeded as National Party leader by FW de Klerk, but remains state president. Botha meets Mandela. De Klerk takes over as state president and releases some senior ANC figures from jail. The Berlin Wall falls. SWAPO wins a landslide victory in Namibia's independence elections.

1990: De Klerk announces the unbanning of the ANC, SACP and PAC at the opening of Parliament. Mandela walks from prison on 11 February. ANC exiles start returning. The ANC and the NP sign the Groote Schuur Accord, committing themselves to an end to violence and a negotiated solution. Namibia becomes an independent republic.

1991: All negotiating parties sign the National Peace Accord. The political violence continues. The first meeting of the Conference for a Democratic South Africa (CODESA) takes place.

1992: A referendum for whites gives De Klerk a strong go-ahead for negotiations. Forty people are massacred at Boipatong and the ANC breaks off all negotiations. The ANC's Cyril Ramaphosa and the NP's Roelf Meyer form a "special channel of communication" and resume negotiations that lead to the signing of a Record of Understanding.

1993: On 10 April popular ANC and SACP leader Chris Hani is assassinated by a right-winger. Former SADF chief General Constand Viljoen mobilises tens of thousands of white men countrywide for possible military intervention, and they embark on a limited sabotage campaign. The multiparty conference ratifies an Interim Constitution.

1994:   Ciskei and Bophuthatswana collapse. An abortive invasion of Bophuthatswana by the AWB convinces Viljoen to shelve his military plans and register for the elections. On 27–28 April South Africa's first non-racial elections take place and the ANC wins almost two thirds of the vote. Nelson Mandela is sworn in as the first democratic president.

1996:   The final text of the Constitution of South Africa is agreed to by Parliament and ratified by the Constitutional Court. The Truth and Reconciliation Commission starts its hearings.

1999:   Nelson Mandela retires as president after a general election and is succeeded by Thabo Mbeki.

Bibliography

Arbousset, Thomas. *Missionary Excursion*. Lesotho: Morija Museum and Archives, 1991.

Becker, Peter. *Hill of Destiny: The Life and Times of Moshesh, Founder of the Basotho*. London: Panther, 1969.

———. *Path of Blood: The Rise and Conquest of Mzilikazi, Founder of the Matebele*. London: Granada, 1975.

———. *Rule of Fear: The Bloody Story of Dingane, King of the Zulu*. London: Granada, 1972.

Bezdrob, Anné Mariè du Preez. *Winnie Mandela: A Life*. Cape Town: Zebra Press, 2003.

Boeseken, Anna. *Slaves and Free Blacks at the Cape*. Cape Town: Tafelberg, 1977.

Brookes, Edgar, and Colin de B Webb. *A History of Natal*. Pietermaritzburg: University of Natal Press, 1994.

Bruwer, JP. *Manne van die Bantoe*. Johannesburg: Afrikaanse Pers Boekhandel.

Burman, Jose. *Shipwreck! Courage and Endurance in the Southern Seas*. Cape Town: Human & Rousseau, 1986.

Cassalis, Eugéne. *The Basutos* (facsimile reprint of the 1861 edition). Lesotho: Morija Museum and Archives, 1997.

Clingman, Stephen. *Bram Fischer: Afrikaner Revolutionary*. Cape Town: David Philip, 1998.

Coates, Austin. *Basutoland*. London: Her Majesty's Stationery Office, 1966.

Cope, John. *King of the Hottentots*. Cape Town: Howard Timmins, 1967.

Couzens, Tim. *Murder at Morija*. Johannesburg: Random House, 2003.

Davenport, Rodney, and Christopher Saunders. *South Africa: A Modern History*. London: Macmillan, 2000.

Deacon, Harriet (ed.). *The Island: The History of Robben Island 1488–1990*. Cape Town: David Philip, 1996.

Deacon, HJ, and Jeanette Deacon. *Human Beginnings in South Africa: Uncovering the Secrets of the Stone Age*. Cape Town: David Philip, 1999.

De Klerk, FW. *Die Outobiografie*. Cape Town: Human & Rousseau, 1999.

De Klerk, WA. *The Puritans in Africa: A Story of Afrikanerdom*. Harmondsworth: Penguin, 1976.

De Villiers, HHW. *Rivonia – Operation Mayibuye*. Johannesburg: Afrikaanse Pers Boekhandel, 1964.

De Wet, CR. *Die Stryd tussen Boer en Brit*. Cape Town: Tafelberg, 1999.

Du Toit, André, and Hermann Giliomee. *Afrikaner Political Thought: Analysis and Documents, Vol. 1. 1780–1850*. Berkeley: University of California Press, 1983.

Ebrahim, Hassen. *The Soul of a Nation: Constitution-making in South Africa*. Cape Town: Oxford University Press, 1998.

Eldredge, Elizabeth A. *A South African Kingdom: The Pursuit of Security in Nineteenth-Century Lesotho*. Cambridge: Cambridge University Press, 1993.

Ellenberger, D Fred. *History of the Basuto – Ancient and Modern* (facsimile reprint of 1912 edition). Lesotho: Morija Museum and Archives, 1997.

Elphick, Richard. *Khoikhoi and the Founding of White South Africa*. Johannesburg: Ravan Press, 1985.

Elphick, Richard, and Hermann Giliomee (eds.). *The Shaping of South African Society 1652–1820*. Cape Town: Maskew Miller Longman, 1979.

Furlong, Patrick J. *Between Crown and Swastika: The Impact of the Radical Right on the Afrikaner Nationalist Movement in the Fascist Era*. Johannesburg: Witwatersrand University Press, 1991.

Gandhi, Ela. *Mohandas Gandhi: The South African Years*. Cape Town: Maskew Miller Longman, 1994.

Gandhi, MK. *An Autobiography*. London: Penguin, 1982.

Germond, RC. *Chronicles of Basutoland*. Lesotho: Morija Sesuto Book Depot, 1967.

Giliomee, Hermann. *The Afrikaners: Biography of a People*. Cape Town: Tafelberg, 2003.

Golan, Daphna. *Inventing Shaka: Using History in the Construction of Zulu Nationalism.* London: Lynne Rienner Publishers, 1994.

Gordon, RE, and CJ Talbot. *From Diaz to Vorster: Source Material on South African History.* Goodwood: Nasionale Opvoedkundige Uitgewery, 1983.

Grundlingh, AM. *Die Hensoppers en Joiners.* Pretoria: Haum, 1979.

Heese, HF. *Reg en Onreg, Kaapse Regspraak in die 18de Eeu.* Bellville: University of the Western Cape, 1994.

Hill, Stephen J. *A Short History of Lesotho: From the Late Stone Age until the 1993 Elections.* Lesotho: Morija Museum and Archives, 1993.

Hunt, James D. *Gandhi and the Nonconformists: Encounters in South Africa.* New Delhi: Promilla & Co Publishers, 1986.

Kathrada, Ahmed. *Memoirs.* Cape Town: Zebra Press, 2004.

Kruger, DW. *The Age of the Generals.* Johannesburg: Dagbreek Book Store, 1958.

Laband, John. *Rope of Sand: The Rise and Fall of the Zulu Kingdom in the Nineteenth Century.* Johannesburg & Cape Town: Jonathan Ball, 1995.

Le Cordeur, Basil. *The Politics of Eastern Cape Separatism 1820–1854.* Cape Town: Oxford University Press, 1981.

Leibbrandt, Robey. *Geen Genade.* Pretoria: Bienedell Uitgewers, 1993.

Mandela, Nelson. *Long Walk to Freedom: The Autobiography of Nelson Mandela.* Randburg: Macdonald Purnell, 1994.

Mandela, Winnie (edited by Anne Benjamin). *Part of My Soul Went with Him.* Harmondsworth: Penguin, 1985.

Mbeki, Govan. *The Struggle for Liberation in South Africa: A Short History.* Cape Town: David Philip, 1992.

Meer, Fatima. *Apprenticeship of a Mahatma.* Phoenix: Phoenix Settlement Trust, 1994.

Meredith, Martin. *Fischer's Choice: A Life of Bram Fischer.* Johannesburg & Cape Town: Jonathan Ball, 2002.

Morris, Donald R. *The Washing of the Spears.* London: Cardinal, 1973.

Mostert, Noël. *Frontiers: The Epic of South Africa's Creation and the Tragedy of the Xhosa People.* London: Jonathan Cape, 1992.

Muller, CFJ (ed.). *500 Years: A History of South Africa.* Pretoria: Academica, 1975.

Nathan, Manfred. *The Huguenots in South Africa.* Johannesburg: Central News Agency, 1939.

Oliver, Roland. *The African Experience.* London: Pimlico, 1994.

Pakenham, Thomas. *The Boer War.* London: Abacus, 1991.

Peires, Jeff. *The House of Phalo: A History of the Xhosa People in the Days of their Independence.* Johannesburg & Cape Town: Jonathan Ball, 2003.

Penn, Nigel. *Rogues, Rebels and Runaways: Eighteenth-Century Cape Characters.* Cape Town: David Philip, 1999.

Potgieter, Coenraad. *Skipbreuke aan Ons Kus.* Cape Town: Tafelberg, 1969.

Raath, AWG. *Siener van Rensburg en die Rebellie.* Pretoria: Kontak Uitgewers, 1994.

Raath, AWG, and N van Zyl. *Die Vierkleur Wapper Weer: die visioene van Siener van Rensburg.* Bloemfontein: Vierkleur Uitgewery, 1995.

Reitz, Deneys. *Commando: A Boer Journal of the Boer War.* Harmondsworth: Penguin, 1988.

Ritter, EA. *Shaka Zulu: The Rise of the Zulu Empire.* London: Longmans Green & Co, 1955.

Rosenthal, Eric. *General de Wet: A Biography.* Central News Agency.

Ross, Robert. *A Concise History of South Africa.* Cambridge: Cambridge University Press, 1999.

Sampson, Anthony. *Mandela: The Authorised Biography.* London and Cape Town: Harper Collins and Jonathan Ball, 1999.

Sauer, Hans. *Ex Africa.* London: Geoffrey Bles, 1937.

Schoeman, Agatha E. *Coenraad de Buys, the First Transvaler.* Pretoria: JH de Bussy, 1938.

Selby, John. *Shaka's Heirs.* London: George Allen & Unwin, 1971.

Snyman, Adriaan. *Siener van Rensburg – Boodskapper van God.* Mossel Bay: Vaandel Uitgewers, 2003.

Sparks, Allister. *Tomorrow Is Another Country: The Inside Story of South Africa's Negotiated Settlement.* Johannesburg & Cape Town: Jonathan Ball, 1995.

Steyn, H, R van der Walt and J van Loggerenberg. *Armament and Disarmament: South Africa's Nuclear Weapons Experience.* Pretoria: Network Publishers, 2003.

Strydom, Hans. *Vir Volk en Führer: Robey Leibbrandt en Operasie Weissdorn.* Johannesburg & Cape Town: Jonathan Ball, 1983.

Theal, George M. A *History of South Africa Since 1795.* London: Swan
    Schonnstein, 1908.
Tutu, Desmond. *No Future Without Forgiveness.* London: Rider
    Books, 1999.
Uys, Ian. *Survivors of South African Oceans.* Pretoria: Fortress
    Publishers, 1993.
Van Jaarsveld, FA. *From Van Riebeeck to Vorster: An Introduction to the
    History of the Republic of South Africa.* Johannesburg: Perskor, 1975.
Waldmeir, Patti. *Anatomy of a Miracle: The End of Apartheid and the
    Birth of the New South Africa.* Harmondsworth: Penguin, 1998.
Watson, RL. *The Slave Question: Liberty and Property in South Africa.*
    Johannesburg: Witwatersrand University Press, 1990.
Worden, Nigel. *Slavery in Dutch South Africa.* Cambridge: Cambridge
    University Press, 1985.

Glossary

dominee:	reverend
drostdy:	residence and official headquarters of the landdrost
impi:	a body of Zulu warriors
kraal:	animal enclosure or traditional rural settlement of huts and houses
landdrost:	magistrate
lobola:	bride price
sangoma:	traditional healer
uitlander:	foreigner
vastrap:	stand firm
veldkornet:	field cornet
veldwagtmeester:	field guard
VOC:	Dutch East India Company (Vereenigde Oost-Indische Compagnie)
volkstaat:	nation state

Index